DESIGN
PRESENTATION

DESIGN PRESENTATION

**Techniques
For Marketing
And Project
Proposals**

McGraw-Hill Book Company

New York St. Louis San Francisco
Aukland Bogotá Hamburg
Johannesburg London Madrid
Mexico Montreal New Delhi Panama
Paris São Paulo Singapore Sydney
Tokyo Toronto

Ernest Burden

Library of Congress Cataloging in Publication Data

Burden, Ernest E., date.
  Design presentation.

  Includes index.
  1. Architectural design — Audio-visual aids.
  2. Communication in architectural design.   I. Title.
  NA2750.B86   1983   720′.28′4   83-14918
  ISBN 0-07-008931-0

ISBN 0-07-008931-0

34567890 HAL/HAL 897654

The editors for this book were Joan Zseleczky and Esther Gelatt.
the designer was Ernest Burden, and the production
supervisor was Thomas G. Kowalczyk. It was set in Claro
by Karen Burden.

Printed and bound by Halliday Lithograph.

CONTENTS

ACKNOWLEDGMENTS

Design presentations precede the actual building by several years. Some projects may never become realities for one reason or another. Others may undergo such extensive revisions that the design, as originally conceived and presented, may not resemble the finished product.

It is with this in mind that I thank all the firms listed in the "Design Credits" for permission to publish their presentations.

I appreciate the assistance of those directly concerned with the production of this book, including Jeanmarie McGovern who helped make and remake the photographs and complete the mechanicals.

Many thanks to the editors at McGraw Hill who have made this book a valuable experience.

Thanks to my wife Karen for her ongoing understanding and encouragement during this project.

Ernest Burden

PREFACE

Visual communication has been around for nearly 25,000 years — from the cave paintings of France to the rock cut tomb frescoes of ancient Egypt, where hieroglyphics combined art and storytelling forms of communication.

Medieval painters depicted scenes with seemingly primitive concepts of space rendition, yet variations of some of these techniques are being used today with great success. It took the painters and architects of the Renaissance to apply mathematical rules of perspective and studies in light and shade to give us a recognizable facsimile of reality.

Many of the presentation techniques developed during the Renaissance are still in use today in a slightly updated form. Since the days of the beaux arts school, there have been many different styles of presentation, which have altered the course of presentation techniques. Even today, many architects are developing their own styles of drawing that best describe their architecture.

One of the most popular styles of presentation drawing today does not rely on the skills of the perspective artist or architectural delineator. Many designers have skillfully used orthographic projection and anonometric project drawing to present their designs. This book displays the many techniques used by the designer-artist.

With the adaptation of the easier style, many more architects can depict their own designs without the aid of perspective. However, few people will have the time or the patience to master the three-point perspective technique, and among those who do, even fewer will be able to apply it to the design of the three-point sectional perspective as seen in this book.

Competitions always stimulate architects to use their best combination of drawing techniques. Some of the best-known projects are included in this section, plus many not published previously. The chapter on print media describes how design concepts are presented in brochures, design portfolios, newsletters, and other forms of mass-distributed printed publications.

Projected visual presentations are one of the major forms of presentation in use today. They include nearly all the elements found in direct-viewing presentations, such as plans, renderings, and models, but they can include much more. By their nature, they can present visual information otherwise inaccessible to the presentation. They can overcome the limitations of time and space and present a lot of information in a short time frame.

Due to the unlimited possiblities of the media, good planning becomes a necessity. Once the concepts and formats have been considered, certain guidelines are needed to prepare the material to accomplish the objectives of the presentation.

Since few things can be learned by the theoretical approach, this book applies a case study approach. Many sample visual presentations are included in the final chapter to show each project sequentially, with coordinated words and pictures.

The presentation of design will continue to see new forms of artistry, particularly as computers become more capable of simulation. What computer technology will find difficult to replace is the kind of magic that the human hand can bring to a drawing.

Ernest Burden

PART ONE:
Direct Viewing Visuals

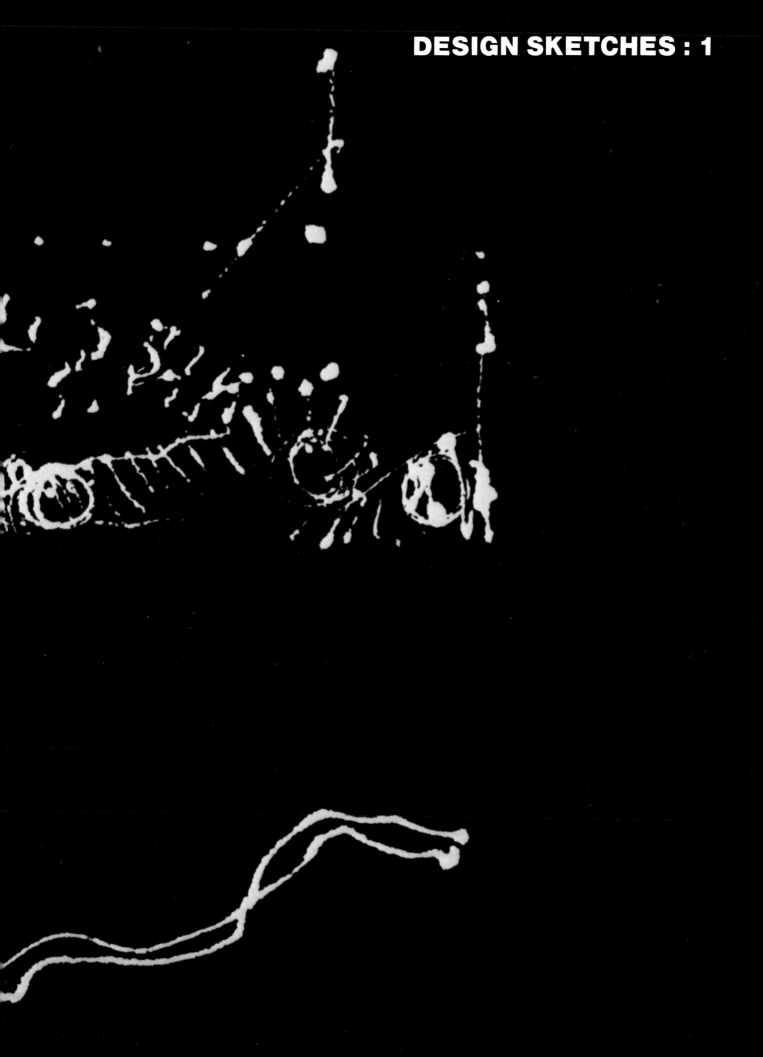

Design Scroll

Design study sketches are often done on tracing paper. Each sketch is torn off the tracing paper roll, thus losing the continuity of ideas as they are sketched out. By leaving the sketches on the roll, you produce a continuous scroll with the design progression very clearly shown. This is very useful when making presentations to clients in the early design stages. Unroll the scroll as you progress through the evolution of your design ideas.

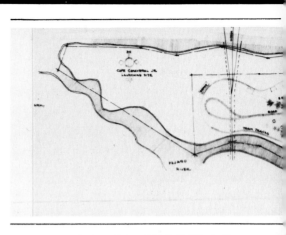

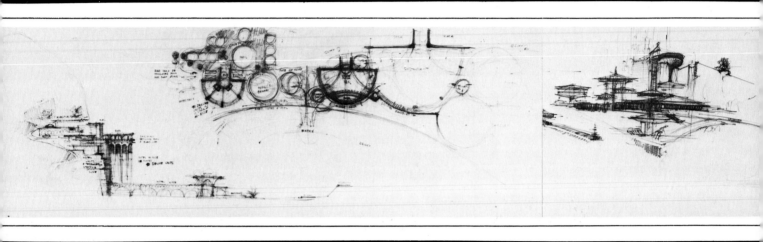

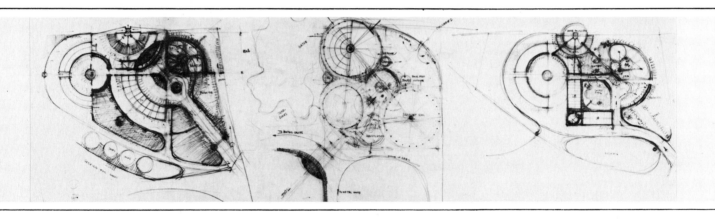

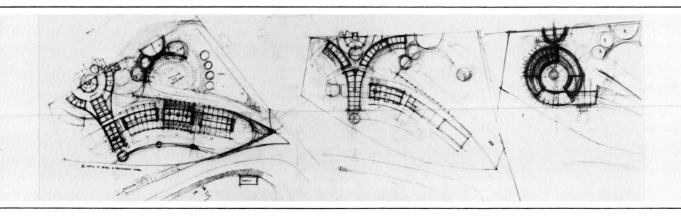

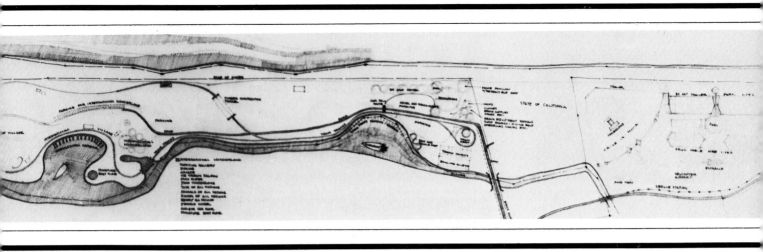

Design Study Sketches

Design study sketches for the State of Illinois Center were drawn by the architect. These sketches were later assembled into a chronological sequence for presentation. Most often, the concept of the structure is quite evident in these sketches and can become a basis for the design development drawings.

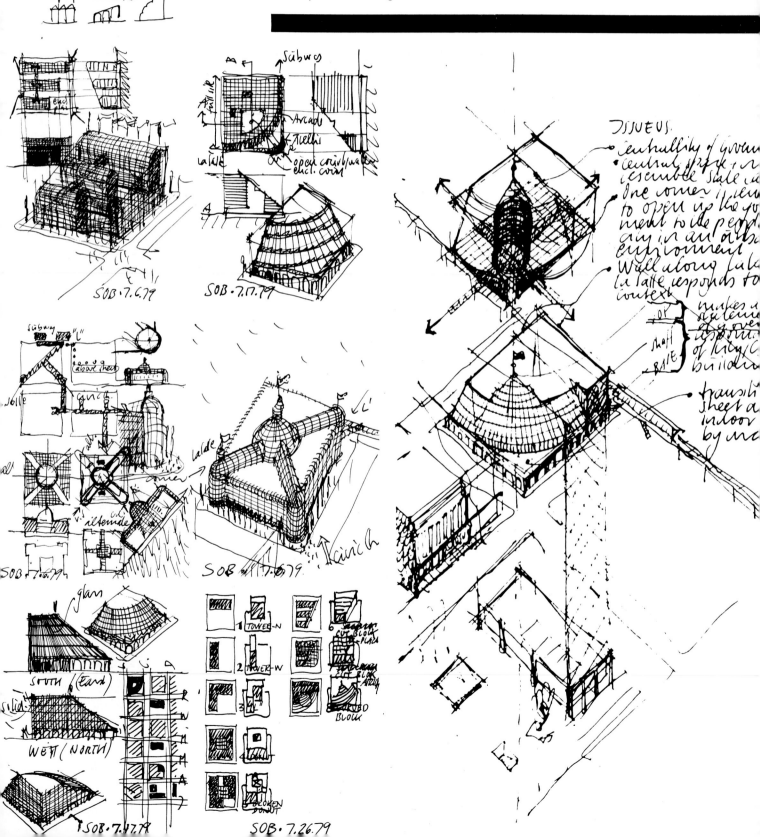

SOB·7.6.79

SOB·7.17.79

SOB·7.06.79

SOB·7.6.79

SOB·7.47.79

SOB·7.26.79

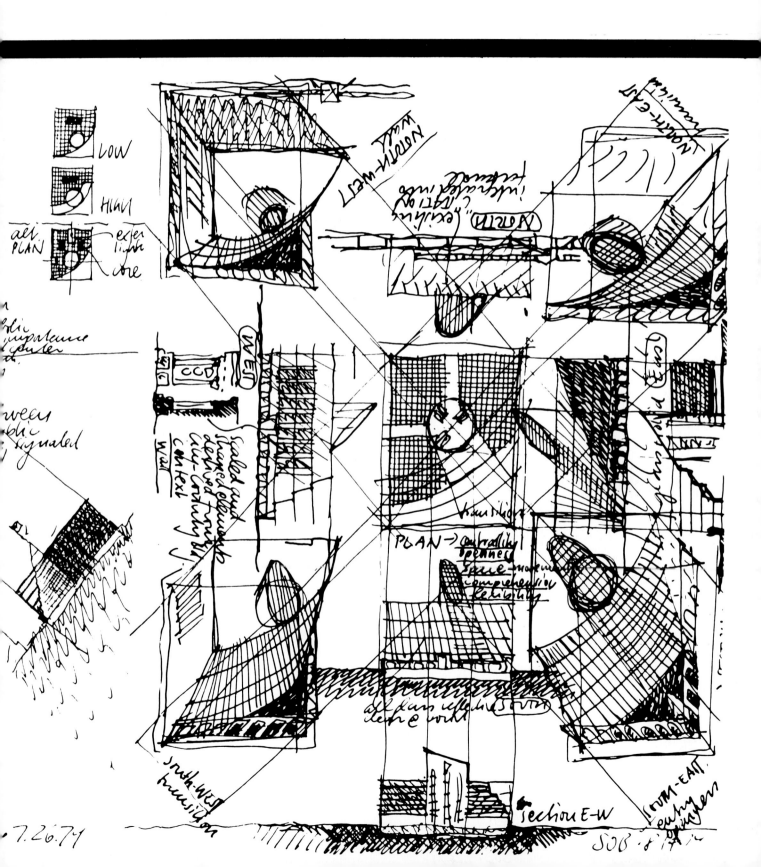

Gulfport

The concept sketch for the design of an urban plaza was drawn on a napkin. This sketch played an important part in the design development. Since the project was in a coastal town, but not on the shore, the configuration of the shoreline (shown in the sketch left) became a major design element of the plaza. It was reproduced by a walkway and pergola design. The other design sketches show the concept in three dimensions. Several overlapping sketches are shown in the drawing below.

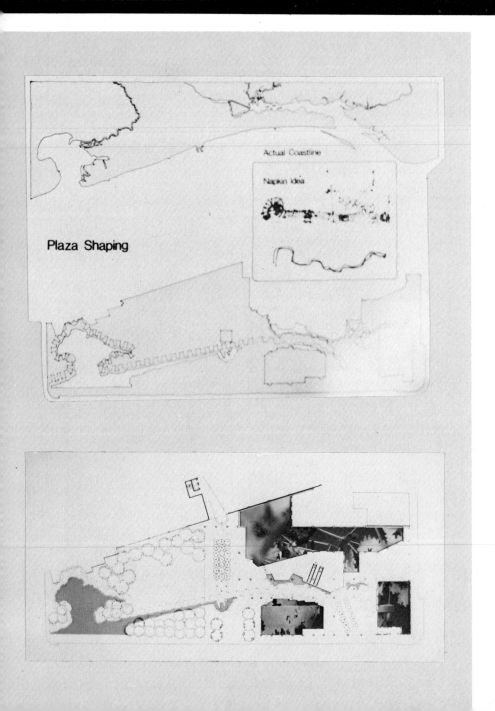

Actual Coastline

Napkin Idea

Plaza Shaping

St. Charles Ave.

Environmental sketches of street scenes such as these are effective in showing urban change. If sketches are done over projected images of slides or photographs, the scale will be accurate and the detail will be appropriate to the location.

While an overall view is often helpful in describing the overall project, it is the ground level views that are the most impressive. These always relate to the view most people get of the project. Details and sketches of the street furniture are also helpful in describing the project.

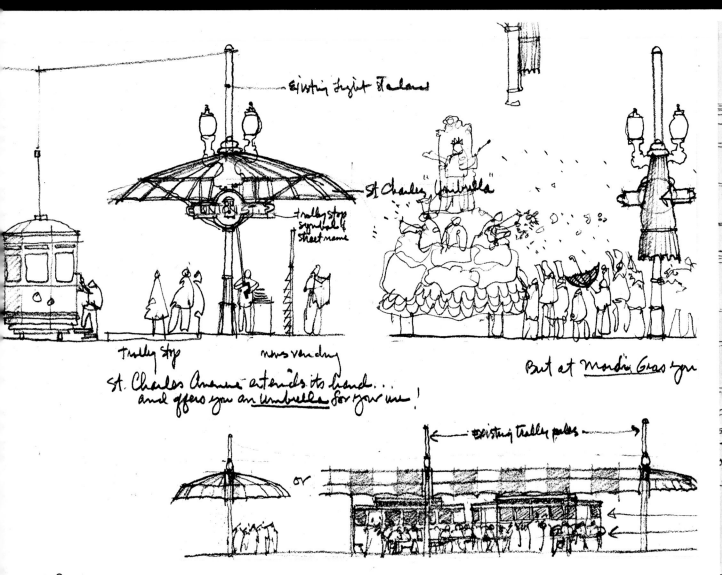

Existing light standard

trolley stop symbol & street name

St. Charles "Umbrella"

trolley stop   news vendor

St. Charles Avenue extends its hand...
and offers you an umbrella for your use!

But at Mardi Gras you

Existing trolley poles

or

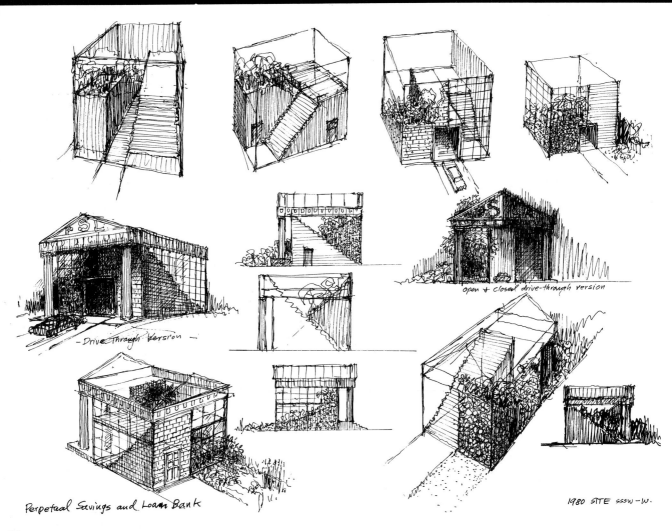

Perpetual Savings and Loan Bank

— Drive-Through Version —

open & closed drive-through version

1980 SITE SSSW-W.

Savings And Loan Bank

Oftentimes the simple method of orthographic projection describes the concept better than an elaborate perspective. Although some design concepts are sketched out first the method of presentation is the plan and elevation. The addition of an axonometric helps to point out the unusual, but clearly classical, approach to the design of a savings and loan bank building.

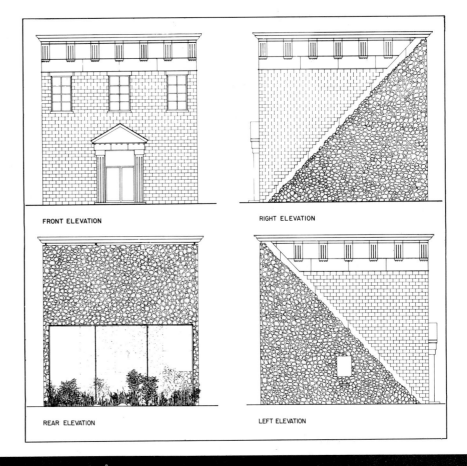

FRONT ELEVATION

RIGHT ELEVATION

REAR ELEVATION

LEFT ELEVATION

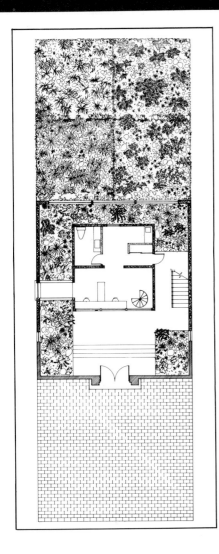

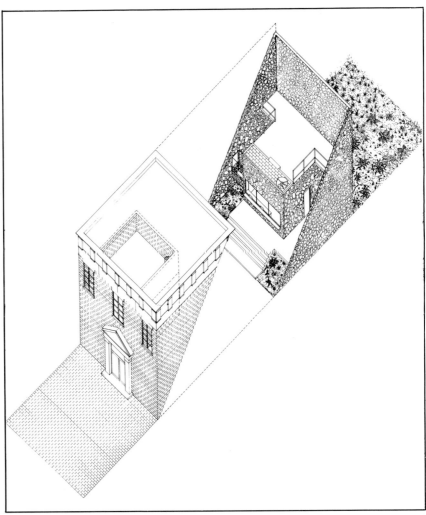

Jaffe Residences

The use of bold and sketchy line work adds drama to these drawings of residential buildings. The drama is further heightened by the selection of perspective angle. It is immediately clear how much the sketches tell you about the structures.

DR. AND MRS. TURETSKY.
OLD WESTBURY, LONG ISLAND N.Y.

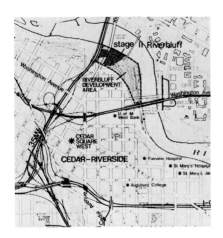

Cedar Riverside

Loose environmental sketches of many large scale projects can be very effective in describing the buildings. What is more important is that spatial relationships are more easily stated in the sketch than in any other form of presentation.

Model photographs of more refined designs do not always have the same representation of space.

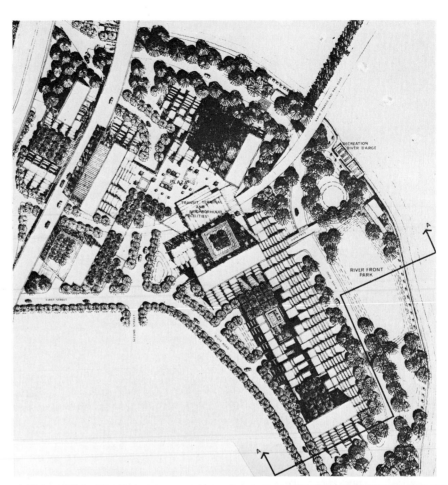

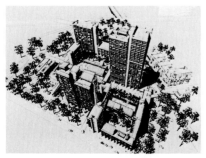

14

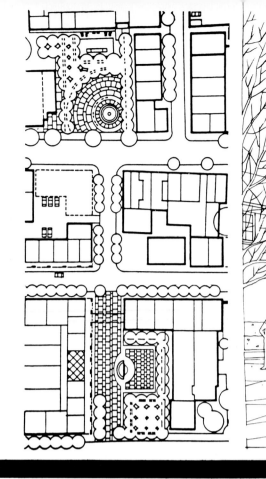

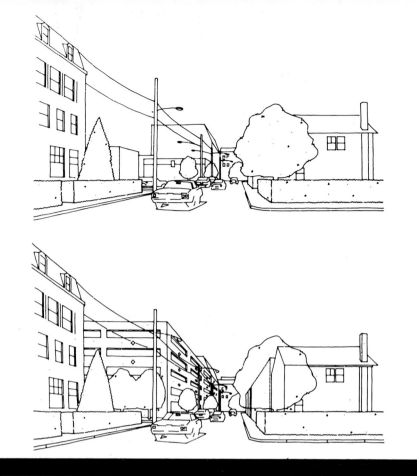

Princeton Urban Design Study

Urban design studies are most often done months, even years, ahead of actual development. Therefore, the technique used to present these schemes should not be the same as a final project drawing. Here the studies are executed in a simple line style and certain features are shown in a comparative study format. The existing neighborhood is shown and the same scene is repeated with the new project inserted.

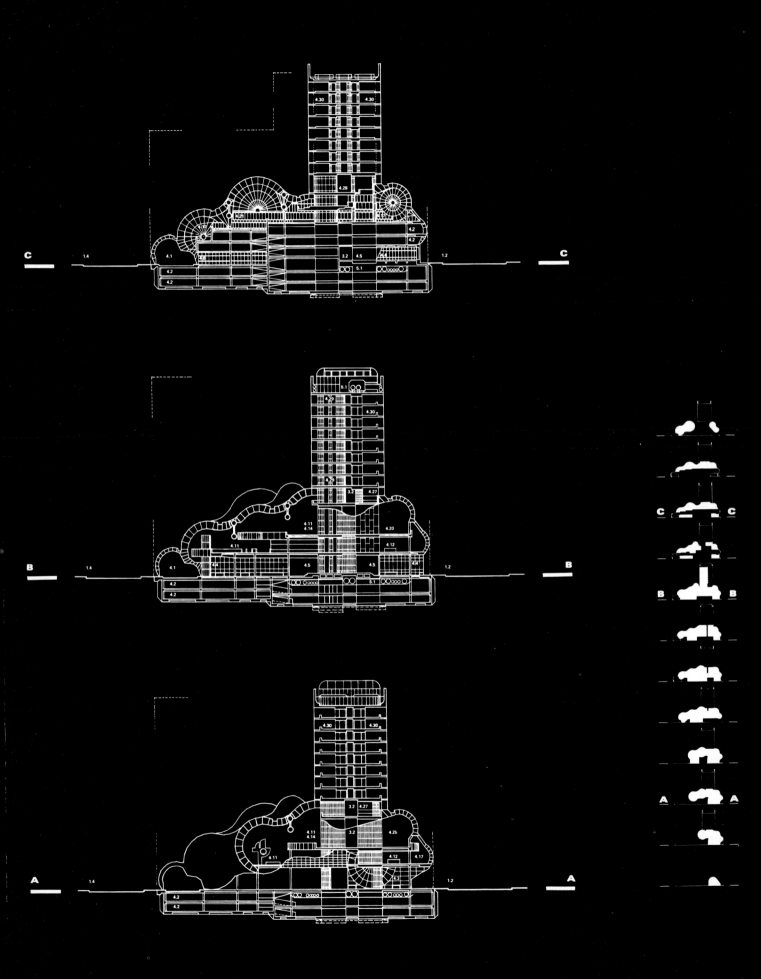

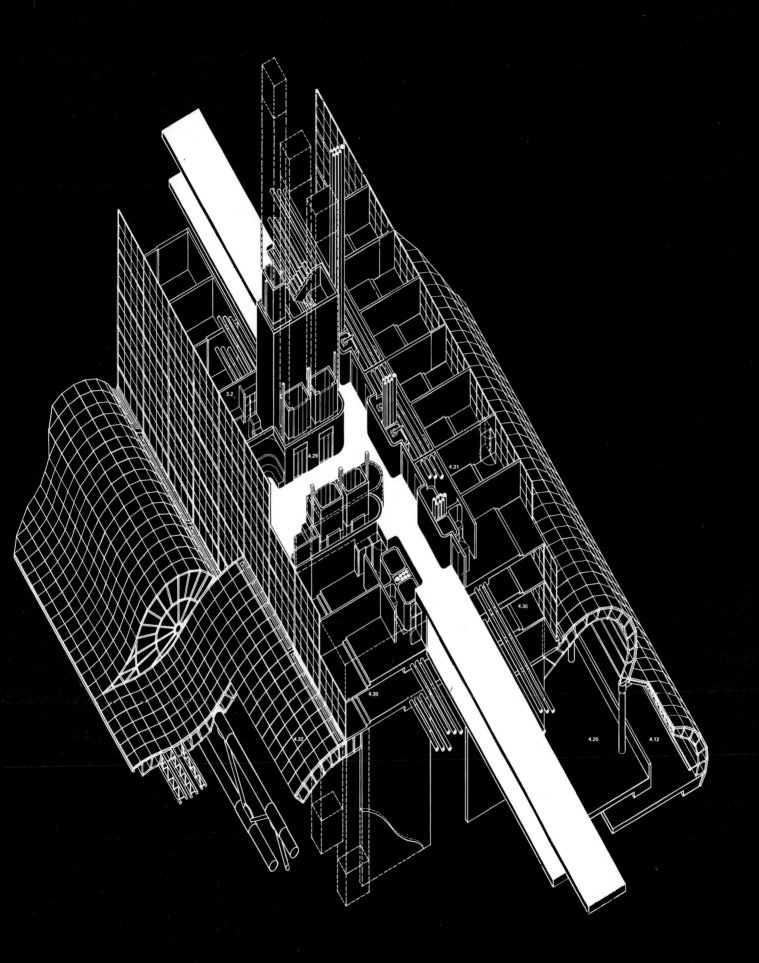

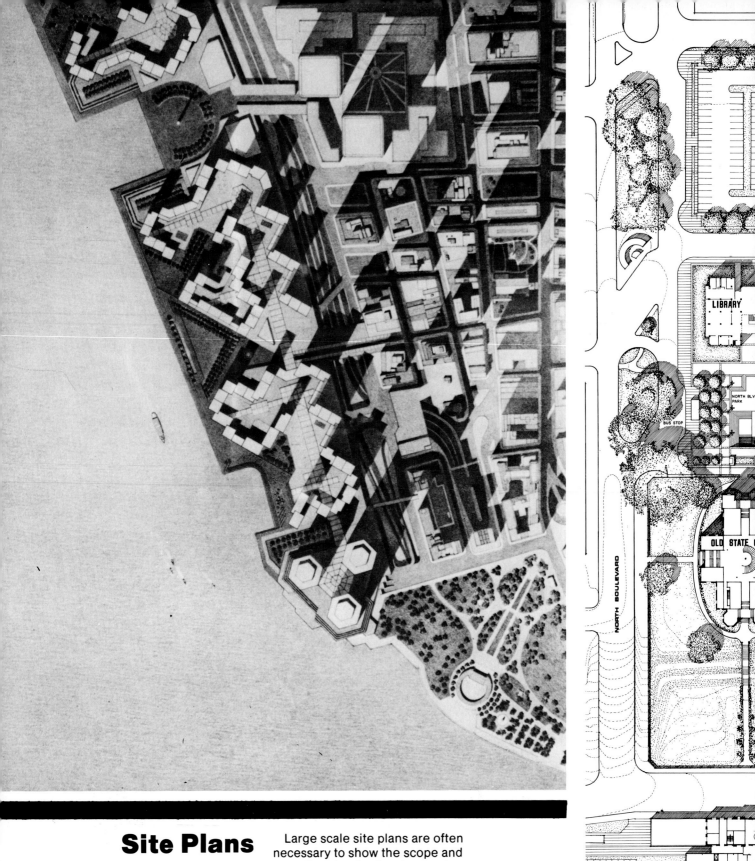

Site Plans

Large scale site plans are often necessary to show the scope and overall scale of a development project. Detail is not necessary, but the forms of the structures must be distinct. Shadows cast by the buildings can be a key to their shape and even their height. In the example on the right, the shadows of the structures are cast on the ground floor plan, giving the illusion of three-dimensional shapes.

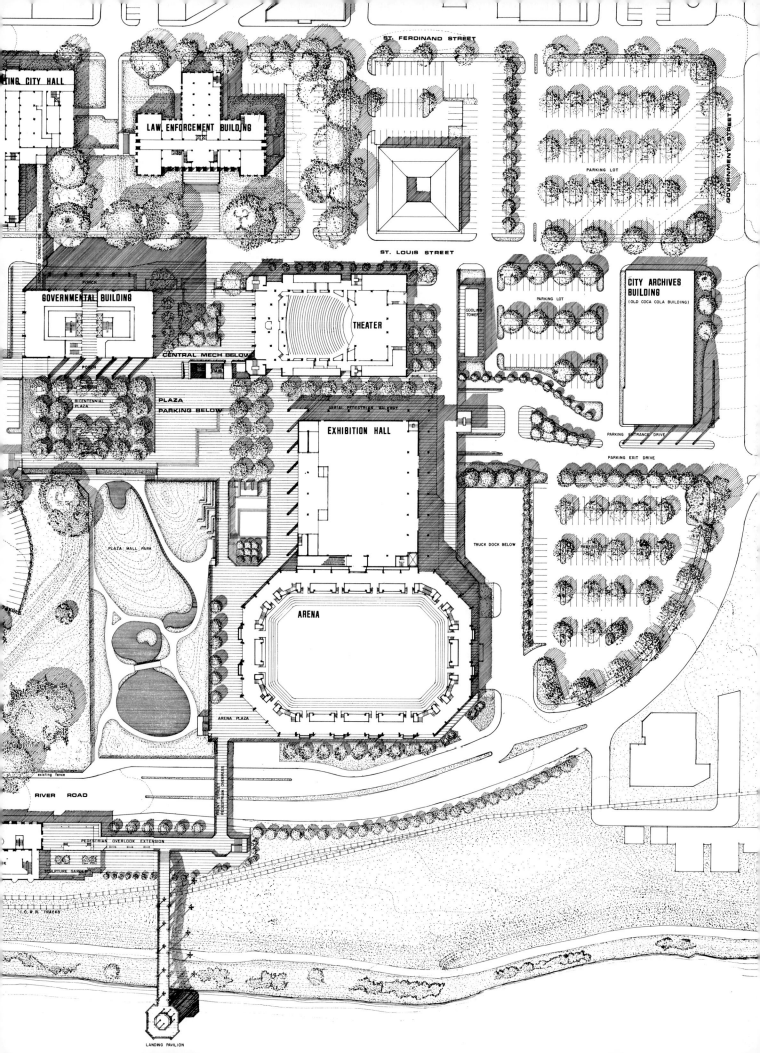

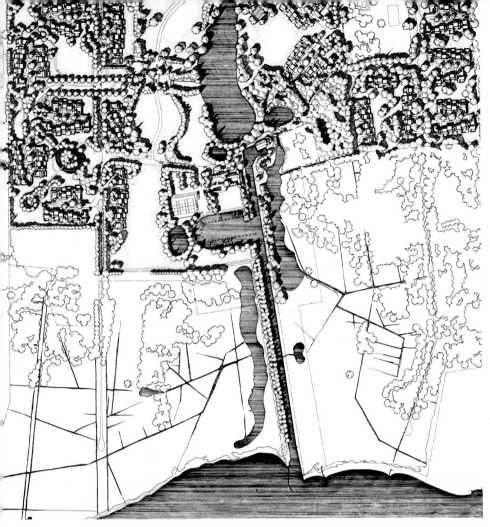

Rendered Plans

The readability of the plan of a project can be greatly enhanced by the technique used to give it the proper scale. This, of course, differs from small scale to close-up scale. For example, in overall site drawings the trees are shown in groups without detail. In closer site plans the trees are delineated more carefully and ground textures become more important. Finally, in detailed plans the trees are shown with branch detail and paving patterns become more dominant.

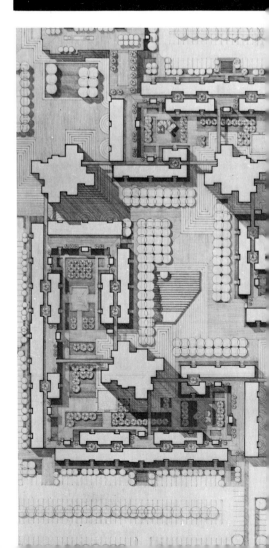

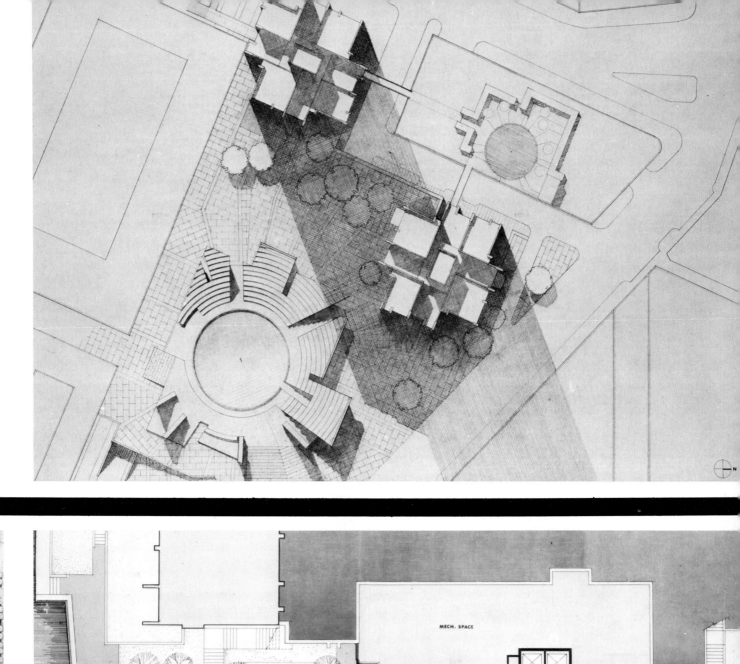

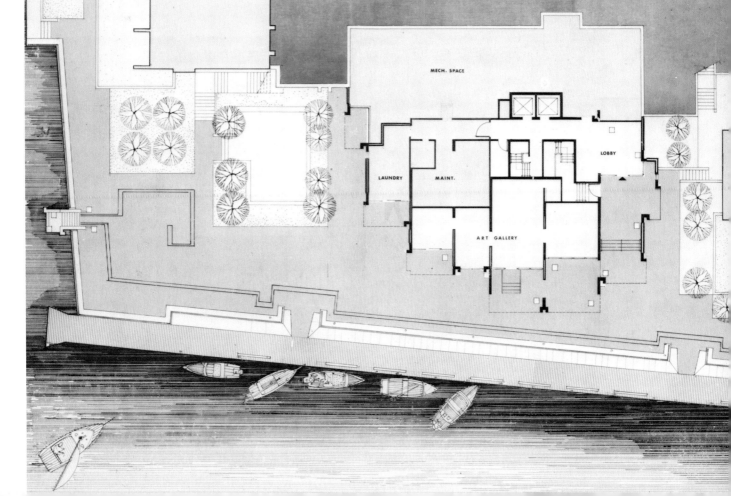

MECH. SPACE

LAUNDRY

MAINT.

LOBBY

ART GALLERY

Landscape Plans

The focus of landscape plans is very naturally on the tree forms and ground cover patterns. The buildings are, therefore, reduced to block forms without detail and the pattern of tree placement dominates. Most landscape plans are more graphic in form, emphasizing the abstract nature of foliage that is designated for installation.

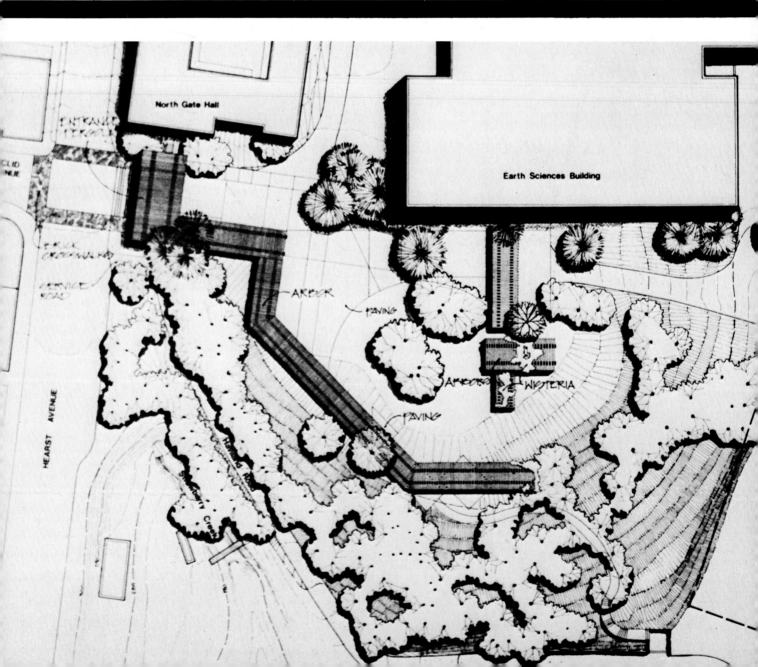

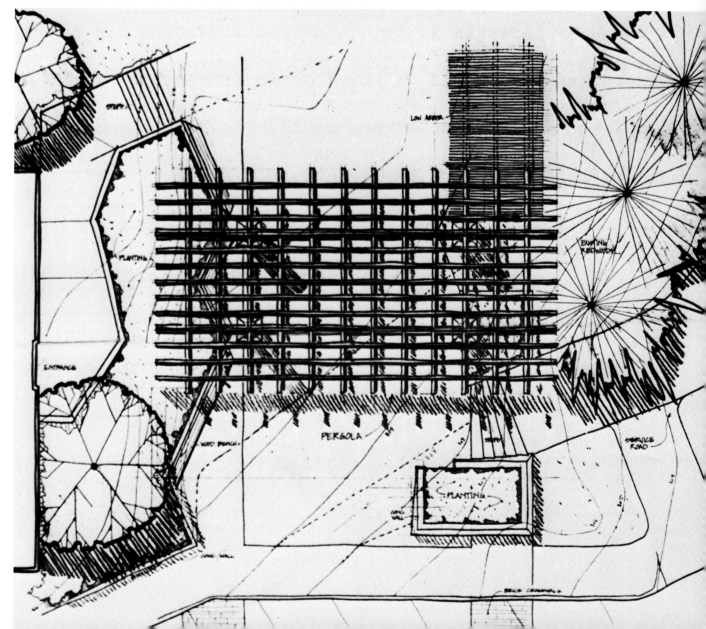

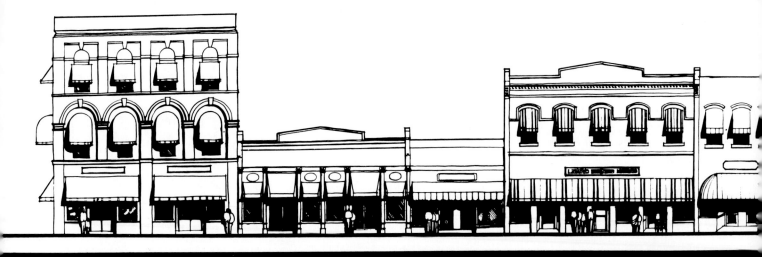

Photodrawings

Concepts in facade renovation are easily expressed in frontal views. But if the project covers several blocks in a small urban area, you might turn to photography for assistance. These elevations were drawn to the correct scale and configuration by tracing over individual photos taken of each building. The detail was very apparent and extremely accurate. Presentation drawings were made from these photographs by a simple overlay technique. The scale of the original photodrawings is kept large so that the scale is sufficient to record all detailed notes.

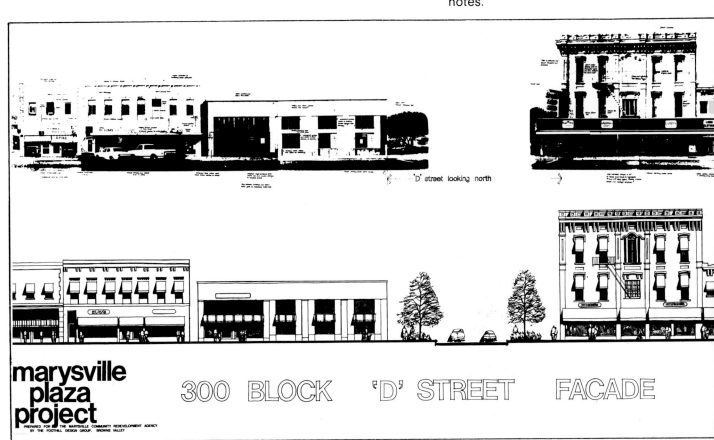

'D' street looking north

marysville plaza project
PREPARED FOR THE MARYSVILLE COMMUNITY REDEVELOPMENT AGENCY
BY THE FOOTHILL DESIGN GROUP. BROWNS VALLEY

300 BLOCK 'D' STREET FACADE

remove stucco and
restore brick facade

remove sign support

retain windows and expose window cornices

remove stucco &
restore brick

remove vent

open
original
windows

Paint out drainwater
pipes if still functioning

Remove stucco and return
to original facade

Remove
beer signs &
other graphics

IDEAL BAKERY

remove
tile

restore steel columns
and continue down to sidewalk.

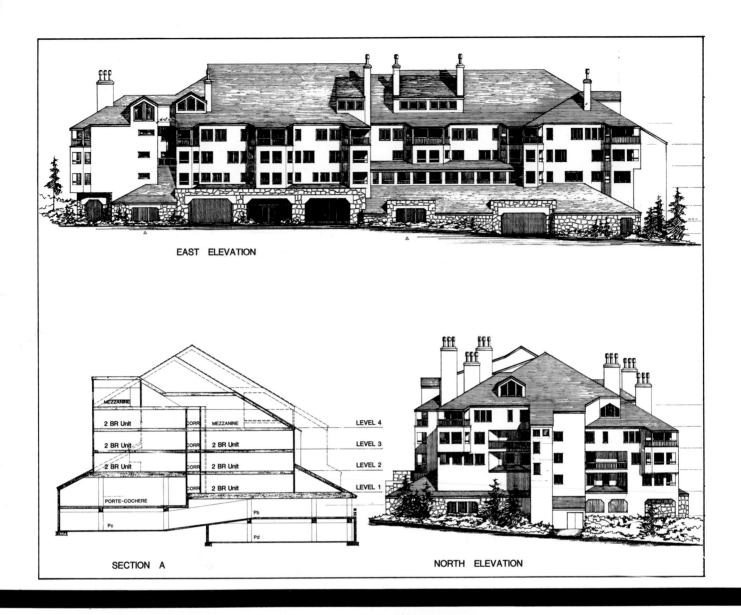

EAST ELEVATION

MEZZANINE

2 BR Unit | CORR | MEZZANINE | LEVEL 4

2 BR Unit | CORR | 2 BR Unit | LEVEL 3

2 BR Unit | CORR | 2 BR Unit | LEVEL 2

CORR | 2 BR Unit | LEVEL 1

PORTE-COCHERE

Pb

Pc

Pd

SECTION A

NORTH ELEVATION

Schematics

The schematic drawing is a stage between the design and production drawing. It is usually the final design study and often is used for presenting the final scheme to the client. Therefore, shades, shadows, and textures are very important elements.

Sometimes perspective renderings or axonometric drawings are done at this stage to supplement the two dimensional views. The elevation on the lower right was drawn first by the computer and the tones and shadings were added later by a draftsman.

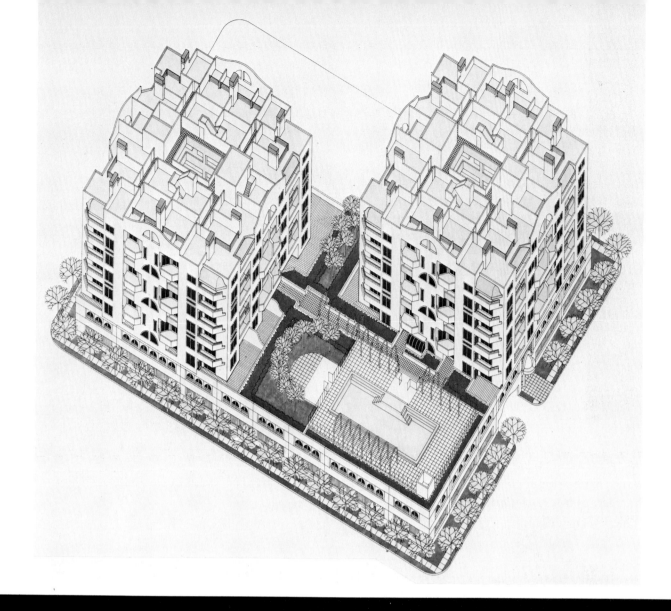

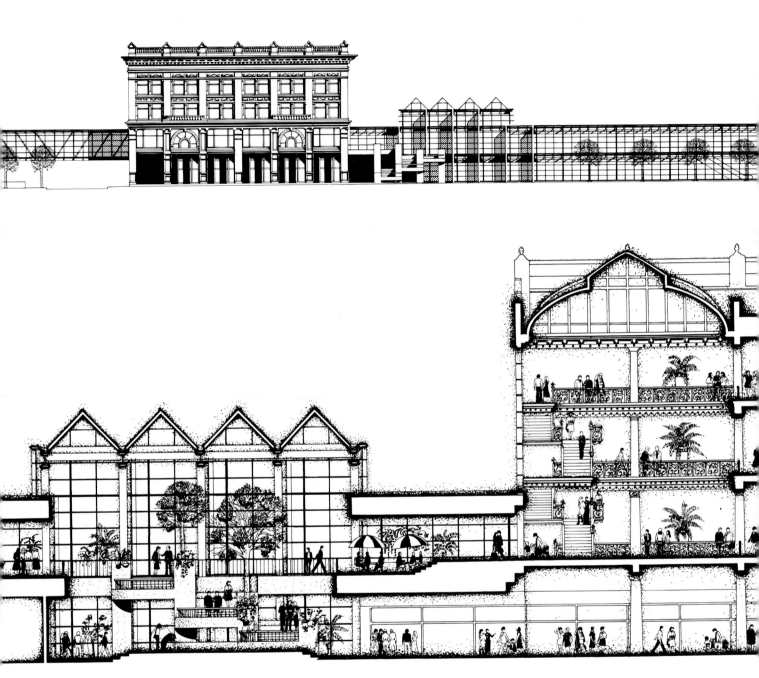

Rendered Sections

A combination of section and perspective can show many elements of a project that are not possible by any other means. It can show the relationship between inside and outside and show areas and shapes that would otherwise be hidden. The simple sketch technique is useful where vignet-ting and can help to focus attention to the main space. In large, complex, multi-storied structures the sectional perspective is particulary helpful in showing the space relationships from floor-to-floor. The extent of detail is optional, but the more active and alive the space looks, the more appeal it will have.

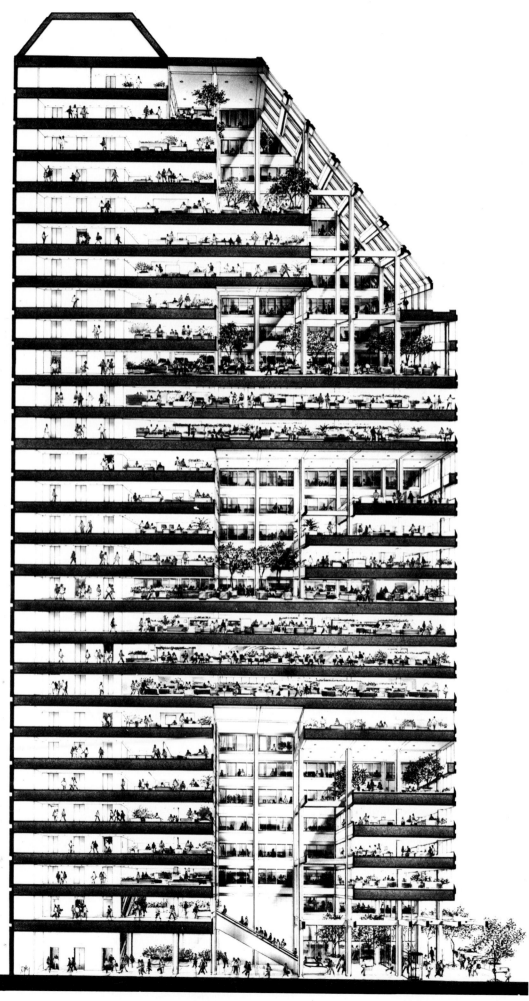

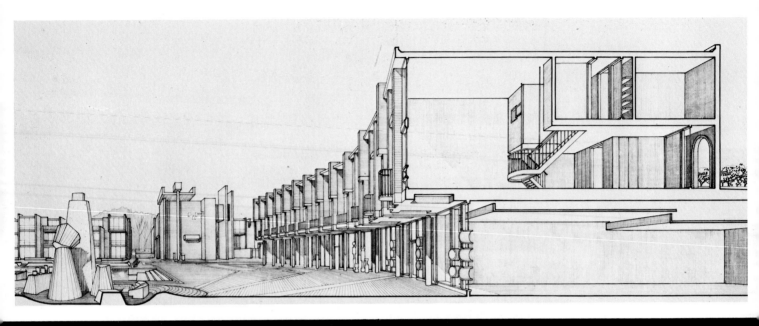

Sectional Perspectives

Sectional perspectives are often drawn in a two-dimensional or one-point format. This makes it a combination orthographic and perspective drawing. The section area of the building is a scaled plane where dimensions can be easily established. The drawing can then be completed either by completing the planes behind the section, as in the case above, or in extending from the plane in both directions, as in the case below.

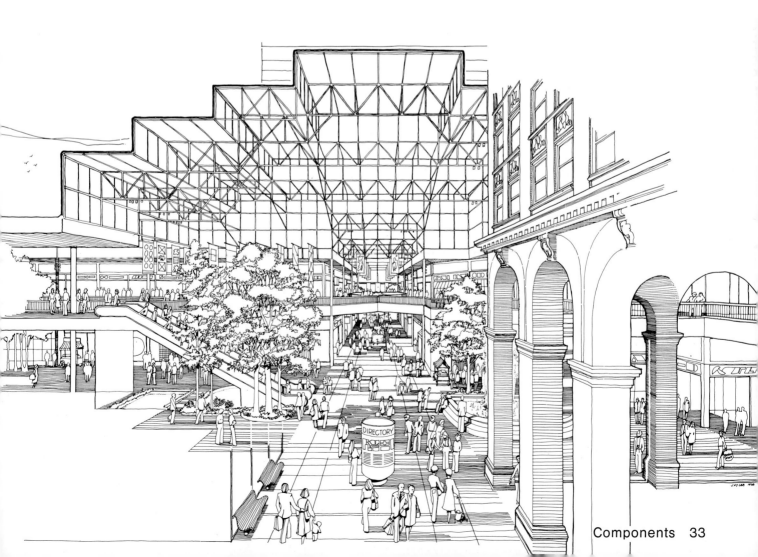

Components 33

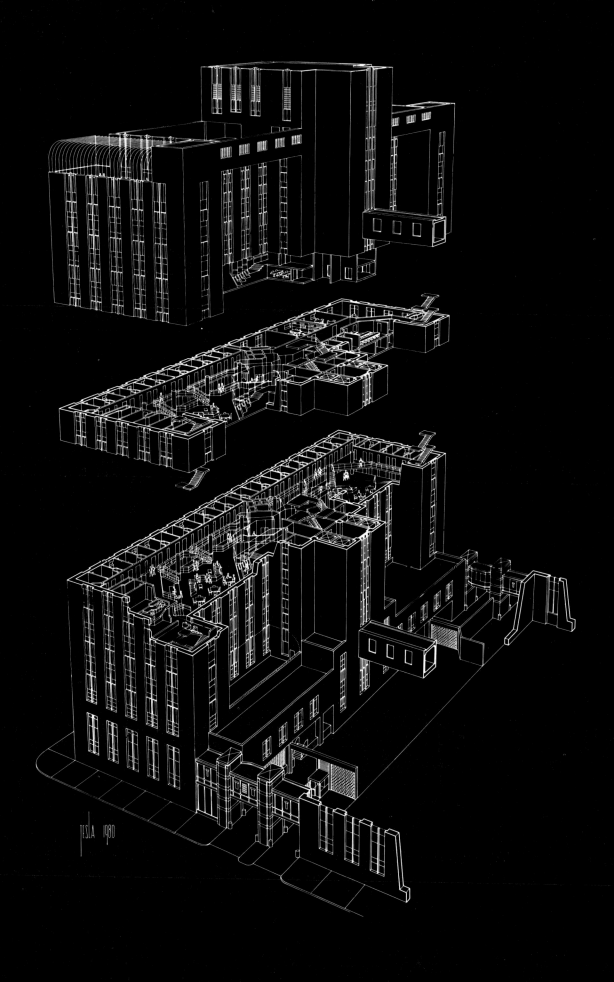

3-Point Sectional Perspectives

Sectional perspectives are seen throughout this book and are normally one-point perspectives. What makes these unique is that they involve three vanishing points. The third vanishing point overcomes some of the optical illusions that are inherent in some orthographic projections. For example, any structure below eye level tends to look bigger at the base if drawn without the third point. The perspective artist Tesla uses the third vanishing point on most of his major work.

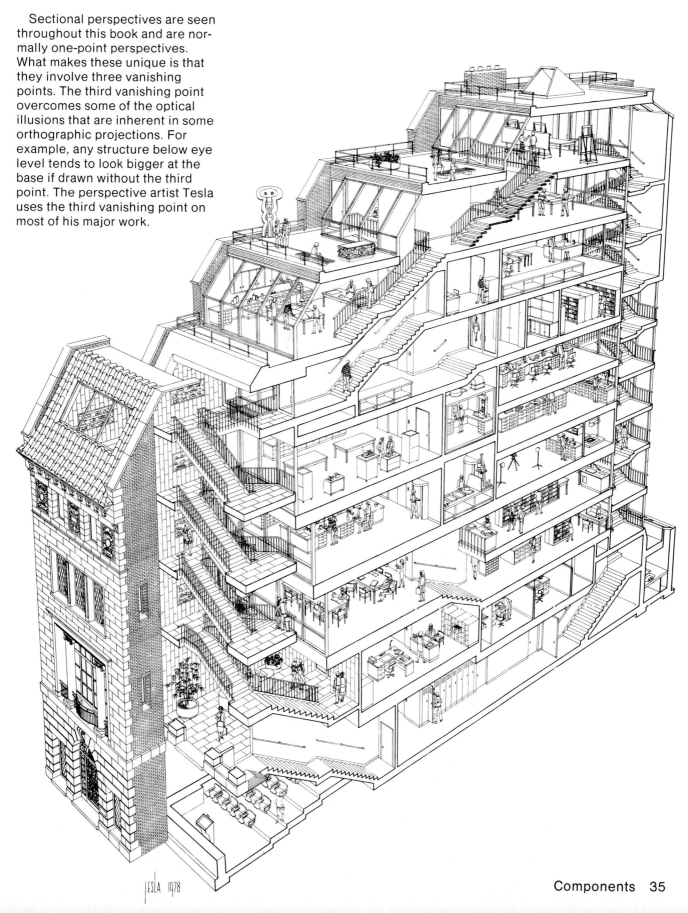

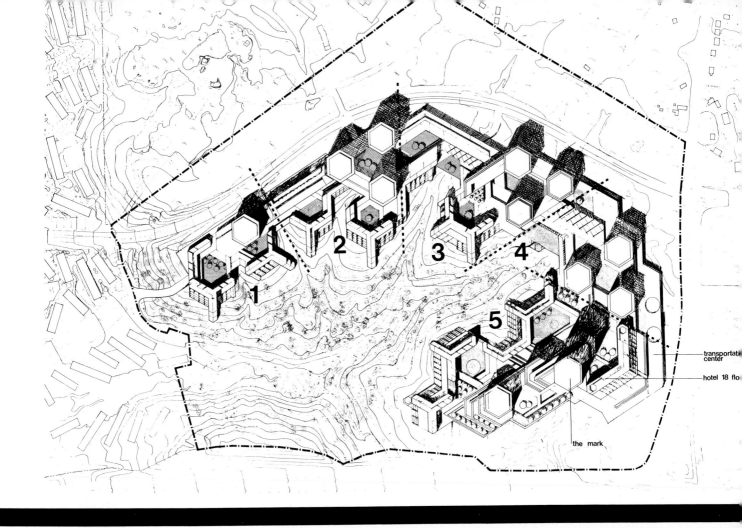

transportati
center

hotel 18 flo

the mark

Staging Models

The staging of development of a project can be shown by many methods, including the one illustrated here using simple mass models. If the model is constructed in units, it can be photographed as it is being assembled. Finally, the mass model can be photographed in its fully developed stage. These pictures are usually taken from a fixed camera position. Once completed, the model can be photographed from any number of oblique views.

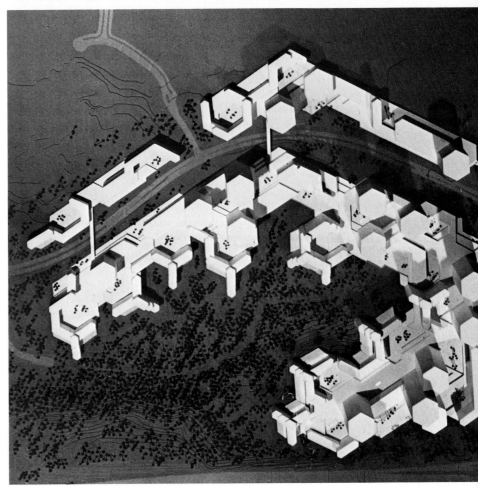

Photo Composites

The combination of photographs and drawings can add a new dimension of realism for presentation drawings. In this sequence (left) the aerial photo shows the surrounding urban setting. By placing black line prints of the building on the projected site, the project could be studied and presented to others in a more realistic manner.

If the same concept is carried into three dimensions, many more options are available. For example, if a model of the project is placed on an aerial photo-map of the site, it can be photographed in plan view and also in oblique views. Obviously the scale of the flat photo does not match the three-dimensional model. However, the photo has a somewhat dimensional aspect to it by virtue of the cast shadows. It will give a sense of realism much greater than placing a model on a flat un-scaled background.

The model can then be photographed from many different angles and it will always have the correct relationship to its surroundings.

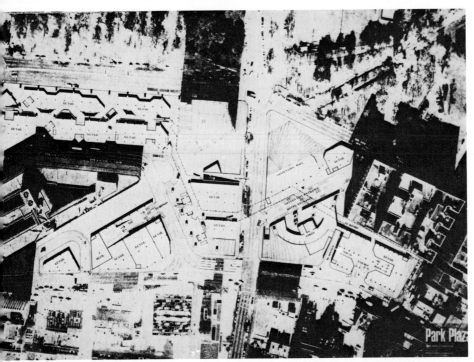

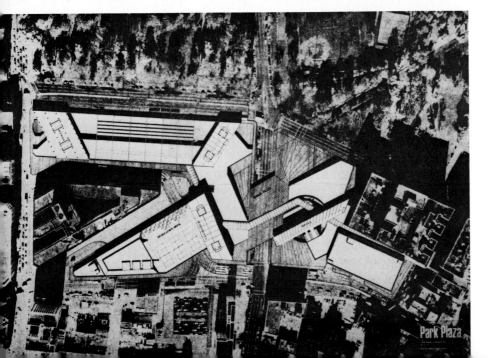

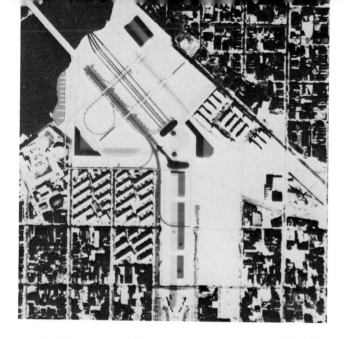

Airbrush Rendering

The most realistic drawing in appearance is the fully rendered airbrush drawing. Tones can be applied in layers and they can be varied in intensity. Though somewhat more involved than the drawn or painted picture, the results are worth the expended effort. For example, one single element in the drawing can be emphasized, leaving the surroundings in single line.

Photo Superimpositions

Full scale realism is usually appropriate for projects planned in urban settings. Here the actual relationships between site and building and neighboring structures is of prime importance.

One technique for achieving a high sense of realism and accuracy of scale, is to use photographs superimposed over actual sites. The photos can either be of colored renderings or of architectural models. Whichever method is used, it must be prepared with the same vantage point and perspective angles as the original photo.

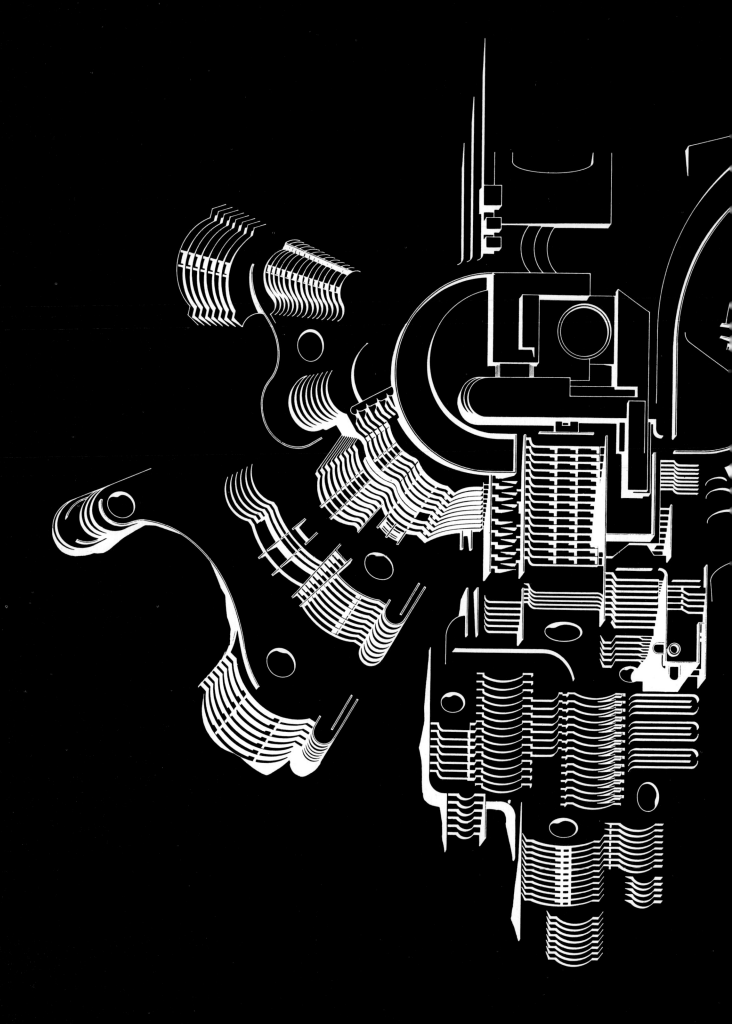

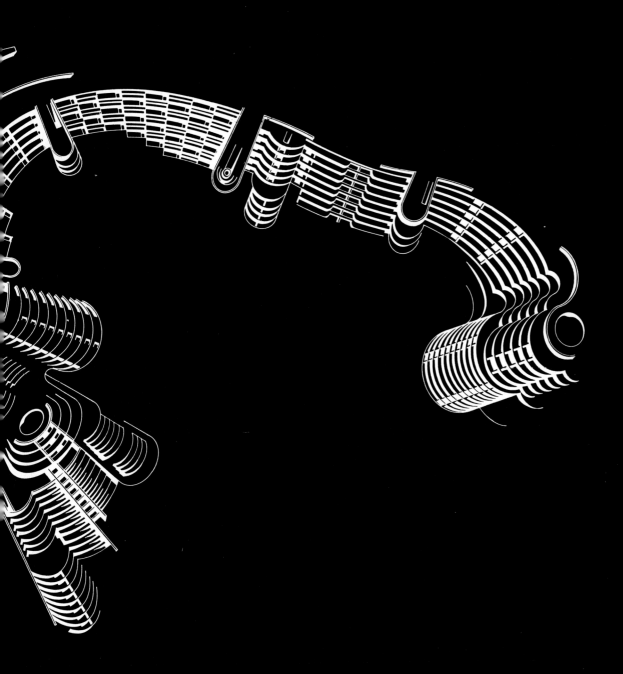

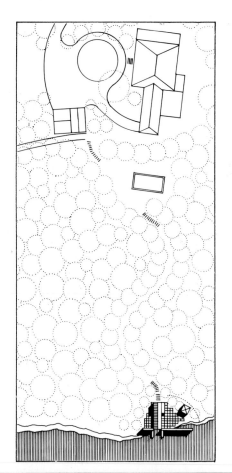

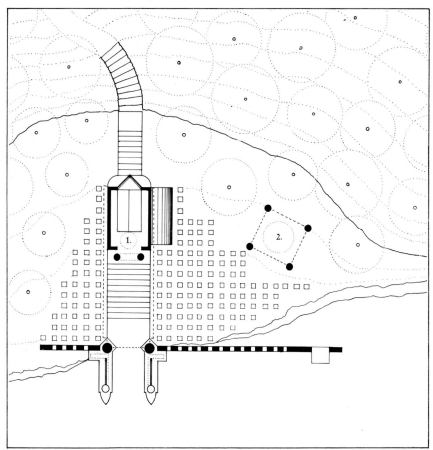

Mausoleum

The combination of orthographics and axonometrics clearly describe this mausoleum and its relationship to its pristine site. The use of highly stylized rendering techniques adds further to the crispness of the structure by its contrast. Surrounding foliage is outlined with a lightweight stipple technique. The conical shape of the foliage is an interesting counterpoint to the angularity of the structure itself, depicted with a crisp linear quality. The reflections in the water, also delineated by a dot technique, further soften the surroundings.

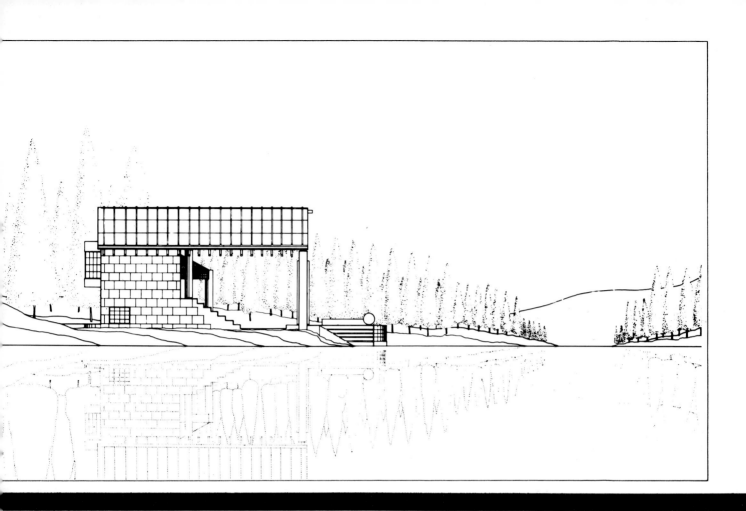

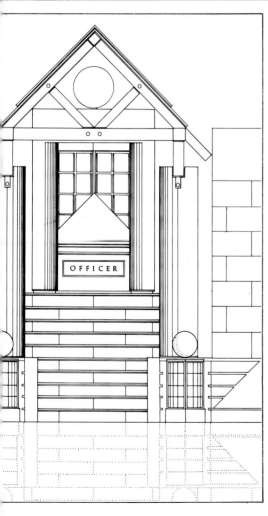

OFFICER

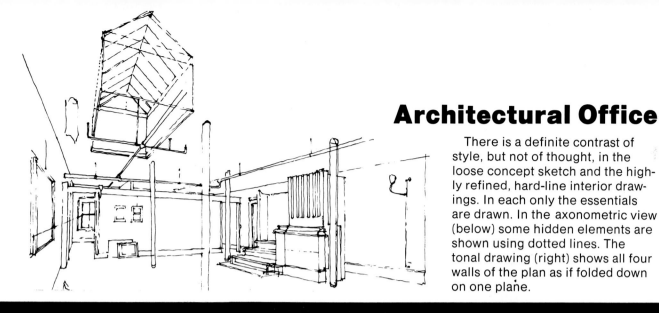

Architectural Office

There is a definite contrast of style, but not of thought, in the loose concept sketch and the highly refined, hard-line interior drawings. In each only the essentials are drawn. In the axonometric view (below) some hidden elements are shown using dotted lines. The tonal drawing (right) shows all four walls of the plan as if folded down on one plane.

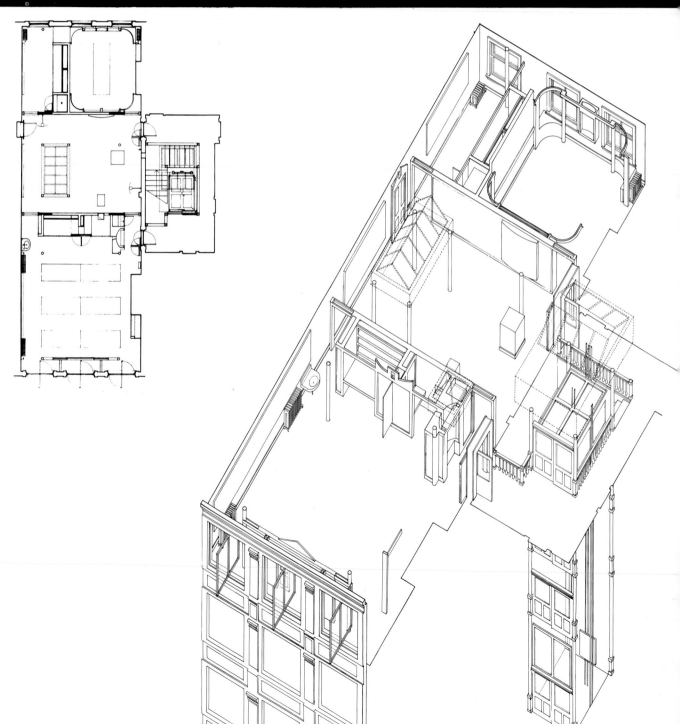

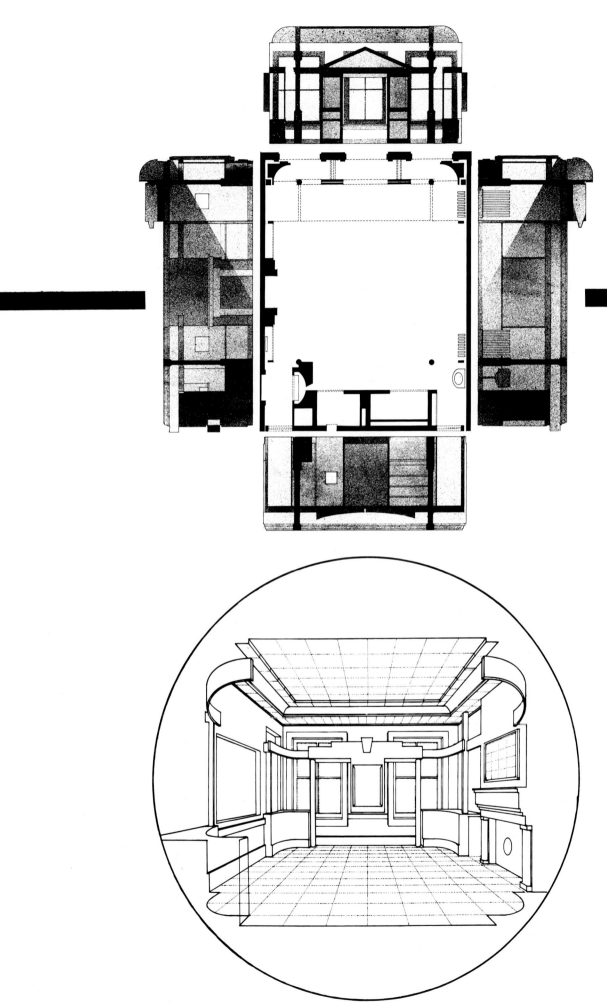

Bulova Watch Factory

A rendered sectional perspective is a very effective way of showing the inner workings of a building. This is particularly true when the interior is a large atrium-covered courtyard. The drawing is then more of an exterior view than an interior one.

Steve Oles has skillfully rendered the play of light filtering into the courtyard and into the sturcture. By placing the drawing in a totally darkened base, he has heightened the effect of the play of light and shade within the building.

Expedition House

These drawings depict an expedition house for an ongoing research project near the Karnak temple complex in Egypt. The structures will be built using the local mud-brick techniques. The drawings depict this style through the use of cross-sections through the buildings. The exterior ground level view depicts the brilliant sun through the use of shading, and the aerial view describes the open courtyards.

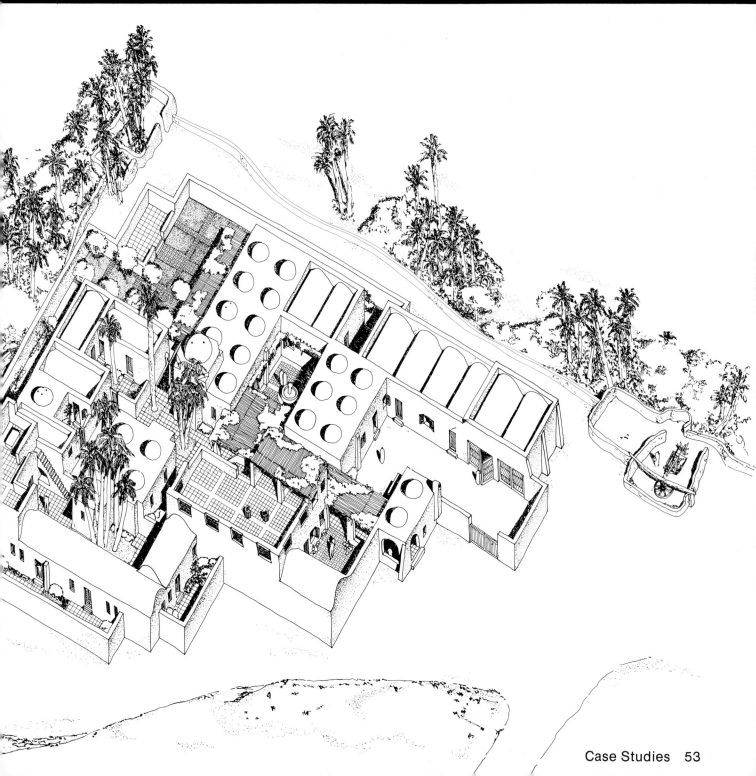

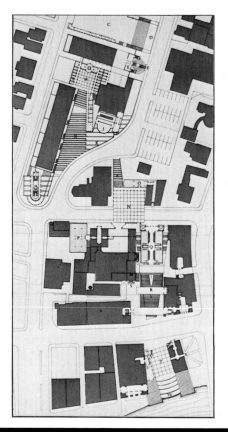

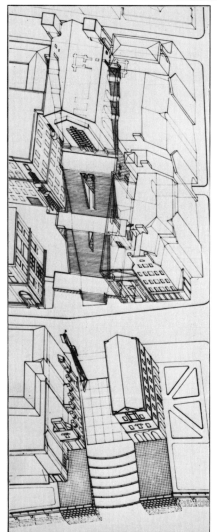

"The Steps of Providence"

The power of simple line drawing is evident in this project. The purpose was to illustrate the urban space created by linking parts of the Rhode Island School of Design campus. The site was a steep slope in the oldest part of the city. The "steps" would tie the buildings together from the bottom of the hill at the river to the top of the slope, where the last RISD building is located.

Because RISD is an art and architecture school, the spaces were purposefully "exemplary." The drawings demonstate a clean clear architectural style.

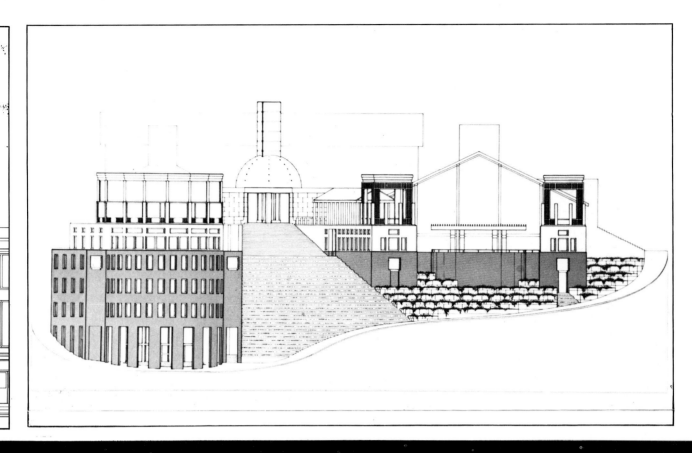

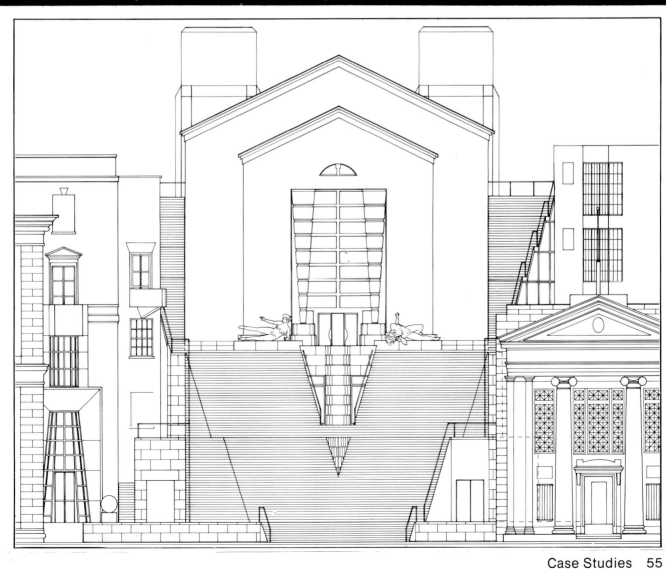

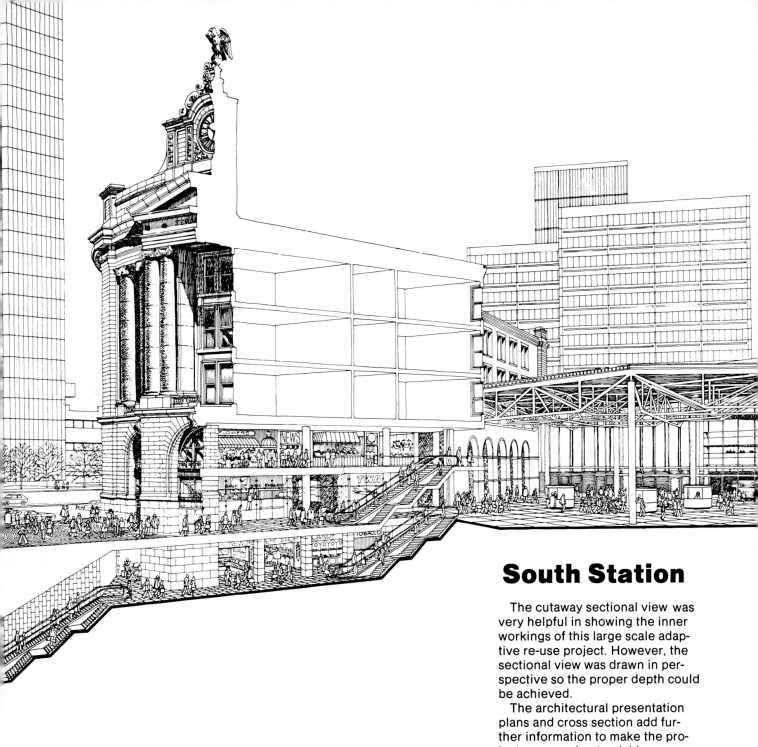

South Station

The cutaway sectional view was very helpful in showing the inner workings of this large scale adaptive re-use project. However, the sectional view was drawn in perspective so the proper depth could be achieved.

The architectural presentation plans and cross section add further information to make the project more understandable.

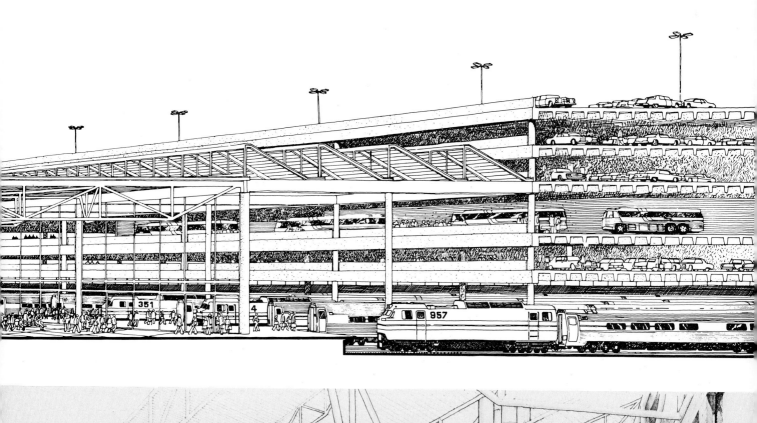

Country Club

This seemingly contemporary design is actually more than two decades old.

The medium is lead pencil on tracing paper. The pencil was used in a variety of ways to establish a wide range of tonal qualities. First, the elements were plotted and drawn in hard-line outline, then areas were toned in, using softer pencils. The sky was rendered with powdered pencil shavings, applied with cotton balls. Tones in the cloud area were removed using a soft eraser.

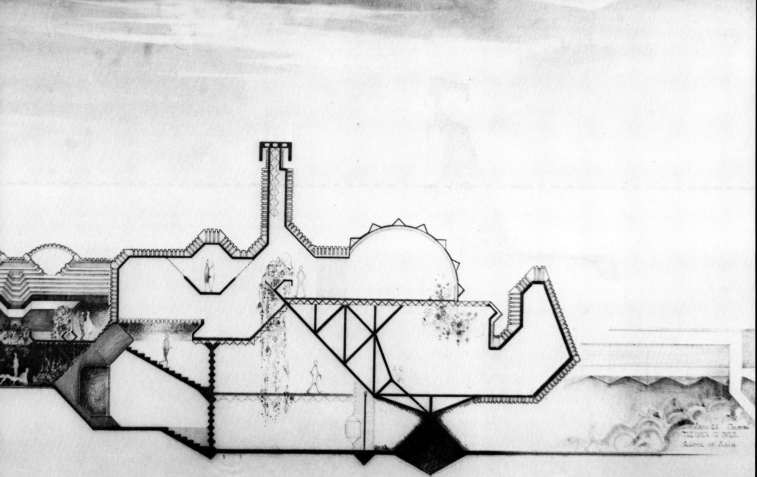

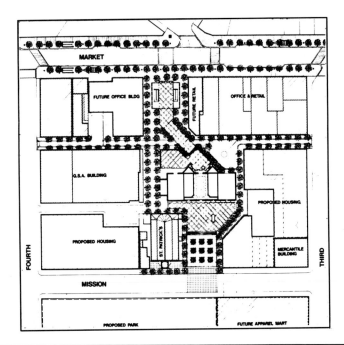

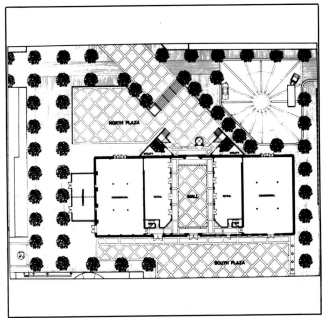

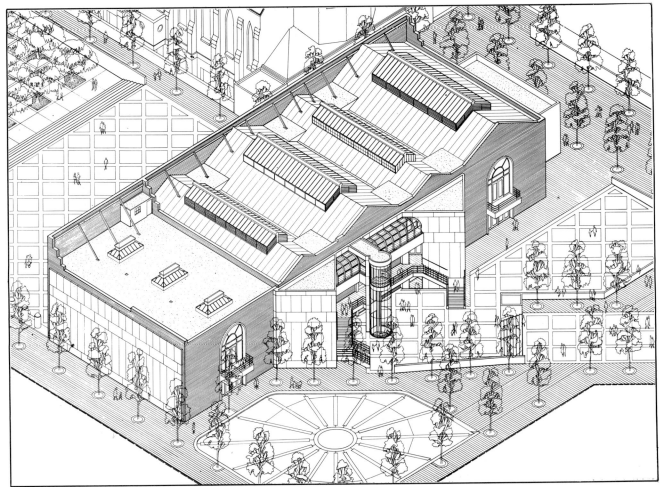

Substation

These drawings were part of a report and presentation on a renovation of a utility company's building, designed originally by architect Willis Polk. The series consisted of a location map, which placed the site within the city, an important public use consideration. The site plan showed relationship to the landscaping and the new paving patterns of the public space. The section through the structure showed the scale and the axonometric drawing showed the completed building on the newly developed site. The interior space was shown in a circular format and featured a viewpoint showing the intricate roof structure.

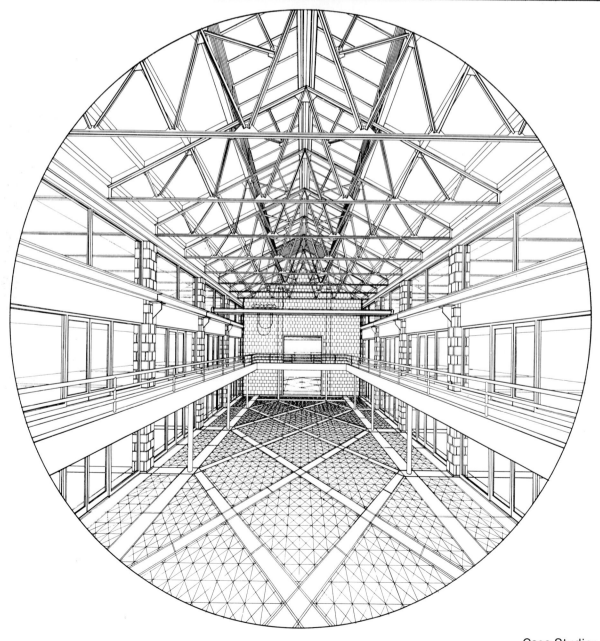

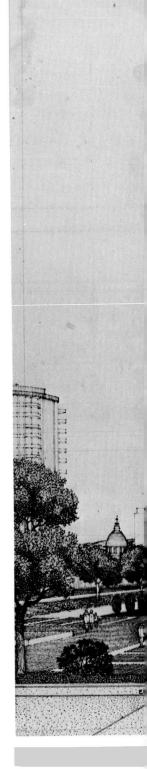

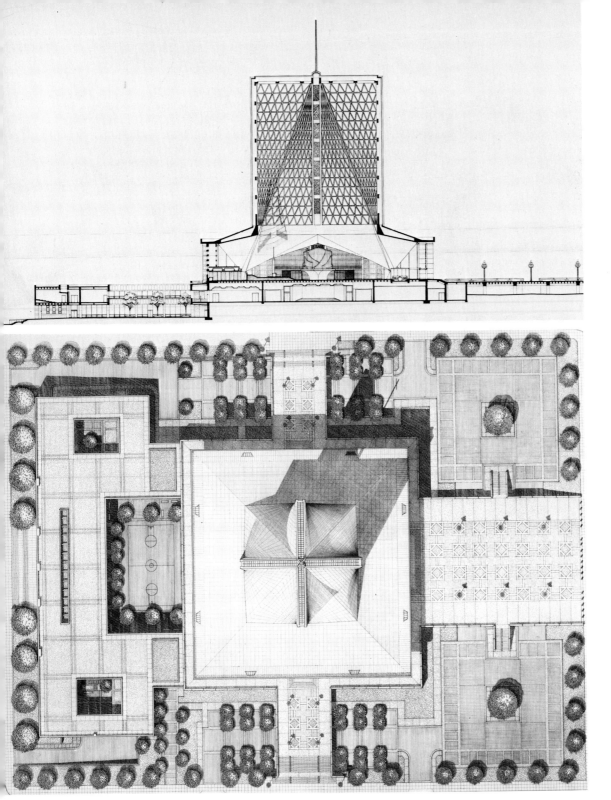

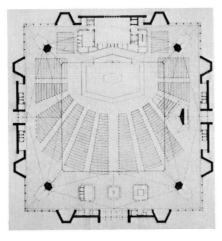

St. Mary's

Rendered and landscaped site plans are very good for giving the sense of order in a plan. When you combine a cross section and detail of the plan, as was done here, coordination is much easier to achieve. They should be done to the same scale so that the relationships are immediately apparent. The exterior perspective view, taken from the edge of the site, adds the finishing touch.

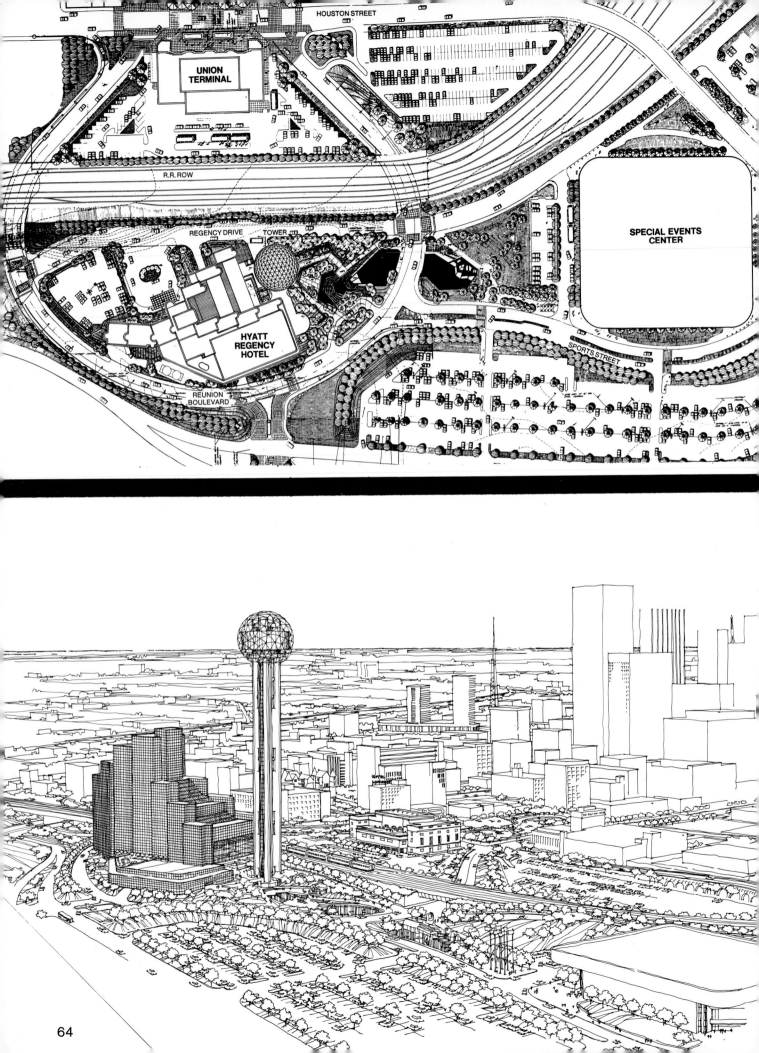

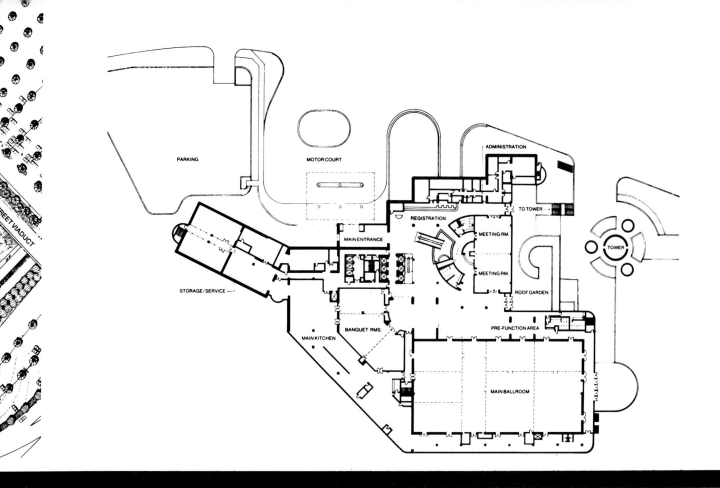

Hyatt Regency At Reunion

Any structure as prominant as this one must be shown in the early presentation stage in relation to its neighbors. Thus the elaboratly developed and rendered site plan provides the context, while the sketch of the project relates it to the fabric of the existing city skyline. The architectural drawings were done in a clean crisp ink-line style.

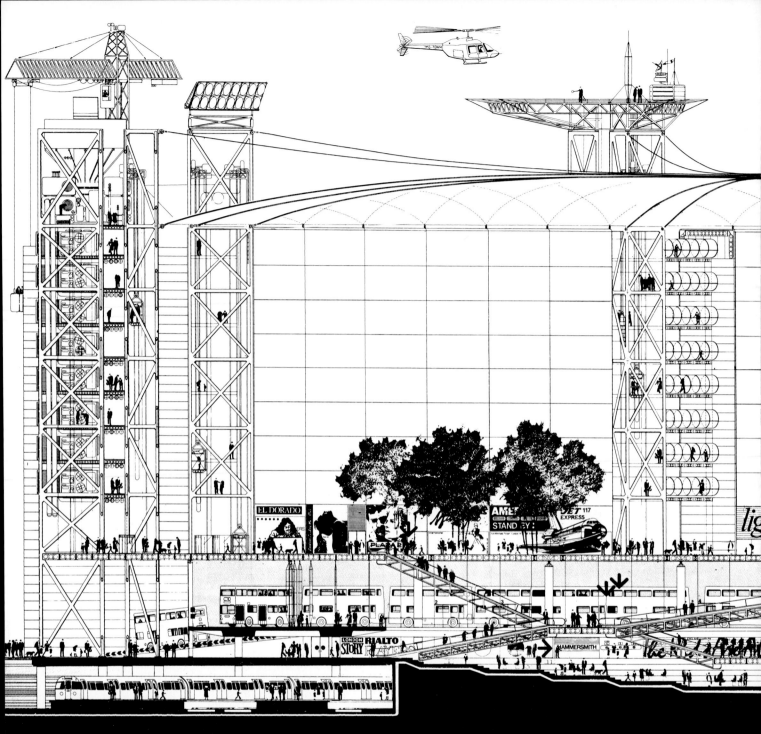

London Center

Large scale spaces are shown best by orthographic means. In this sectional perspective each point can be located orthographically without tedious perspective methods. This type of depiction usually simplifies the space and a great amount of detail can be added very easily.

Although this style of drawing can show many layers of activity at the base of the structure, it can become confusing if the planes overlap in the level of detail. Quick free-hand sketches are a good supplement to the exactness of the architectural drawing.

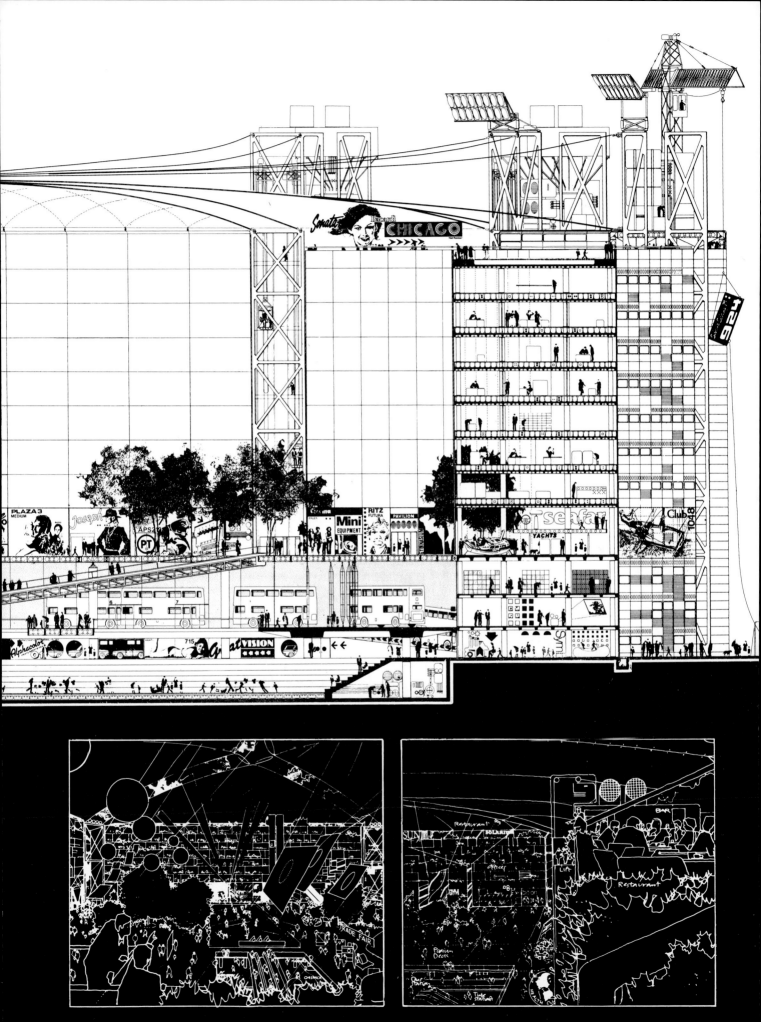

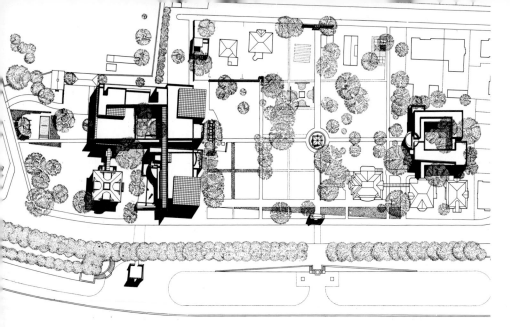

Museum For The Decorative Arts

The crisp delineated lines of the structure are contrasted sharply with the use of old engravings of trees. In the rendered site plan the more traditional method of representing trees was used, whereas the other drawings use the landscape forms as means of contrast. They are also used to help define planes and open spaces.

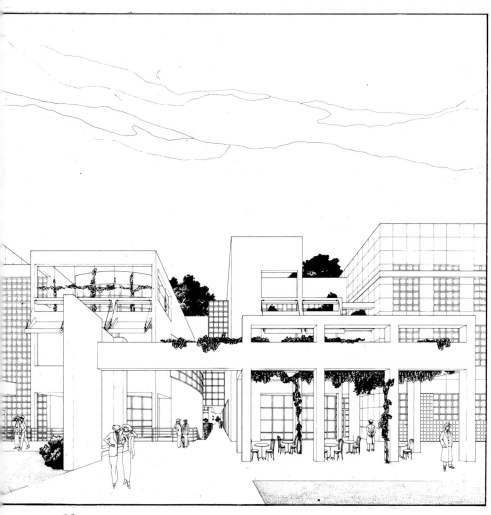

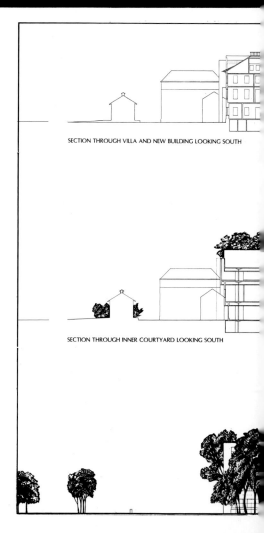

SECTION THROUGH VILLA AND NEW BUILDING LOOKING SOUTH

SECTION THROUGH INNER COURTYARD LOOKING SOUTH

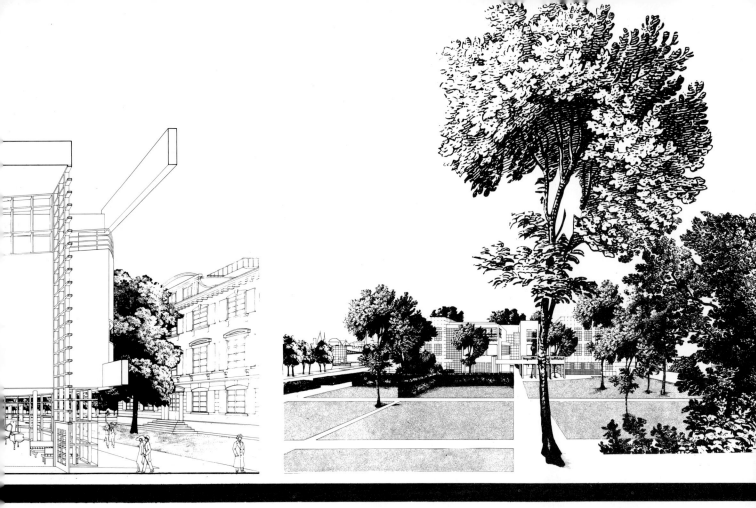

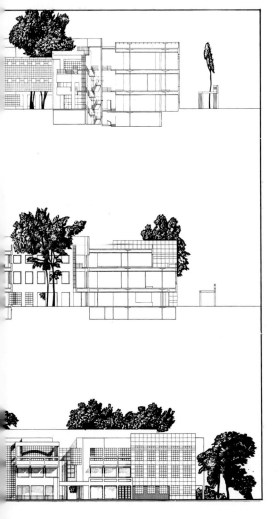

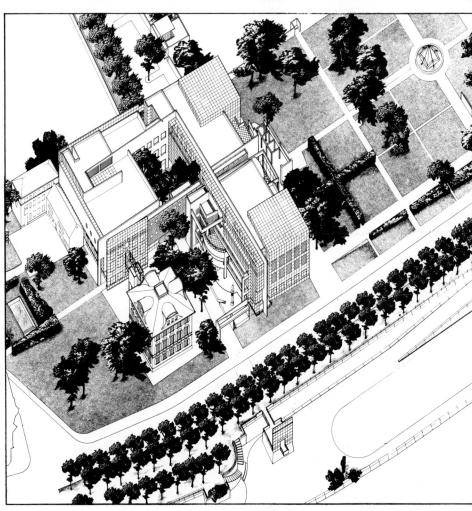

Radio City

This series of drawings was prepared to study the use of air rights over Radio City Music Hall for a new tower. The Music Hall had just received landmark status so regulations were severe and influenced the solution.

The proposal was made with cross sectional drawings and phantom-line axonometrics. The problem was to show the relationship of the proposed tower to the large structural grid necessary to span the Music Hall and leave its interior intact. The drawings also show an atrium space 22 floors high between the new structure and existing one. The plans feature the Music Hall and the garden level 14 floors above the street.

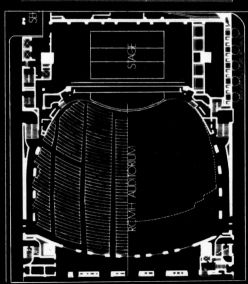

HOTEL

OFFICES

6th AVENUE

51st STREET

AMAX BLDG

RESTAURANT

RETAIL

ATRIUM

ROOFTOP GARDEN

APRIX

6th AVENUE

RESTAURANT

RETAIL

SHUTTLE LOBBY

50th STREET

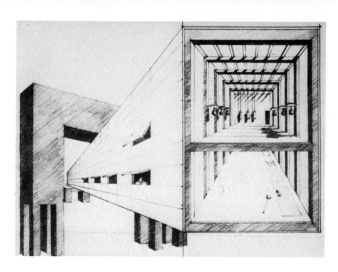

Gymnasium-Bridge

Strong design statements can often be explained best through plan and elevation drawings. With the addition of textured tones and shading, the shapes can be more clearly delineated.

By combining the plan view and the elevational view in close proximity, the design is more clearly defined. The flatness of the elevation view can be very helpful in simplifying the concept and the added tonal values can make it an interesting drawing.

Telescope House

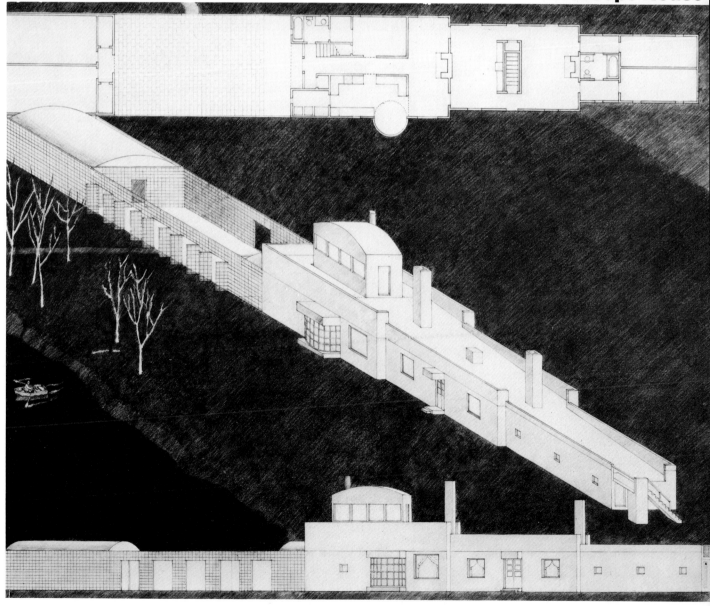

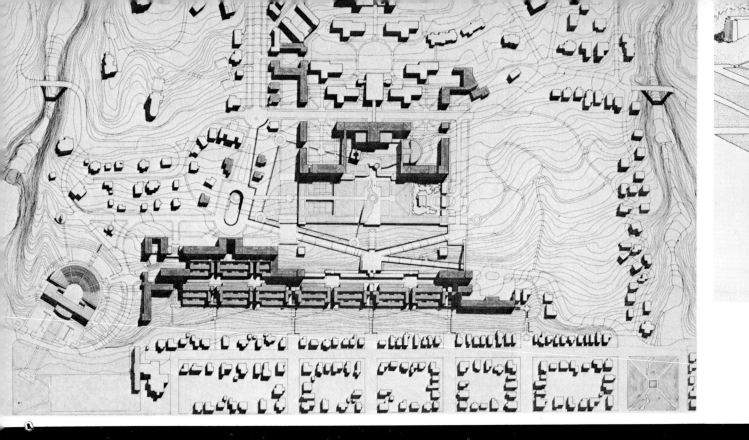

University Avenue

The overall aerial is the best means of showing large scale developments relating to an existing site. Oftentimes the single line approach is the best way to describe the concept of the project without distracting detail.

Here the foliage masses were treated in the same manner; as simple blocks of equal height. By doing this they became more of an integrated form with the proposed structures. The strong axial solution of the design is evident in all the viewpoints chosen for the drawings.

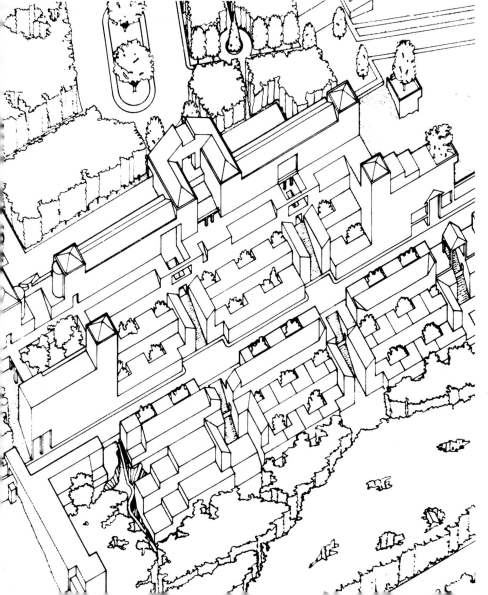

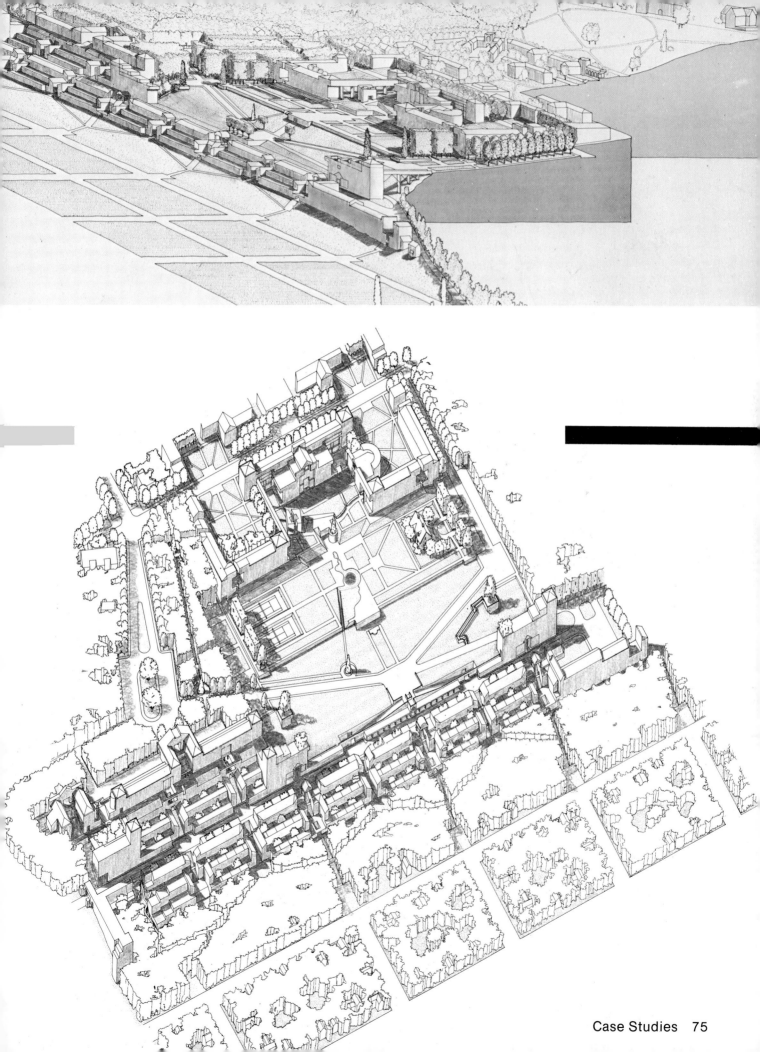

Makkah

Freehand sketches done over an accurately laid out perspective have a softening effect. In this series of drawings for the King Abdul Aziz University in Egypt, the effect of the brilliant sun and the architectural solution to it were clearly demonstrated. All the drawings contained extreme contrasts. The exteriors were bathed in light while the interiors showed light being screened. By using this sketch technique, there was detail even in the shaded areas of the drawings.

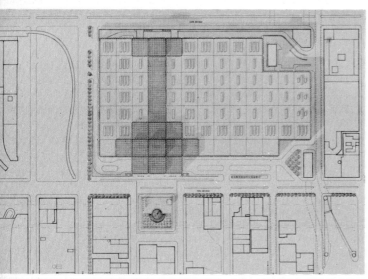

Convention Center

A large scale model was built for presentation and many photographs were taken, both exterior and interior views. But these drawings by Steve Oles give a sense of scale and activity on the level of the user.

The two exterior views show the identical scenes, one daytime and one nighttime. In each drawing the identical figures, cars, and trees are there. The building is reflective during the day and transparent at night.

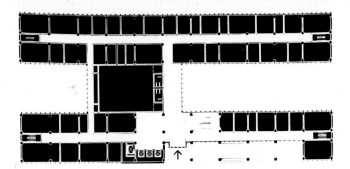

U S Embassy — Tokyo

A clean-cut graphic approach was taken in defining the plan and elevations of this structure. The floor structure was emphasized by using this technique. On the exterior elevation the drawing depicts the graphic pattern that the chosen architectural elements will make. This pattern is very visible in the exterior rendering which was done in tempera, whereas the other drawings were done with crisp ink-line.

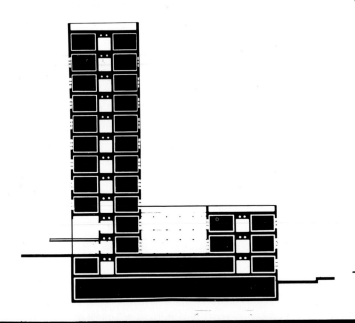

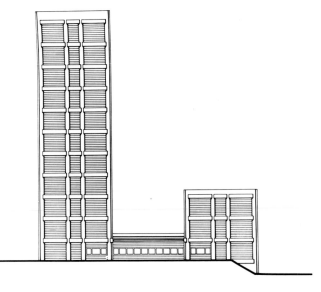

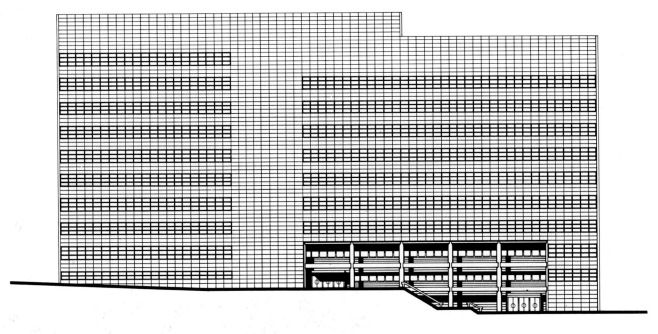

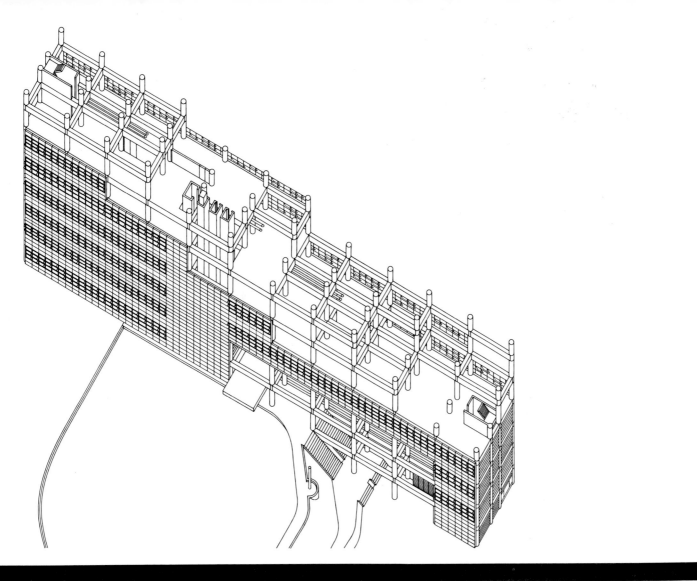

Courthouse Center

A number of elements were used to present an early scheme of this project, which has since been built. The tonal aerial rendering relates the project to some local landmarks.

Rough sketch sectional perspectives show the intricacy of the space in the seemingly long low building. One of the drawings used graphics quite creatively to indicate activities of people.

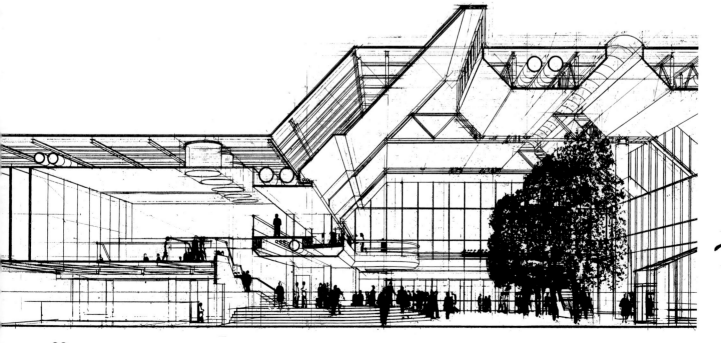

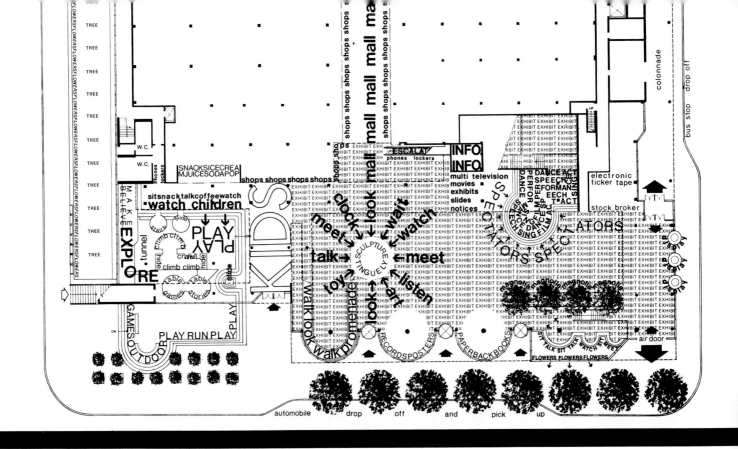

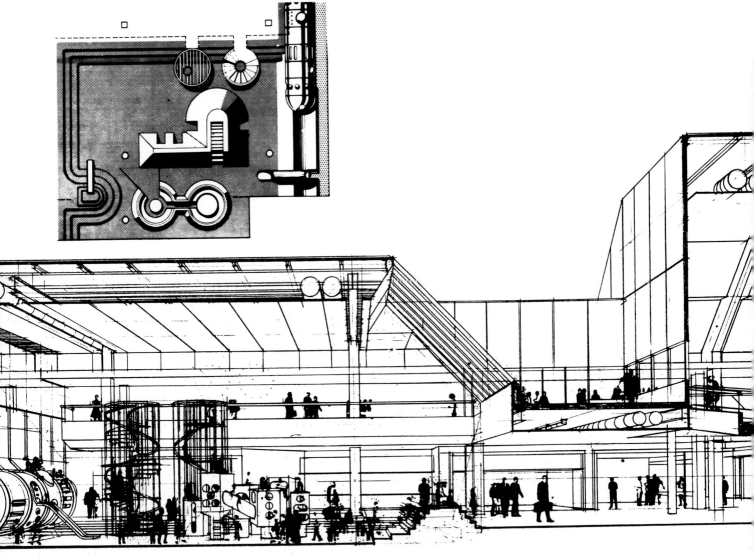

Kiva Lodge

The architectural persentation drawings, executed in pencil, were enhanced with the addition of an ink-line drawing of the interior of the lodge, which shows the multi-level space with retail shops.

The exterior overall depicts the structure in its mountain setting and gives a more exact scale to the large complex.

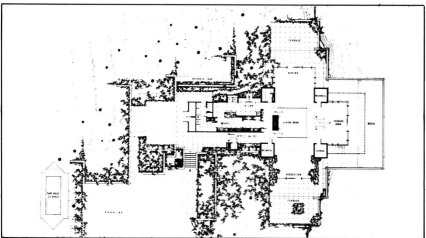

House In Central Arkansas

The architectural drawings are designed to explain the concept and spatial relationships of this residence. The sections are outlined in heavy tones, which delineate the space beyond.

The symmetry of the building is captured in the photograph from the lake, where the building is reflected in the water. Photographs of the interior show the angular height in the main living area.

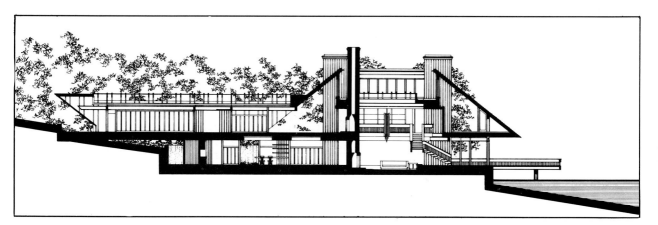

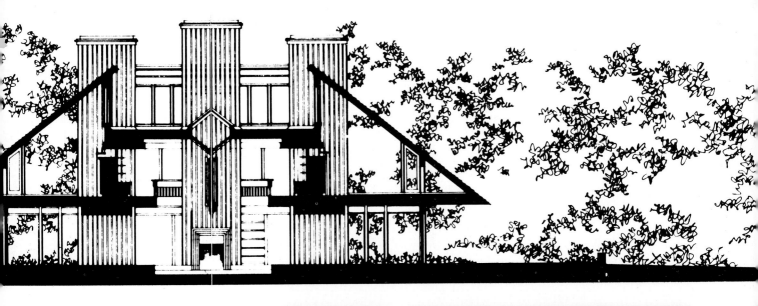

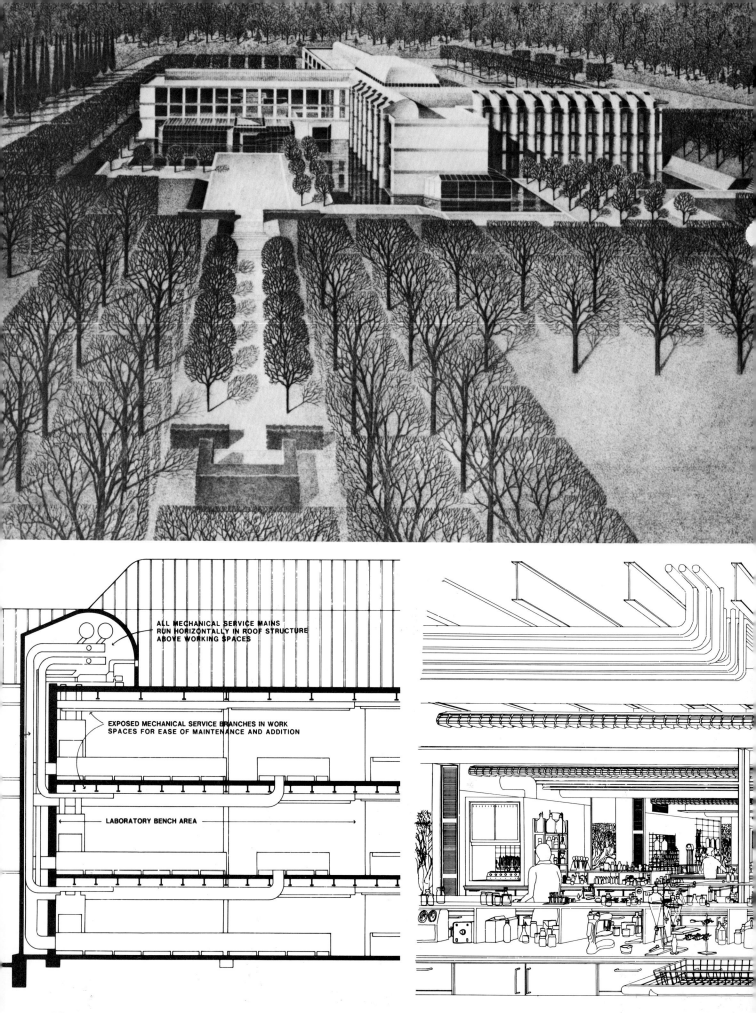

ALL MECHANICAL SERVICE MAINS
RUN HORIZONTALLY IN ROOF STRUCTURE
ABOVE WORKING SPACES

EXPOSED MECHANICAL SERVICE BRANCHES IN WORK
SPACES FOR EASE OF MAINTENANCE AND ADDITION

LABORATORY BENCH AREA

Standard Brands

This high-tech laboratory building was rendered in a very stylized manner. This applies to both the low-angle aerial view and the alternate view point from the interior. The axis of view in the aerial drawing is identical to that of the interior. From the executive conference rooms, which are housed in glass prisms, the views are framed by elegant ranges of trees and pathways.

The working spaces and the mechanical rooms are explained in a sectional diagram and in the interior sectional perspective. This perspective is a three-dimensional interpretation of the mechanical diagram.

The Centennial

Many visual elements are used to portray this large condominium structure near Vail, Colorado. The 7-story complex has the look of a grand resort hotel.

The sketches show a main entry drive (left) and a view of the pool area (far right). The interior space shows bridges crossing the lobby on upper levels. The plan and elevation are drawn in simple ink-line (below left) as well as the exterior view (below right).

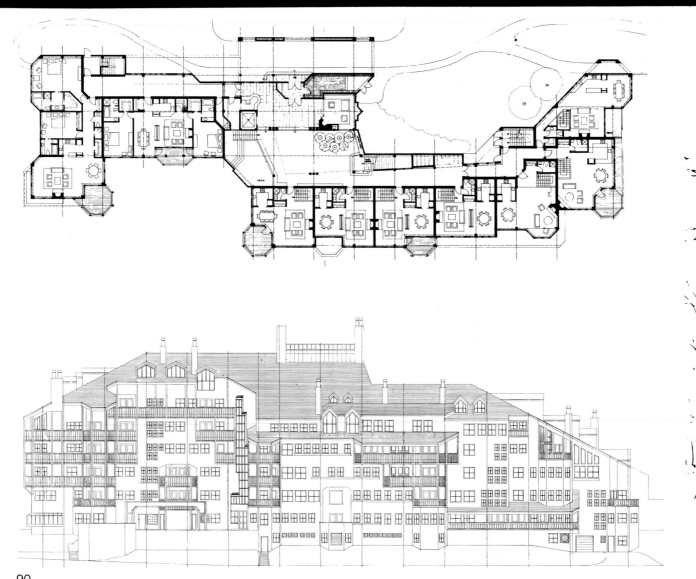

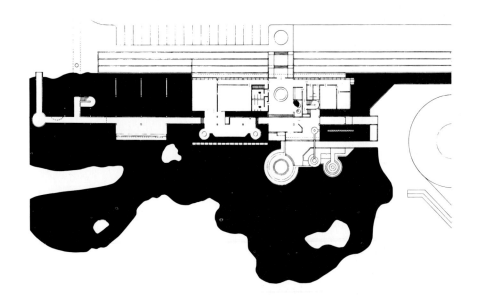

Water Reclamation Plant

This plant is located on an 88-acre site and contained a complete treatment facility and administration building. The client requested that a Japanese garden be incorporated into the remaining site and developed as a park and recreation area. The administration building is depicted in a graphic plan diagram and in rendered cross section, which explains the various levels of the visitors center.

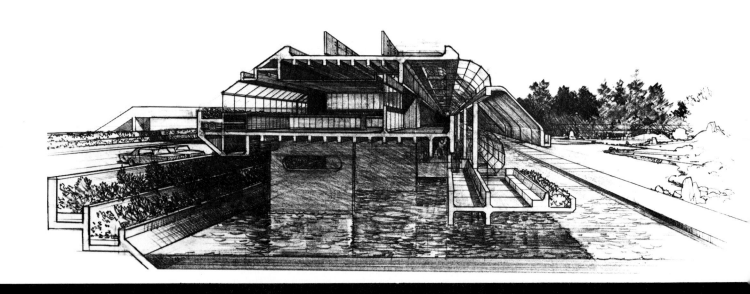

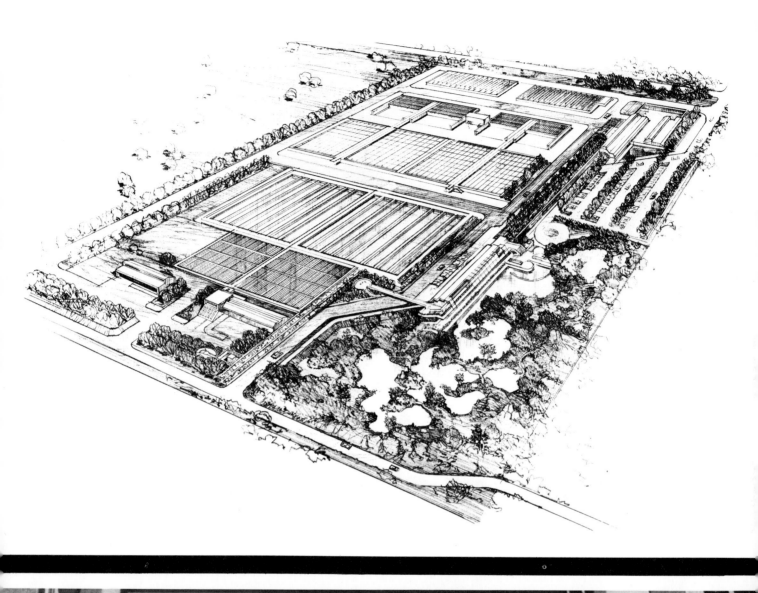

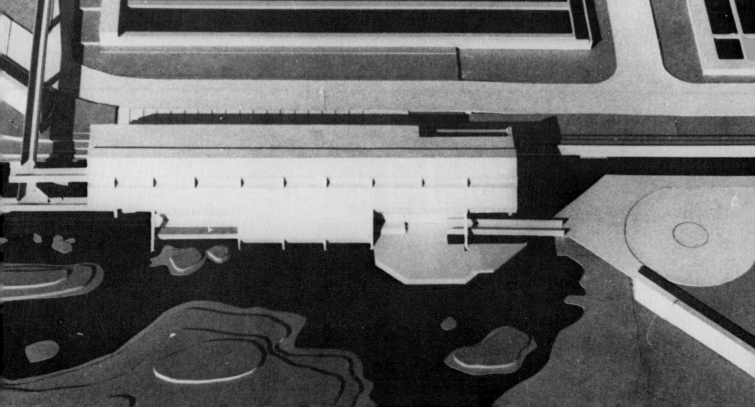

An urban project should be shown in its total context and the aerial view is best for this. Street level views are necessary to give detail and illustrate the environmental elements in the design. Interior views can show activity within the project. But the key drawing in this series and the most exciting is the nighttime view.

Playhouse Square

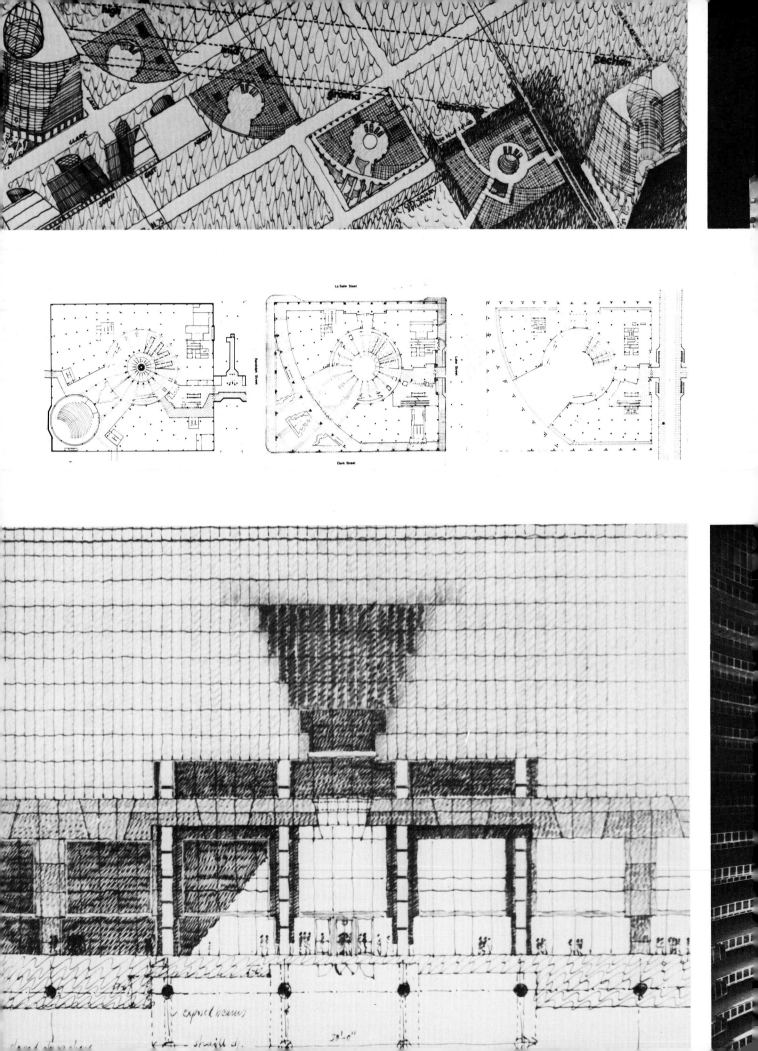

La Salle Street

Randolph Street

Lake Street

Clark Street

State Of Illinois Center

The early conceptual studies for this 17-story building in downtown Chicago show a concern for contextual and historic implications, as well as image and orientation of the building to its urban site. The rich facade and central atrium-covered with skylights calls for 18 varieties of glazing materials. The building is further depicted in model photographs, with an exterior and interior view of the atrium.

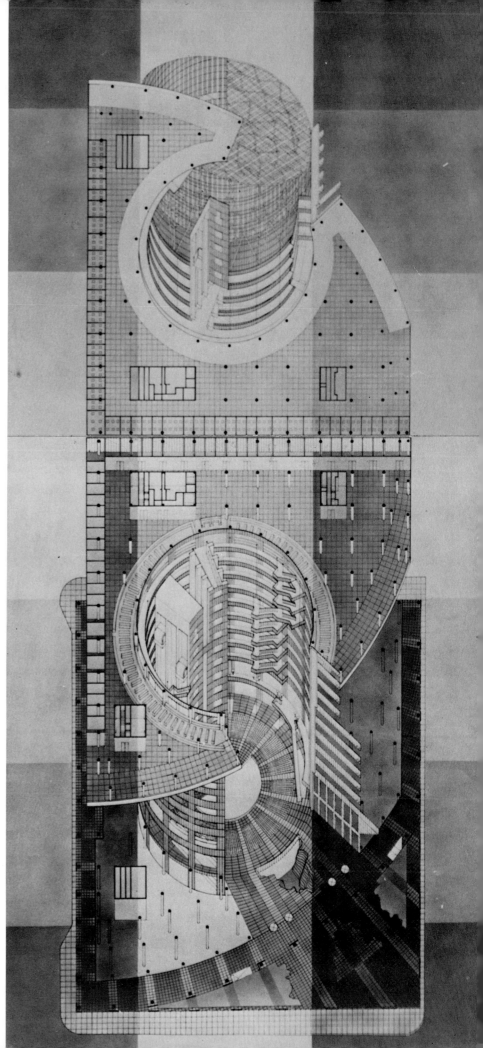

Michigan Plaza

An excellent example of the difference between models and renderings is seen in this project. The model photo, of course, lacks the full range of elements of entourage that are so easy to include in renderings. These include neighboring buildings far and near, detail in the street level activity, and more subtle modeling of the reflective glass surface. The model photo is on the left and the rendering, done from a similar angle, is on the far right.

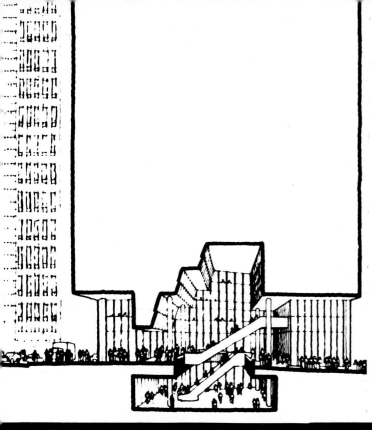

100 William Street

One of the original conceptual sketches on this project, in crowded downtown Manhattan, featured an interior of several stories. As the design progressed, models were built which featured this space. Scale figures were included in the models and the lighting was carefully controlled to provide the same drama that would be in the finished space.

Upon completion, a series of photos was taken using similar vantage points as those in the earlier design model. It is interesting to see how a design concept in rough sketch form can simulate the finished project.

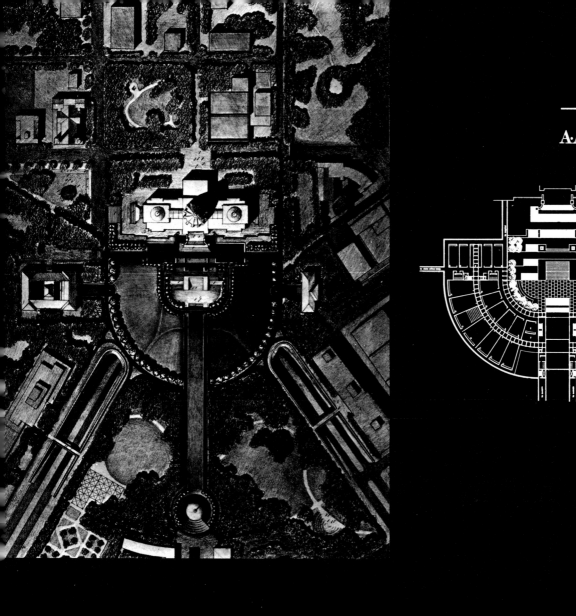

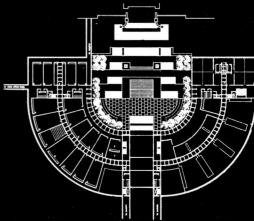

A·A

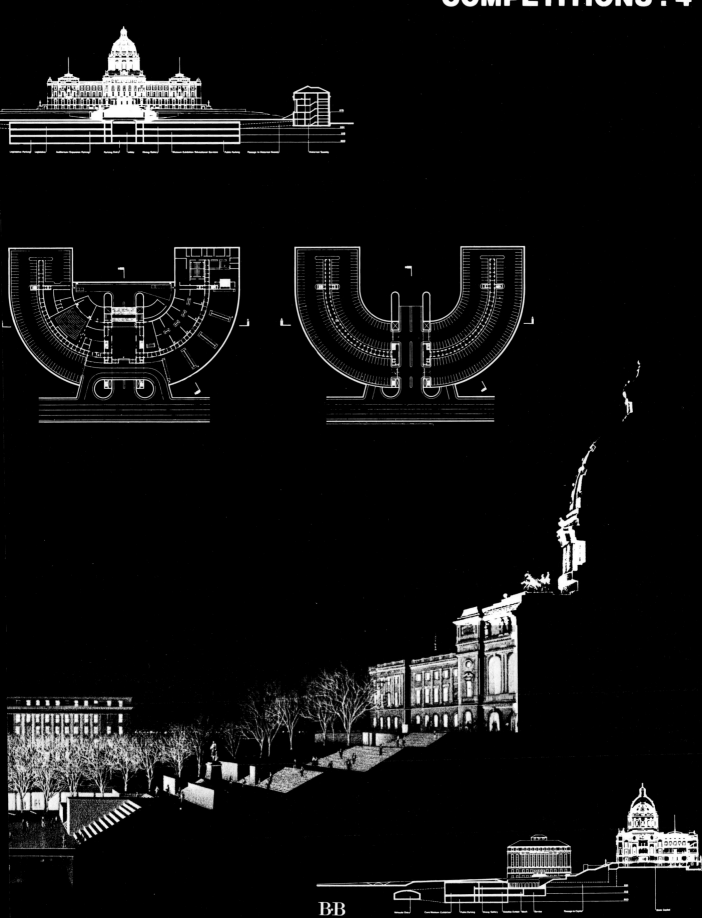

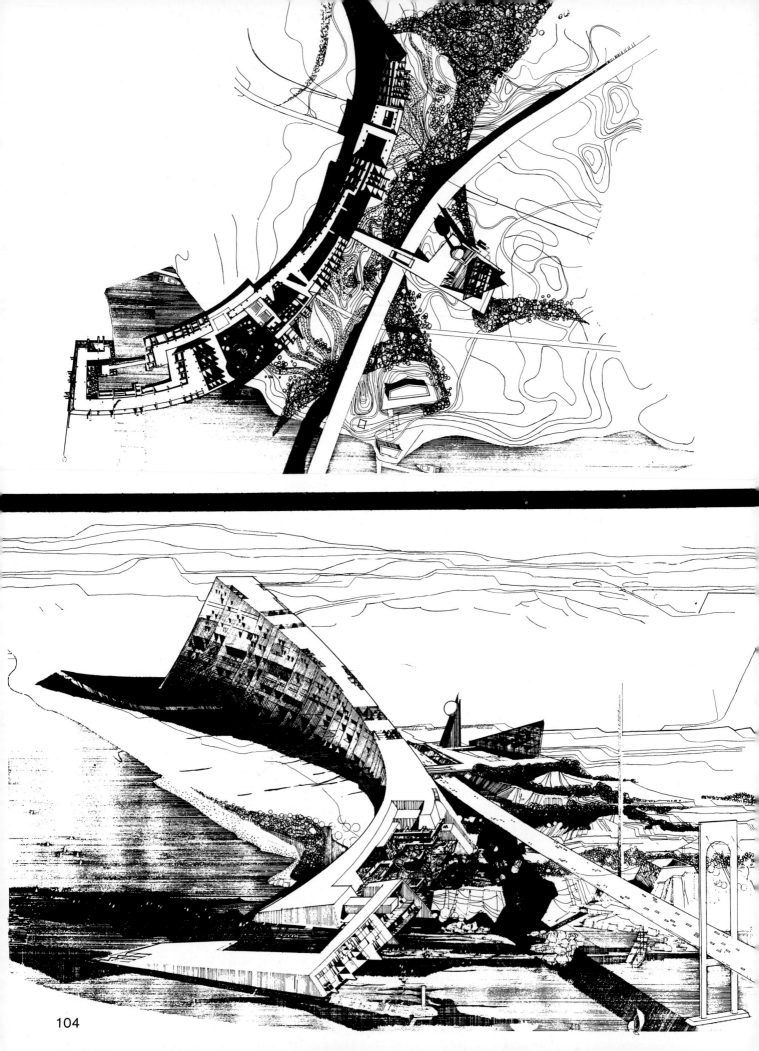

104

NIAE Competition

Of the various competitions that the National Institute of Architectural Education (NIAE) sponsor each year, the Paris Prize (Lloyd Warren Fellowship) is best known and the one that has drawn the widest response from students around the country. Having its roots in the beaux-arts tradition, its real influence is in the number of programs influencing architectural students. The most conspicuous of these ways is through the number and variety of design competitions it sponsors each year.

Subjects for these competitions run the gamut from regional planning problems to studies for the reuse of existing structures.

The competitions are based on designs and the methods of depicting them.

GALLERY

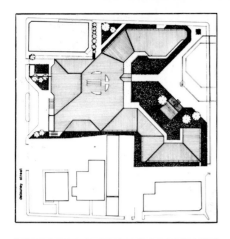

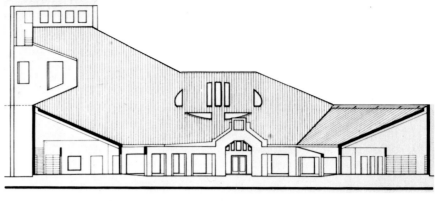

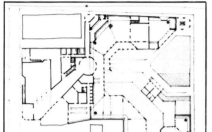

Biloxi Library

The old historic city of Biloxi, Mississippi decided in 1976 to erect a new library and cultural center. Six professionals teamed up with students for a design festival and competition.

The winning scheme presents a walled garden, opening up from the street and across from City Hall. The simple ink-line technique gives a light and airy feeling to the interiors. A phantom view, isometric drawing further explains the structure.

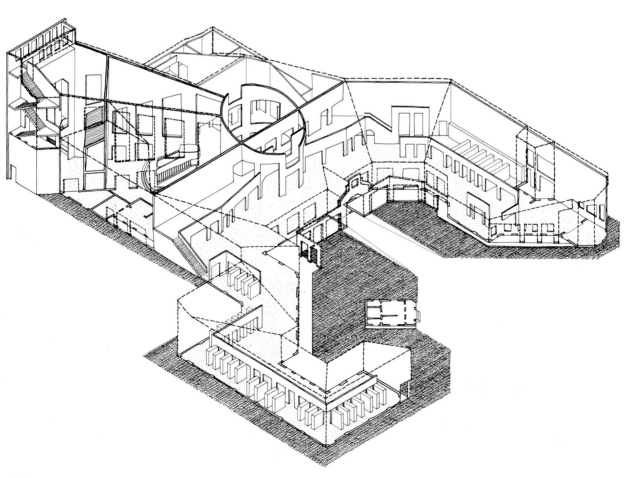

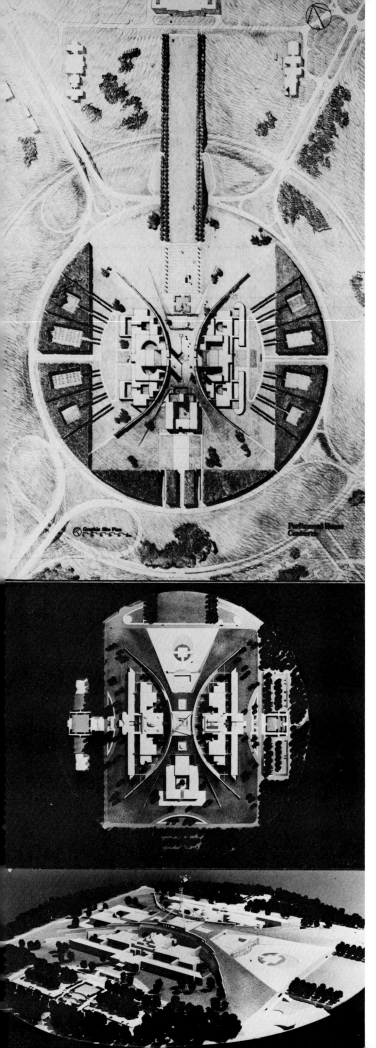

Parliament House

This winning design was selected from over 300 entries submitted for this competition. Among some of the presentation drawings were the rendered site plan of stage one (left), and the detailed elevation view of the structure showing the Australian flag (right).

The model was photographed both in plan and oblique view. In addition, vignette sketches done by the architects showed the members hall (above) and the house chamber (below).

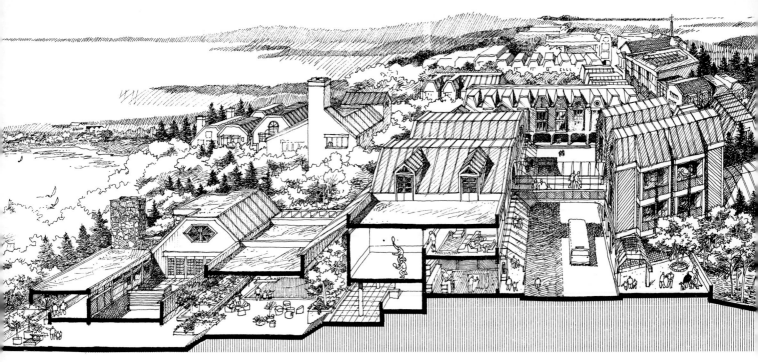

New Alaska Capital City

The field of contenders for this project was 150 firms. As one of the 11 finalists, the architects presented a conceptual scheme. Later they presented more refined plans in an open forum, and once selected, they prepared more detailed drawings to present to the Alaskan Legislature.

The early schemes focused on the town center and an indication of the life style and environmental quality was stressed. Many of the drawings prepared were published in a 28-page full-color newspaper report to the people of Alaska.

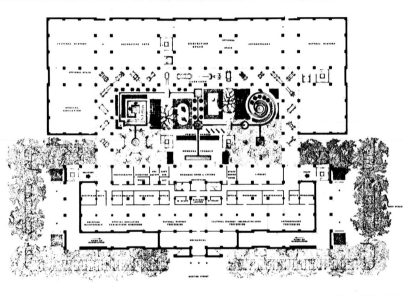

Charlestown Museum

Repetition of motif and emphasis of the main architectural form is characteristic of this series of drawings. The major site plan strongly delineates the building proper, showing the interior courtyard. The section further delineates the space (top right). The aerial perspective echoes all the elements that are shown in the site plan, including surrounding historic and residential buildings.

The one typical elevation is drawn at a large scale and shows the harmonic proportions in relation to other historic buildings.

112

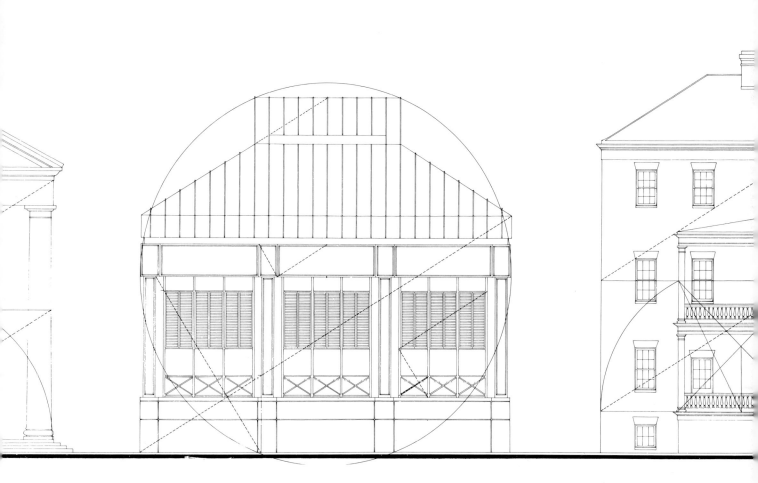

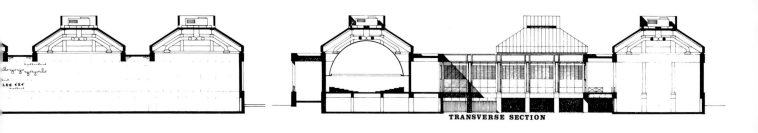

TRANSVERSE SECTION

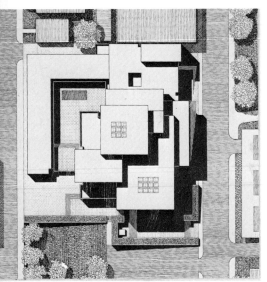

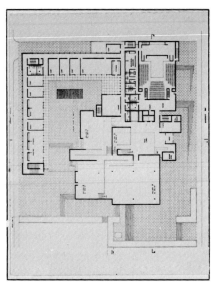

Art Center

Two plans are used to describe this building. The roof and site plan uses shadows to emphasize the overlapping of forms. The rendered elevation (above) and the photograph of the model (below) were taken from the same vantage point. The dark background behind the model further emphasizes the solidity of the building.

Once inside the main lobby, you get a view of the 3-story space with a view into one of the upper galleries. The drawings are executed with a tonal pencil technique.

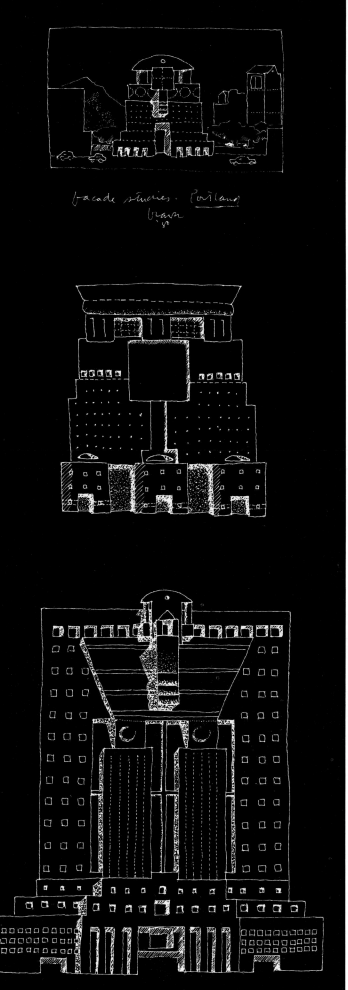

facade studies. Portland
braun
'80

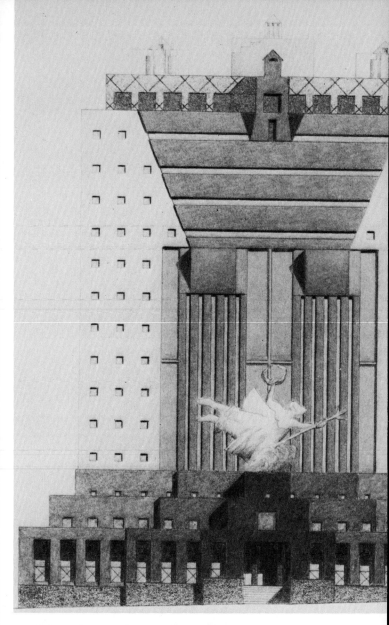

Portland Building

Three styles of drawings are shown here. The first is a series of design study sketches (far left). The building's exterior was rendered in a single ink-line style (above). The sparse treatment of the entourage and surrounding buildings provides an elegant touch. The same is true of the interior meeting room.

The architect's elevations were very colorful and rendered mostly with colored pencils and pastels to display the rich palette of color he envisioned for this important public building.

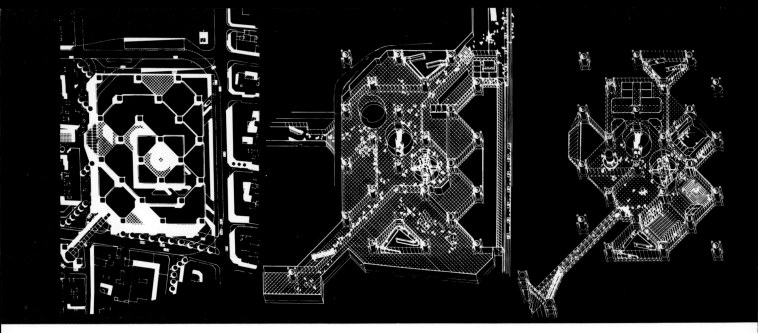

Plateau Beaubourg

This award winning concept for a new cultural center in Paris, France used a combination of visual material to describe the intricate structure. First, there were the traditional plans of each level and an overall site plan. Next, each level was developed into an axonometric drawing of that level only. Cross sections showed the elaborate space frame that would distribute the facilities internally. Model photos, dramatically lit, gave the structure its futuristic look.

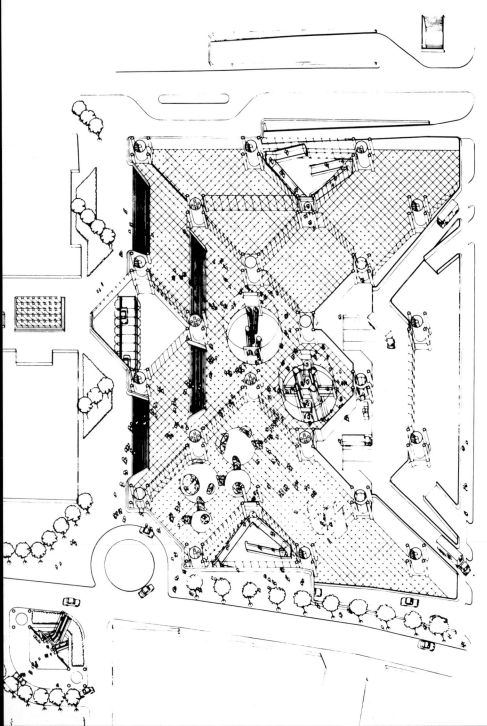

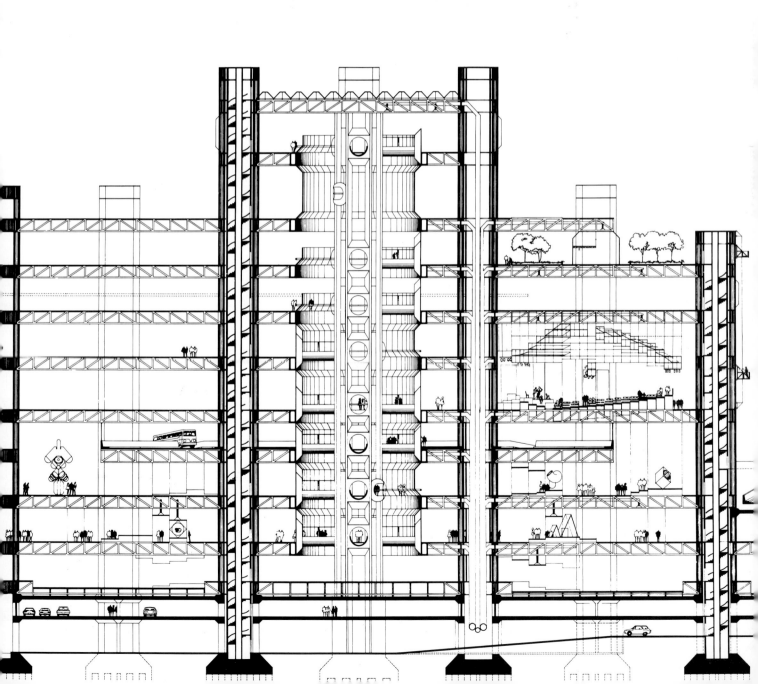

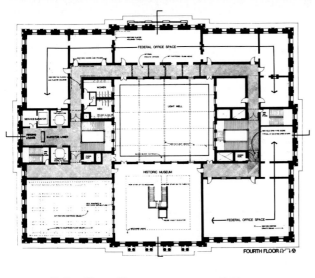

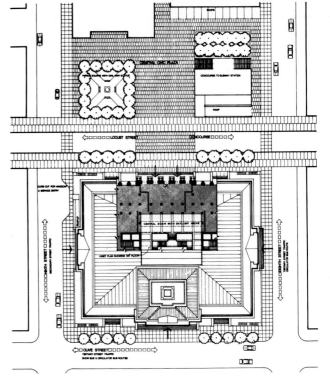

U.S. Custom House

The winning proposal for adapting this grand structure involved removing all unnecessary elements that had been added since 1884 and getting the structure back to basics. The view shown here depicts the existing skylight hovering in the light well, which will be renovated, and new balcony-like esplanades and staircases, which were added to heighten appeal and access. The straight ink-line drawing makes use of cross-hatching to build up the tonal values, which are darkest at the bottom and back of the building.

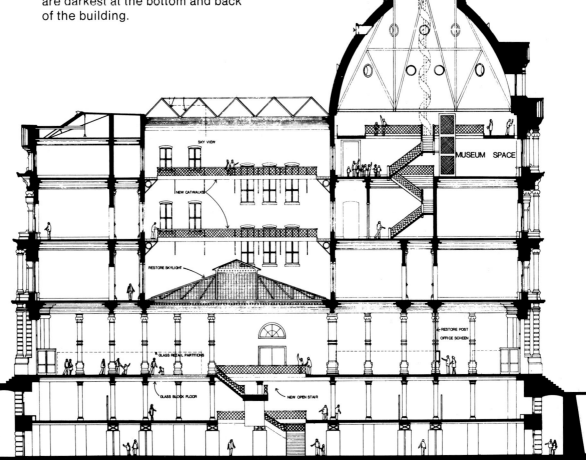

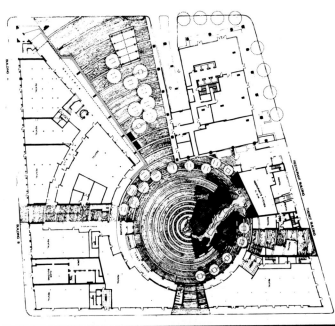

Piazza d'Italia

The winner of this urban plaza competition produced many forms of visual material, including models and architectural drawings. Since the fountain was the focal point of the plaza, it was played up in the presentation drawings. A single line rendition of the classical elements seemed to be the best method of depicting this urban space.

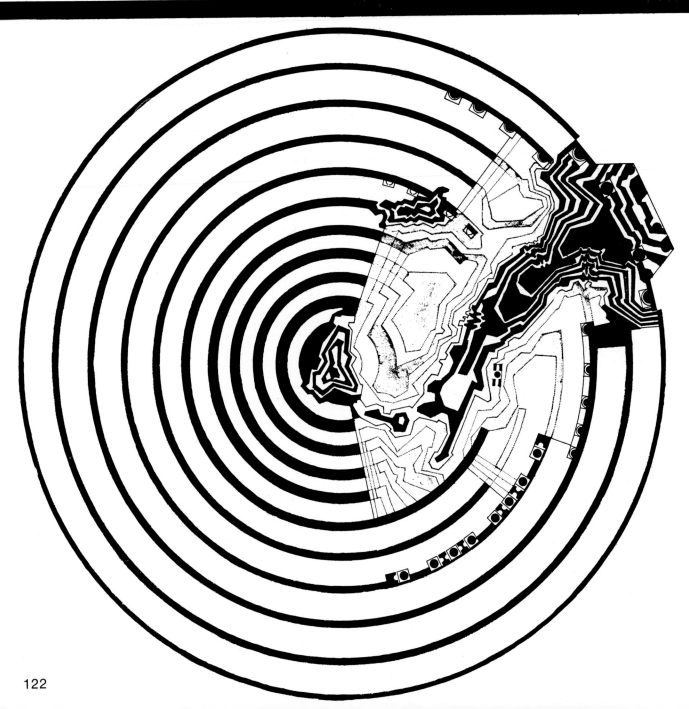

122

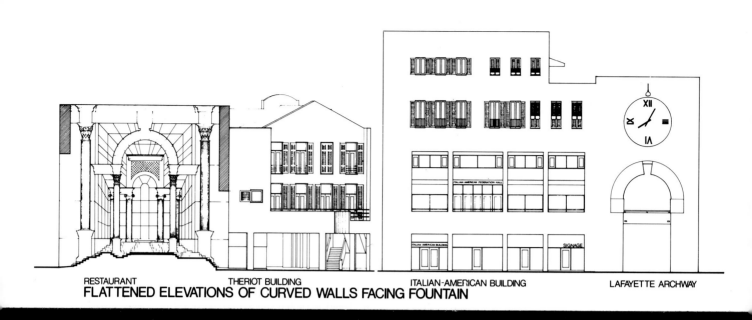

RESTAURANT   THERIOT BUILDING   ITALIAN-AMERICAN BUILDING   LAFAYETTE ARCHWAY

FLATTENED ELEVATIONS OF CURVED WALLS FACING FOUNTAIN

A Minnesota II

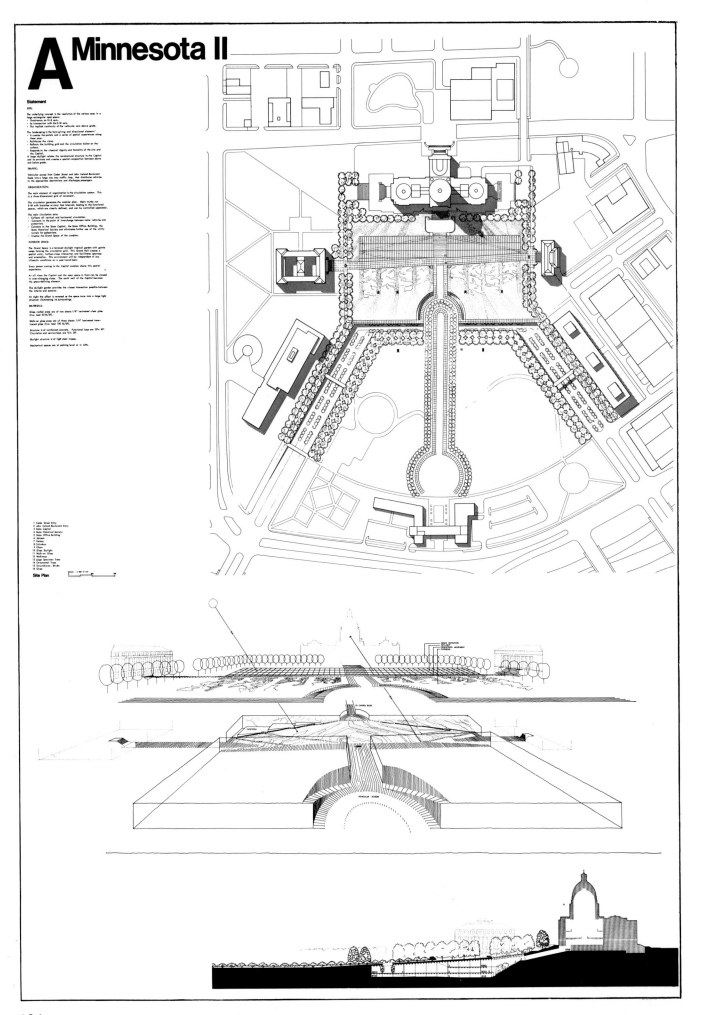

St. Paul Competition

The original design for the State Capitol was obtained through a competition won by St. Paul architect, Cass Gilbert in 1893. In 1976 a program was announced for an annex building to be built underground. There were 476 entries, 256 submitting designs, and 5 finalists.

The winning scheme illustrated very clearly the underground and connecting link concept. Board A (left) followed competition requirements, whereas the perspective views described the vista over the new building and a view from below.

Roosevelt Island

Of the many entries, these two are perhaps the closest to opposite approaches as one could find. The crisp line of quality of the stepped-back structure (below) makes a clear architectural statement. The other approach uses a technique simulating a picture scrapbook (complete with missing picture). It presents a design, which is a mirror to the city, and depicts in the stipple technique a mirror to life in the new project, rather than an architectural treatment. Both are striking in their own way.

mirror to manhattan: our home reflects the city, yet it's an island apart...

context: the square across from the arrival deck is really a triangle...from there begin main street shops and arcade under the upper income housing...

livability: we chose to design our own apartment...this is probably the only place in the world you can do that...we may be able to add a unit after the new baby...

maintenance: short sunny halls and convenient laundries are always spotless...everybody on the floor knows everybody else and takes pride in them...

tunnel: everybody likes to walk past here over the bridge under the building past flower gardens and shaded sitting area

security: it's real nice having the management right in the lobby...except on the first of the month...

glass elevators: you can't get mugged in our elevators, and you can always tell where you are in relation to the ground only problem at first was people taking joyrides...

hill: this is the only place on the island for sledding...they probably built the hill with earth from the tidal pool...

swimming pool: the pool is right at the water's edge even though it's inland...it's open all year and is a great place to meet people...

CAPITOL
HILL

NORTH

PENNSYLVANIA AVENUE

NEW
"AIR RIGHTS"
BUILDINGS

RETAINED

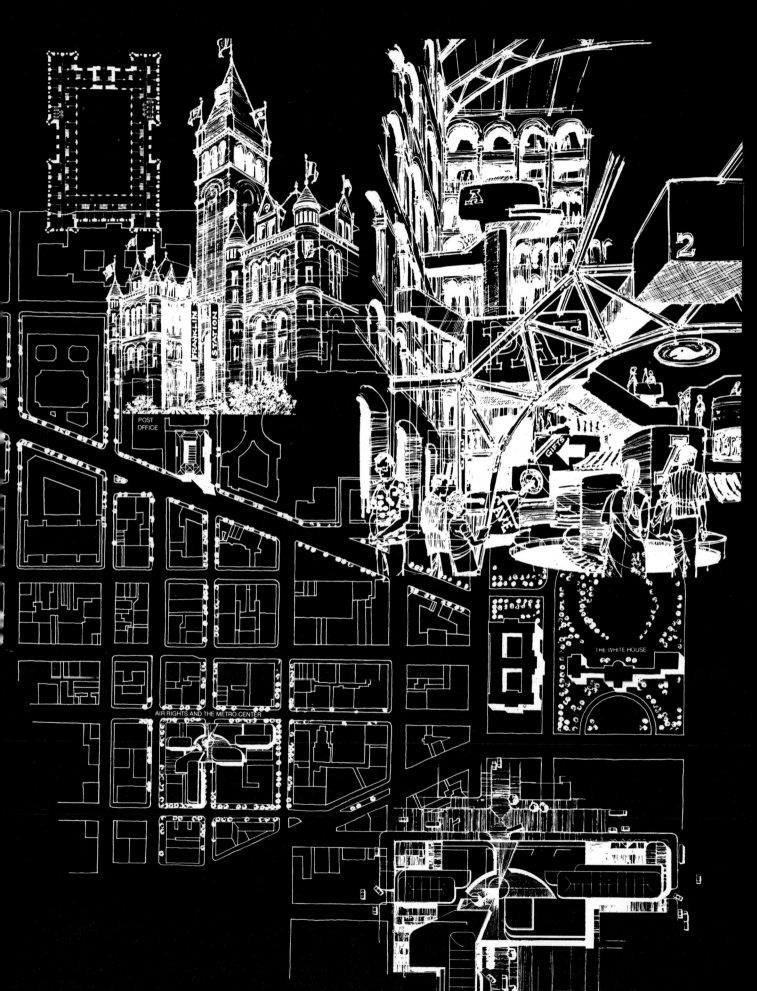

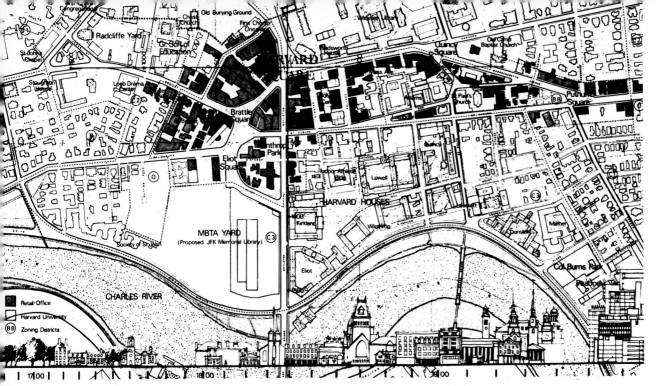

Retail-Office
Harvard University
BB Zoning Districts

CHARLES RIVER

MBTA YARD
(Proposed JFK Memorial Library)

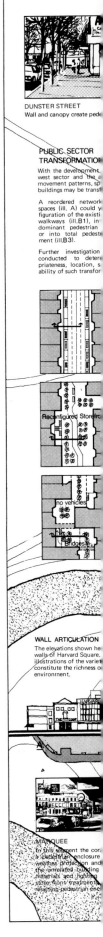

DUNSTER STREET
Wall and canopy create pede...

PUBLIC SECTOR
TRANSFORMATION

With the development...
west sector and the a...
movement patterns, sp...
buildings may be transf...

A reordered network...
spaces (ill. A) could y...
figuration of the existi...
walkways (ill. B1), in...
dominant pedestrian...
or into total pedestri...
ment (ill. B3).

Further investigation...
conducted to deter...
priateness, location, s...
ability of such transfor...

Reconfigured Storefro...

no vehicles

...
Bridges...

WALL ARTICULATION
The elevations shown he...
walls of Harvard Square,...
illustrations of the varie...
constitute the richness o...
environment.

MARQUEE
In this segment the cor...
pedestrian enclosure...
weather protection and...
the articulated building...
materials and lighting...
store front treatment...
resulting pedestrian enc...

Harvard Square

This report was prepared for the City of Cambridge as an investigation in urban design. All the pages of the report are the same size and follow the same basic format. The left-hand column contains the text material. A square format on the right contains a mixture of maps, land use plans, and diagrams.

This mixture of graphic and diagramatic information gives it a richness common to the project area itself — Harvard Square — a subway stop, a traffic intersection, a neighborhood, speciality shops and a dynamic and varied street life. All these ingredients are aptly captured and expertly portrayed visually in this report.

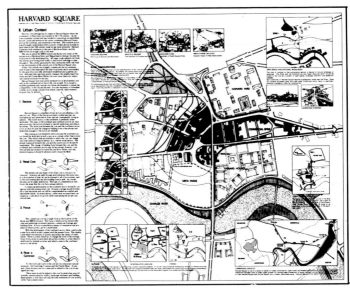

HARVARD SQUARE

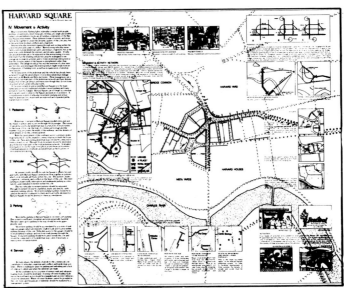

HARVARD SQUARE

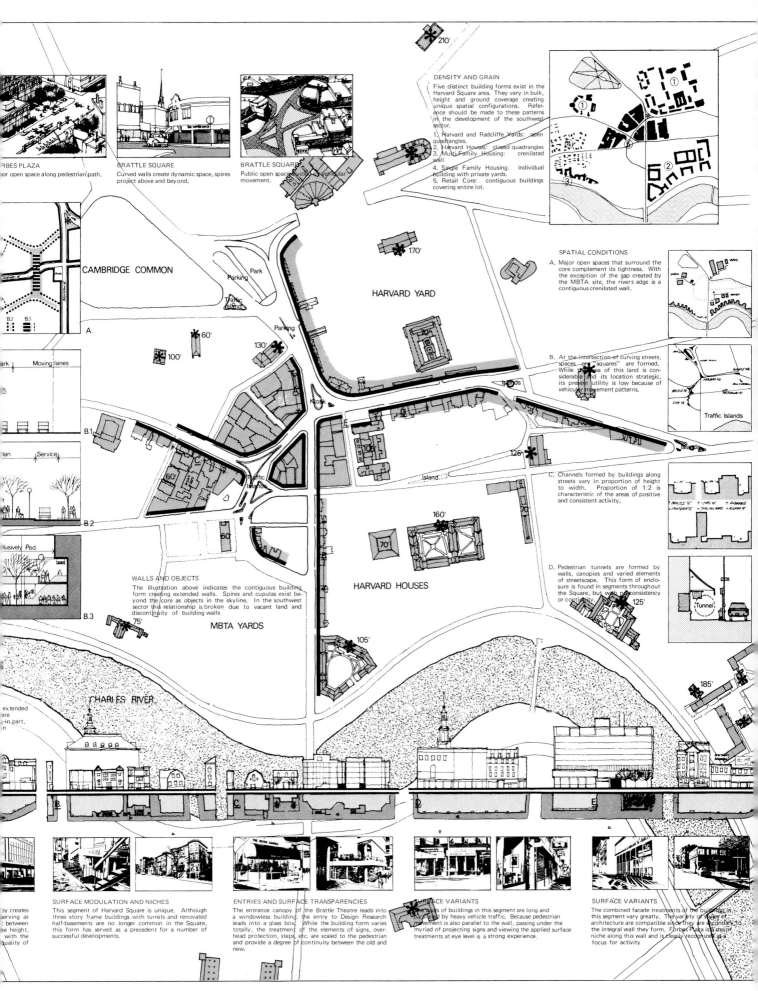

RBES PLAZA
or open space along pedestrian path.

BRATTLE SQUARE
Curved walls create dynamic space, spires project above and beyond.

BRATTLE SQUARE
Public open space with vehicular movement.

DENSITY AND GRAIN
Five distinct building forms exist in the Harvard Square area. They vary in bulk, height and ground coverage creating unique spatial configurations. Reference should be made to these patterns in the development of the southwest sector.
1. Harvard and Radcliffe Yards: open quadrangles.
2. Harvard Houses: closed quadrangles.
3. Multi-Family Housing: crenilated wall.
4. Single Family Housing: individual building with private yards.
5. Retail Core: contiguous buildings covering entire lot.

SPATIAL CONDITIONS
A. Major open spaces that surround the core complement its tightness. With the exception of the gap created by the MBTA site, the rivers edge is a contiguous crenilated wall.

B. At the intersection of curving streets, spaces or "squares" are formed. While the area of this land is considerable and its location strategic, its present utility is low because of vehicular movement patterns.

Traffic Islands

C. Channels formed by buildings along streets vary in proportion of height to width. Proportion of 1:2 is characteristic of the areas of positive and consistent activity.

D. Pedestrian tunnels are formed by walls, canopies and varied elements of streetscape. This form of enclosure is found in segments throughout the Square, but with no consistency or continuity.

Tunnel

CAMBRIDGE COMMON

Parking Park
Traffic Island
Parking

HARVARD YARD

Moving lanes

Service

Kiosk

Island

Islands

HARVARD HOUSES

WALLS AND OBJECTS
The illustration above indicates the contiguous building form creating extended walls. Spires and cupulas exist beyond the core as objects in the skyline. In the southwest sector this relationship is broken due to vacant land and discontinuity of building walls.

MBTA YARDS

CHARLES RIVER

SURFACE MODULATION AND NICHES
This segment of Harvard Square is unique. Although three story frame buildings with turrets and renovated half-basements are no longer common in the Square, this form has served as a precedent for a number of successful developments.

ENTRIES AND SURFACE TRANSPARENCIES
The entrance canopy of the Brattle Theatre leads into a windowless building; the entry to Design Research leads into a glass box. While the building form varies totally, the treatment of the elements of signs, overhead protection, steps, etc. are scaled to the pedestrian and provide a degree of continuity between the old and new.

SURFACE VARIANTS
The walls of buildings in this segment are long and dominated by heavy vehicle traffic. Because pedestrian movement is also parallel to the wall, passing under the myriad of projecting signs and viewing the applied surface treatments at eye level is a strong experience.

SURFACE VARIANTS
The combined facade treatments of the buildings in this segment vary greatly. The variety of styles of architecture are compatible since they are secondary to the integral wall they form. Forbes Plaza is a major niche along this wall and is clearly recognized as a focus for activity

Lexington Center

This 30-page brochure describes a new urban, multi-level project in downtown Baltimore. The project will contain new retail and office space, a commercial mall, a 300-unit residential tower, and parking structure. The format of the presentation begins by describing the project as if you were there as a shopper, as a businessman, as a visitor, and as a resident.

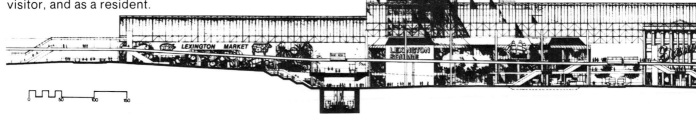

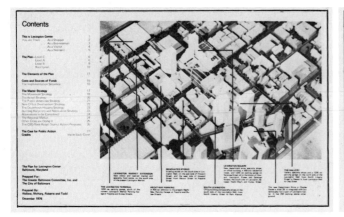

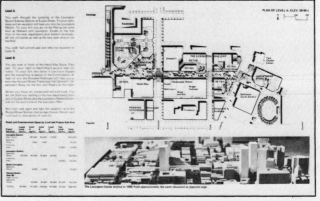

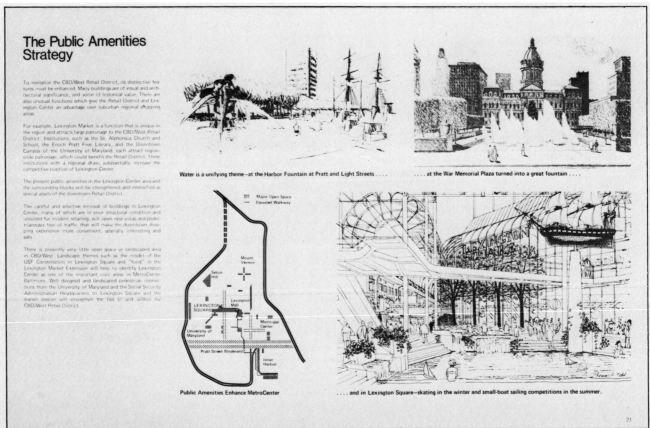

The Public Amenities Strategy

To revitalize the CBD/West Retail District, its distinctive features must be enhanced. Many buildings are of visual and architectural significance, and some of historical value. There are also unusual functions which give the Retail District and Lexington Center an advantage over suburban regional shopping areas.

For example, Lexington Market is a function that is unique in the region and attracts large patronage to the CBD/West Retail District. Institutions, such as the St. Alphonsus Church and School, the Enoch Pratt Free Library, and the Downtown Campus of the University of Maryland, each attract region-wide patronage, which could benefit the Retail District. These institutions with a regional draw, substantially increase the competitive position of Lexington Center.

The present public amenities in the Lexington Center area and the surrounding blocks will be strengthened and intensified as special assets of the downtown Retail District.

The careful and selective removal of buildings in Lexington Center, many of which are in poor structural condition and unsuited for modern retailing, will open new vistas and pedestrian ways free of traffic that will make the downtown shopping experience more convenient, spatially interesting and safe.

There is presently very little open space or landscaped area in CBD/West. Landscape themes such as the model of the USF Constellation on Lexington Square and "food" on the Lexington Market Extension will help to identify Lexington Center as one of the important civic areas in MetroCenter Baltimore. Well designed and landscaped pedestrian connections from the University of Maryland and the Social Security Administration Headquarters to Lexington Square and the transit station will strengthen the ties to and within the CBD/West Retail District.

Water is a unifying theme—at the Harbor Fountain at Pratt and Light Streets....

....at the War Memorial Plaza turned into a great fountain....

Public Amenities Enhance MetroCenter

....and in Lexington Square—skating in the winter and small-boat sailing competitions in the summer.

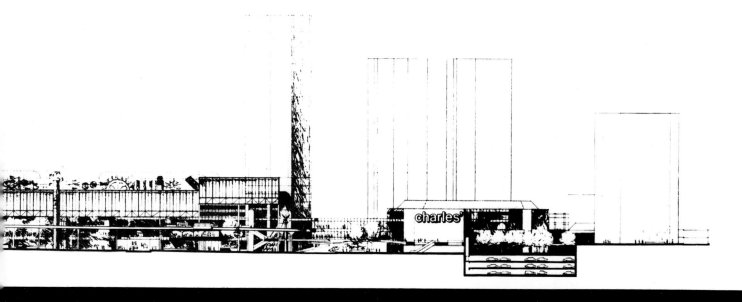

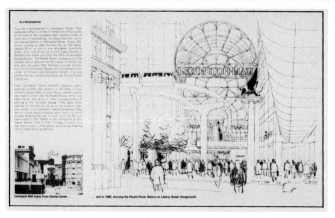

You are There

The Elements of the Plan

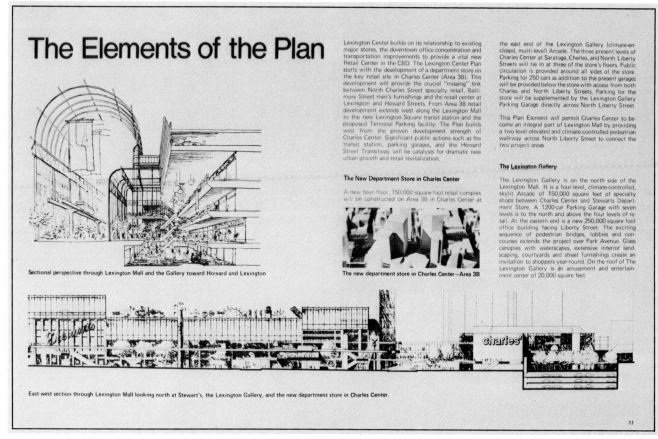

Lexington Center builds on its relationship to existing major stores, the downtown office concentration and transportation improvements to provide a vital new Retail Center in the CBD. The Lexington Center Plan starts with the development of a department store on the key retail site in Charles Center (Area 3B). This development will provide the crucial "missing" link between North Charles Street specialty retail, Baltimore Street men's furnishings and the retail center at Lexington and Howard Streets. From Area 3B retail development extends west along the Lexington Mall to the new Lexington Square transit station and the proposed Terminal Parking facility. The Plan builds west from the proven development strength of Charles Center. Significant public actions such as the transit station, parking garages, and the Howard Street Transitway will be catalysts for dramatic new urban growth and retail revitalization.

The New Department Store in Charles Center

A new four-floor, 150,000 square-foot retail complex will be constructed on Area 3B in Charles Center at

The new department store in Charles Center—Area 3B

Sectional perspective through Lexington Mall and the Gallery toward Howard and Lexington

the east end of the Lexington Gallery (climate-enclosed, multi-level) Arcade. The three present levels of Charles Center at Saratoga, Charles, and North Liberty Streets will tie in at three of the store's floors. Public circulation is provided around all sides of the store. Parking for 250 cars as addition to the present garages will be provided below the store with access from both Charles and North Liberty Streets. Parking for the store will be supplemented by the Lexington Gallery Parking Garage directly across North Liberty Street.

This Plan Element will permit Charles Center to become an integral part of Lexington Mall by providing a two-level elevated and climate-controlled pedestrian walkway across North Liberty Street to connect the two project areas.

The Lexington Gallery

The Lexington Gallery is on the north side of the Lexington Mall. It is a four-level, climate-controlled, skylit Arcade of 150,000 square feet of specialty shops between Charles Center and Stewarts Department Store. A 1200-car Parking Garage with seven levels is to the north and above the four levels of retail. At the eastern end is a new 250,000 square foot office building facing Liberty Street. The exciting sequence of pedestrian bridges, lobbies and concourses extends the project over Park Avenue. Glass canopies with waterscapes, extensive interior landscaping, courtyards and street furnishings create an invitation to shoppers year-round. On the roof of The Lexington Gallery is an amusement and entertainment center of 20,000 square feet.

East-west section through Lexington Mall looking north at Stewart's, the Lexington Gallery, and the new department store in Charles Center.

11

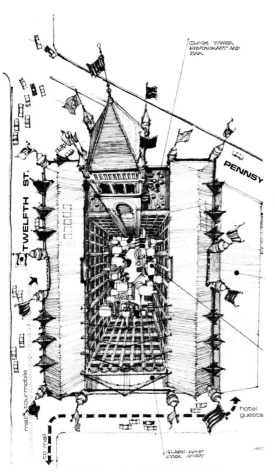

Cities Brochure

This brochure is part of a coordinated series that the firm developed. They all have sleek black covers with dropout white lettering describing the title of each piece. Inside, each double-spread contains one project in one city.

Each project is described by a combination of visual images: land use plans, planning diagrams, environmental sketches, and models. Many aerial views are coordinated with similar views of sketches or models.

Also shown is the winning design for the Old Post Office project in Washington, D.C.

York, Pennsylvania

An essential part of the development of the Codorus Corridor Plan was an attempt to make the planning as open, participatory, and informative as possible. The plan for planning engaged most of the techniques of a grassroots political campaign, as well as thorough use of all the media, and culminated in several town meetings.

Common perceptions of the city needed to be refocused onto its real strengths—its intown housing, its industrial base, and its traditional farmer's markets. Minimal demand for conventional uses necessitated the invention of unique projects to attract some of the region's active tourism trade, which presently bypasses the city. The plan added three new markets patterned after the two farmer's markets, as an economic backbone for the development of the area. ACM/A led a multi-disciplinary team of consultants including hydrology, finance, traffic, engineering, economics, tourism, pollution, and recreation. Special ecological testing and analysis was performed to determine the source of water pollutants causing an unpleasant smell in the creek area. The major feature of the Codorus Creek, susceptible to flooding, was dealt with by water management analysis. As a complement to the land use plan, a moveable bascule-type dam is projected to create an intown lake for recreation, while improving the protection against possible flooding. Both public and private concepts were analyzed in terms of technical and economic feasibility, and the resulting plan is a combination of an urban renewal plan, a general development plan, and an implementation plan.

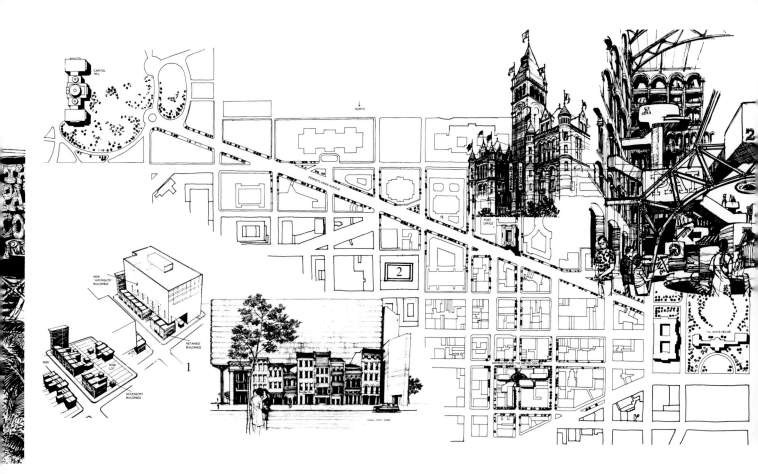

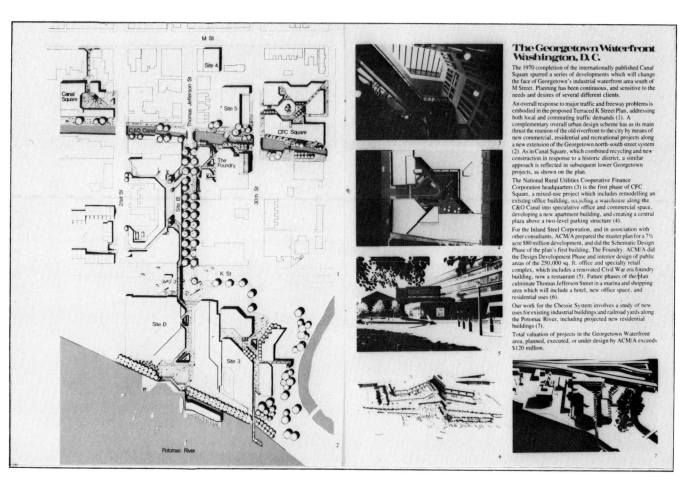

The Georgetown Waterfront
Washington, D. C.

The 1970 completion of the internationally published Canal Square spurred a series of developments which will change the face of Georgetown's industrial waterfront area south of M Street. Planning has been continuous, and sensitive to the needs and desires of several different clients.

An overall response to major traffic and freeway problems is embodied in the proposed Terraced K Street Plan, addressing both local and commuting traffic demands (1). A complementary overall urban design scheme has as its main thrust the reunion of the old riverfront to the city by means of new commercial, residential and recreational projects along a new extension of the Georgetown north-south street system (2). As in Canal Square, which combined recycling and new construction in response to a historic district, a similar approach is reflected in subsequent lower Georgetown projects, as shown on the plan.

The National Rural Utilities Cooperative Finance Corporation headquarters (3) is the first phase of CFC Square, a mixed-use project which includes remodelling an existing office building, recycling a warehouse along the C&O Canal into speculative office and commercial space, developing a new apartment building, and creating a central plaza above a two-level parking structure (4).

For the Inland Steel Corporation, and in association with other consultants, ACM/A prepared the master plan for a 7½ acre $80 million development, and did the Schematic Design Phase of the plan's first building, The Foundry. ACM/A did the Design Development Phase and interior design of public areas of the 250,000 sq. ft. office and specialty retail complex, which includes a renovated Civil War era foundry building, now a restaurant (5). Future phases of the plan culminate Thomas Jefferson Street in a marina and shopping area which will include a hotel, new office space, and residential uses (6).

Our work for the Chessie System involves a study of new uses for existing industrial buildings and railroad yards along the Potomac River, including projected new residential buildings (7).

Total valuation of projects in the Georgetown Waterfront area, planned, executed, or under design by ACM/A exceeds $120 million.

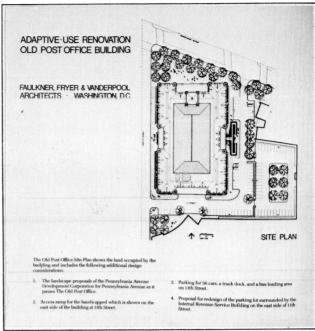

Old Post Office

The brochure was produced for a design competition and the building design scheme was selected as a runner-up. The crisp clean graphic style was evidenced throughout the pages. There was an economy of line-work in the delineation of the plans and sections through the building.

This same austerity and attention to detail was expressed in the interior perspective. Rather than show a ground level view focused on the activity (below) the view focused on the quiet dignity of the space created by the open atrium.

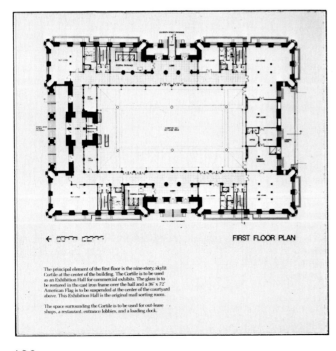

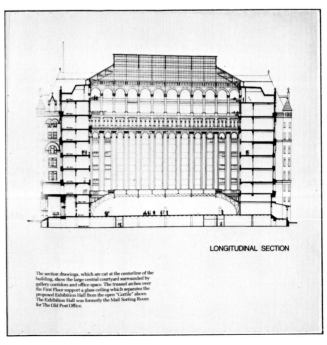

136

Clevernews

Don Clever moved from Canada to San Francisco at age 20 to begin a career as a successful muralist. (Interestingly, he recently supervised the restoration of one of his original murals 42 feet long and 12 feet high

While painting murals, he was often asked for his opinions on other aspects of design. Before long, Don was a full scale interior designer, offering his clients design services on everything from silverware to the graphic design on matchbooks,

With his many clients and major projects through the years, Don's firm has remained small (less than six persons). Yet each project is presented to the client in an elaborate fashion that contrasts with the shoestring budget on which it is produced. The presentations are enhanced by taking place in his office, which is a gallery of Clever designs, a most stimulating setting for a client interested in design.

This demonstrates how his business has developed over the years without a major effort in advertising or developing promotional literature. However, his willingness to procede without such help changed recently.

Don began seeking an appropriate medium to expand information on his services.

What he chose was a newsletter format. Striking in its appearance with a stark, bold black-and-white design, it resembles a newspaper in its 17"x22" unfolded size. Yet it neatly folds into an 8½"x11" size for easy filing.

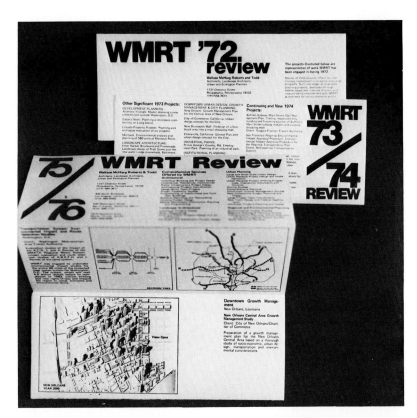

WMRT Reviews

This brochure system utilizes a very flexible format for a yearly review of the firm's work. The accordian-style folder can be of varying lengths, depending on the number of projects shown.

Each fold encompasses a typical project, so the division is a very natural one. On each project panel there is a title and written description of the project. This description includes a statement on the status of the project. An overall site plan, map, or model photograph describes the project visually.

Downtown Buffalo
Comprehensive Plan and Implementation Program for Downtown Buffalo
Buffalo, New York
Client: City of Buffalo, New York
State Urban Development Corporation and Greater Buffalo Development Foundation

The Comprehensive Plan is designed as a strategic program in the revitalization of the City of Buffalo through the implementation of five major elements of its Downtown: an efficient, balanced movement system, a 2500 foot climate-controlled Downtown Mall on Main Street, major new parking structures, new office space development guided in accordance with the Plan, and a new Convention Center.

Status: Since adoption of the Plan by the City, phases of implementation are underway. The subway system has been adopted, and a funding program has commenced; a Convention Center bond issue has been approved and WMRT has been selected as architect for the Main Street Shopping Mall and Downtown Subway Stations.

Los Angeles Downtown General Development Plan
A Central City 1990 Development Plan
Los Angeles, California
Client: Committee for Central City Planning, Inc.

This plan establishes a guide for Downtown Los Angeles' future development, accommodating growth pressures in a manner to reflect long-range regional development goals. One key element of the plan is its regional transportation network implementing an integrated system of rapid transit, people-movers, parking, highways, and pedways. Another important feature is a Title VII new-town-in-town surrounding a large urban park.

WMRT has begun preparation of documents for implementation of the Central City Plan.

Status: Approved by the City Planning Commission; under consideration by the City Council.

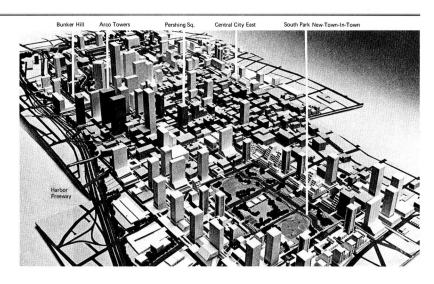

HLW Newsletter

When they began publishing their newsletter in 1974, it concentrated on specific projects. Its format was small (6x9) and its graphics, frankly underwhelming. Looking ordinary, it received only an ordinary response.

Today's newsletter is quite an improvement: four pages on rich, thick 60-pound cover stock. The format follows principles that come a lot closer to print advertising than to standard newsletter fare. The inside page is banded into three elements:
1. Headlines 2. Captions 3. Body.

They know that four out five readers scan only the headlines, so these carry sales messages. Many will peruse only the illustrations, so they've done the captions in bold-face and given their text special attention. The less prominent middle tier of print is in a regular type face. Don't try this deceptively simple format unless you are a writer who enjoys challenges.

Newsletter is a misnomer. They're not "newsy." They don't provide their readers with bulletins about newly assigned commissions. They don't feel fast-breaking stories inspire anyone to buy their services.

They see the back page as the second cover. This one is a favorite. It also drew the biggest response. A telephone building they designed earlier this century sustained a 16-hour fire in its cable vaults. And survived without structural damage. (How's that for prudent design?)

Who wasn't going to read that caption. The story and style were straightforward. 250,000 phones in Lower Manhattan were out for two weeks. They didn't leave the telephone company's side that entire time. The caption was about the fire; the sales message was was about the quality of their service.

• **SELECTIVITY**
There's no waste. They select their targets. They reach them all.

• **CONTROL**
They're in control. They decide the quality and quantity of their materials. They mail when they feel it's best.

• **NO COMPETITION**
Technically, there's no competition. When their letters are opened, they alone command the readers' attention.

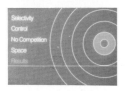

• **SPACE**
They like being able to use as much space as they feel their story needs.

• **RESULTS**
They're reaching their targets with the best shots they can take. That's how they move their message out. Through strategic mail.

There's no doubt that graphically coordinated materials, regularly received, give substance and credibility to your selling effort. They try to be informative, not self-serving, They give readers something useful in their work, write about common problems with uncommon solutions, and answer three questions each reader surely has:

- What do I get from reading this?
- What benefits do HLW's services have for me?
- How are they better than the competition?

They had 12 mailings last year and frequency is steadily rising. They stay in touch with a general mailing list and several specialty lists. Combined, they total 1500 names:

- Past and present clients.
- Friends, people who can influence others to commission them.
- Prospects.
- Fellow professionals, including trade associations.
- The press.
- The firm's partners.

Coordinating, building, and narrowing these lists is a complicated and highly responsible task that they have placed in the hands of their marketing coordinator.

They have four different kinds of printed communications:

- Brochures.
- Announcements.
- P.R. reinforcements.
- List cleaners, Christmas cards.

All these materials have an elegant, recognizable family look. People pay more attention to what they already know. Just like advertising, keeping visually consistent stretches their marketing dollars.

It takes teamwork to turn out this volume of materials. One fourth of the time is spent creating material, planning the campaign for each document and its target market, and managing production. Marching orders come from the marketing staff and the manager of the group for whom the effort is developed. These people advise on target audience, what these prospects need and will buy (sometimes very different) and the best timing for the most impact. The managing partner responsible for business development has the final say.

Their capabilities brochure covers all bases. The cover is entirely embossed. It's terrific. You can feel their logo — like braille — when you leaf through the book.

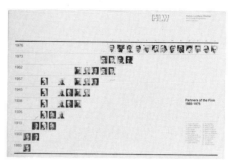

This HLW poster introduced a new graphic style, a new leadership team. It also showed history, continuity, depth.

This 6-page 4-color piece was for their growing landscape architecture and site planning division. The color is dynamite, especially when you realize how very discreet most of their materials are.

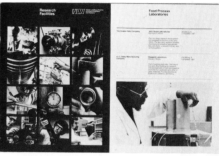

This crisp black-and-white brochure began as a reference piece, designed for skimming. The only photos are of researchers. The unstated message: HLW buildings inspire people to work at their best.

They're in regular touch with trade publications, as this selection of reprints indicates. They provide the artwork for the reprint cover to keep the family look.

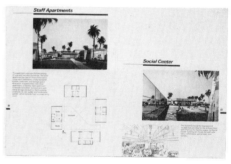

A client used this brochure with the clean Swiss graphics to attract first rate medical people to a clinic in a remote oil-rich desert.

Possibly their most workaday mailing is their SF 254, updated and sent annually to all government agencies for whom they want to design.

A smaller piece that fits into a No. 10 envelope announced the role their graphic designers played in the glorious King Tutankhamen exhibit at the Metropolitan Museum.

Architects Brochure

The time had come for Clark Tribble Harris and Li Architects, to have a new brochure. They were disappointed in the typical format architects usually used — including their own. That is when Jerry Li hit on the idea of a magazine format brochure.

The team was then formed to produce it and the precepts of what makes a magazine a magazine were analyzed. The magazine structure was broken down and approached by sections. Each section is a series of scenarios reflecting different parts of their architectural practice to tell a story.

DEPARTMENTS

These are pages that added continuity to the magazine. The cover, the table of contents, the editor's notes, the postscript, and several other pages were all designed and written to give the illusion of a regularly issued publication. An entire magazine format had to be created as if it was a permanent on-going design. The typefaces, grid systems, graphic elements, along with the varying style of the copy supported the illusion of a previously established and on-going magazine and also held the other diverse elements together.

FEATURES

This section for the most part was viewed as the "fashion" spreads.

"The Partners' Profiles" were short blurbs about each principal presenting their various roles in the firm and some general background material.

"The Shape of Success" was a showcase for architectural awards and comments about award winning buildings.

"The Scope of the Work" section was approached as work in progress at Clark Tribble Harris and Li, work in various stages of design and construction but not finished projects.

"Washington" pages were an introduction to the Washington Office and projects going on there.

ARTICLES

Most magazines have articles filled with information pertinent to their readers. This problem was handled with a series of articles concerning Clark Tribble Harris and Li's approaches to various aspects of architecture, Cost, Energy and Design. They were written and graphically represented as a series in an effort to maximize their impact.

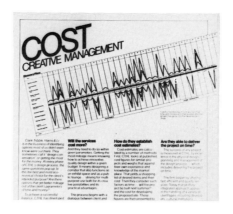

ADVERTISEMENTS

A large portion of any magazine is advertisements. To maintain authenticity Architects required them too. Several approaches were discussed concerning the ads, including the concept of actually selling advertising space. Eventually it was decided that the ads would also play the game of imitation. Two ads were about the office and the rest were "selling" the firm's buildings. These pages were particularly difficult to design because they had to be completely unrelated to each other in concept, feel, and appearance. Magazines, newspapers and other publications were poured over to find types of advertising that could be adapted to our uses. The results were some of the most attractive pages in the magazine.

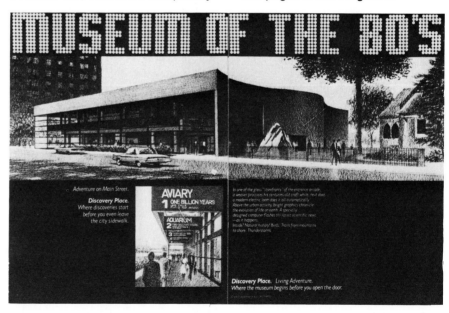

REPRINTS

The reprints make up a good deal of the bulk of the magazine. They are actual articles published about Clark Tribble Harris and Li in other magazines. We changed their sizes slightly in some cases to fit our format and put grey borders around all reprint pages to signal their content. These reprints serve several purposes in Architects. They are objective views about the firm which add credibility. They look like magazine articles which heighten the illusion of being an actual magazine and they present a great deal of information, that in many cases could not have been fit into another section of the format.

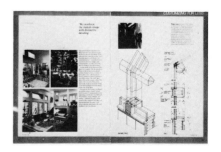

Discovery Place

This 3-fold flier was produced to introduce a new museum, and was designed in a comic strip format. Jerry Li, of Clark Tribble Harris and Li Architects, came up with the innovative format, which was carried to completion by comic strip artist Sam Granger (perhaps best known for his Spiderman drawings).

It was not intended as a joke. It was, in fact, an interesting story about the museum building. It featured the planning and development and use by visitors. The concern for the user was uppermost in their minds.

Flip Chart Presentations

A well-executed flip chart system has never failed to impress the client with the quantity and quality of the thought that's gone into their presentation. It's not as much a series of tablet pages with pictures on them as a system with a very defined strategy, that is very specifically geared toward that one client and his project.

And that's the reason that the free-hand format is preferred to a stenciled or otherwise hard-lettered type of format. It gives the client the feeling that it has been done by hand and that it's been done by someone that's reasonably creative.

It looks like a design professional was sketching. It is something the client enjoys seeing.

And this system allows you to take a security blanket with you to the presentation. You may spend hours working on your presentation but will be assured that in those fifteen, twenty, or thirty minutes, you're going to lay everything on the line in a very orderly fashion.

Flip charts really have two messages. One is the verbal message, the literal message. The other message is maybe more subtle, but has as much impact — it says, "These were done especially for you. It is not something manufactured for a number of different clients. These ideas have been animated for you by my hand." That's the underlying principle in using a free-hand flip chart presentation.

Don Prochaska, architect with Kirkham Michael & Associates, Omaha engages a health facility administrator in a presentation. The flip charts are coordinated with some larger scale diagrams such as the phasing chart shown.

COMPONENTS

Each flip chart has two major components in it. It has the graphic or pictorial component, which is really there to create interest on the part of the client.

Then it has the written or printed component, which is nothing more than the outline for the presentation. You write in sub-titles or phrases or in short sentences on the charts. This becomes your presentation outline, and it's in front of you all the time.

It allows interruptions at any point in time by any number of people. You can always easily return to that point. The words on the chart are not for the client to sit there and read. The words on the charts are there as a built-in flash card for the presenter. The charts are also there for the presenter's convenience. While talking to the client, you can point to the pictures and at the same time read your next line. So there is no fumbling for notes. This naturally increases the smoothness or flow of your presentation.

MODULAR SYSTEM

The presentation sequence is completely flexible. The concept is that it is a modular system. As such it allows maximum flexibility.

When developing the base drawing for flip charts, you have to ask yourself what is common to each presentation that you do.

Make use of generic forms. The site plan shown is generic. It illustrates a site or you can obtain maps of the project site, and have them blown up and added to the flip chart sequence.

The first chart might be a picture of this generic map while you

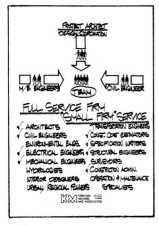

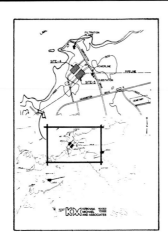

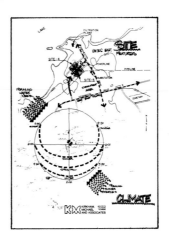

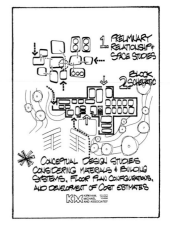

explain how site selection works. The next one can be an actual photograph of the site they've chosen and you have all the hand-lettering on that.

In the schematic design chart, the bubble diagram is drawn one time. The schematic is drawn with the circulation arrows and then the title is changed for each project.

The drawings are printed on mylar — without words. Then you run a blue line print of that and use colored magic markers to hand-letter all the items on each chart, such as location, security, fire safety.

You can rule blue guide-lines for the lettering by using a standard parallel bar, using the width of the bar for spacing. Location of the lettering grid is flexible.

Make the charts very colorful. Use aggressive colors or subtle shades, depending on your personal preference. Or vary it according to the client group. If you're talking to the U.S. Government, tone it down. If it's the local arts commission or someone with a sense of adventure you can be very colorful.

Colorful flip charts will make many of your conventional methods look boring. It's not hard to make a quality-looking flip chart.

PRESENTING HINTS

During the presentation, it is effective to add to the charts. For example, animate the site with simple marks; add some arrows showing traffic flow, both vehicular and pedestrian. It gives you credibility because you're drawing in the same medium as those charts were drawn.

You are a problem solver and a master strategist, but what fascinates clients is when you pick up a marker and sketch right in front of them. It's an aspect of this format that can be extremely effective. It can be pre-planned, but not obviously pre-planned, when you're going to do some sketching.

You want them to know that you drew those charts. That is your message to your client. You want the presentation to appear custom made for him.

It is a high utility, very flexible system. You can use slides just before or just after the flip charts, depending on the nature of the presentation.

USE AS HANDOUTS

It is a customized presentation that allows you to leave something substantial behind. The charts can be left as a package for the client. or they can be reduced to 8½"x11" veloxes and put into a spiral bound book. The client can use them later to refer to your entire presentation.

Generally the reductions should be handed out after the presentation to avoid losing the attention of your audience. However, in very technical presentations or where interaction with your group is desired, the booklet of reductions can be used by them as notebooks during the presentation.

ADVANTAGES

A major advantage to this particular system of flip charts is that it disciplines you in the need to prepare the sheets prior to the presentations. Another major advantage is the incredible speed with which you can put a presentation together.

Flip charts can be prepared in a matter of a few hours. One reason is that the base sheets mentioned earlier have all the pictures on them.

REHEARSAL

No matter how impromptu or informal you want to appear before any group, you must be extremely well-rehearsed. Don't go there with your flip charts and think ideas will pop into your head.

If you've done your preparation correctly, you've already presented this to an in-house audience that has raised doubt with any of the gray areas of your presentation.

You go into battle well-armed. I attribute a lot of it to the basic flip-chart methodology.

This is extremely important because in many presentations done without the assistance of good visual aids, you can inadvertently omit some of your presentation.

The flip charts do a number of things. First they consolidate hours of thought and concern about the project. Therefore, you can speak very articulately and very briefly. Brevity is important.

Another rule of thumb is to mention the client and his problems more times that you mention yourself or your past successes. A simple statement that is universally overlooked.

Don't be quick to judge the merits of a particular presentation format by whether or not you get the first job you use it on, or the first few jobs you use it on.

Practice makes perfect and as you become more practiced with the system, you become smoother and more proficient at communicating your design ideas.

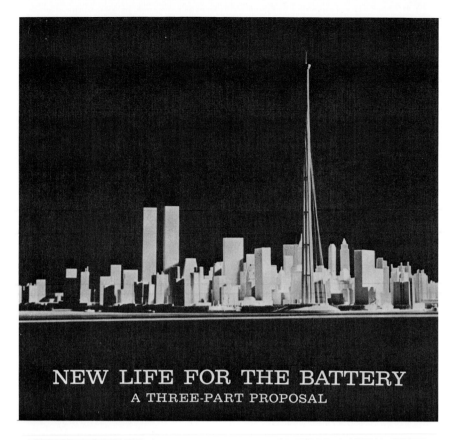

NEW LIFE FOR THE BATTERY
A THREE-PART PROPOSAL

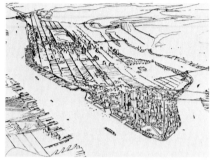

Battery Park

This brochure proposed a new park for the tip of the island of Manhattan. Therefore, the scale of the park and structures had to match the scale of the city. The most visible part of the park design was a tower which was taller than any existing building or monument on the site. The brochure described the new park in relationship to the rich fabric of a major metropolitan city.

Castle Clinton

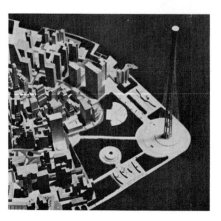

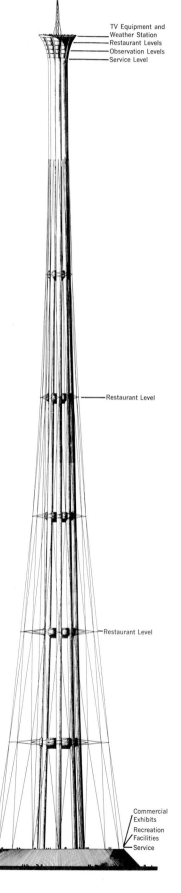

TV Equipment and
Weather Station
Restaurant Levels
Observation Levels
Service Level

Restaurant Level

Restaurant Level

Entrance

Commercial
Exhibits
Recreation
Facilities
Service

THE NEW YORK STOCK EXCHANGE

PART 3: To construct new facilities for the New York Stock Exchange, including related office space, at Bowling Green and Battery Place, utilizing air rights above Brooklyn-Battery Tunnel and adjacent building sites at Numbers 1 and 11 Broadway.

The trading floor of the New York Stock Exchange attracts thousands of visitors. A location at the entrance to Battery Park would be ideal for public access, for proximity to banks and brokerage houses, and to insure the development of Lower Manhattan to its greatest potential.

SECTION LOOKING NORTH

Area of Site:

1 & 11 Broadway	$=\pm$	45,000 sq. ft.
Brooklyn-Battery Tunnel		
Air Rights	$=\pm$	75,000 sq. ft.
Total		120,000 sq. ft.

Zoning Statistics:

F.A.R. 15 x site area	=	1,800,000
10 x plaza area	=	20,000
Total available to F.A.R.	=	1,820,000

Total Height: 60 STORIES

Building Statistics:

52 floors @ 30,000 sq. ft.	= 1,560,000 sq. ft.
Exchange floor and under-floor services	
(clear space 60,000 sq. ft.)	= 180,000 sq. ft.
Members' facilities and Bond room	= 30,000 sq. ft.
Gallery floor	= 25,000 sq. ft.
Lobby floor	= 40,000 sq. ft.
Ground floor facilities	= 35,000 sq. ft.
4 Mechanical floors	= 120,000 sq. ft.
4 Basements	= 160,000 sq. ft.
TOTAL GROSS BUILDING	2,150,000 sq. ft.

ENTRANCE LEVEL

UNDER FLOOR FACILITIES

TRADING FLOOR 90,000 Square Feet

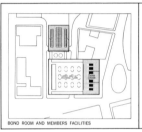

BOND ROOM AND MEMBERS FACILITIES

VISITORS FLOOR Overlooking Trading Floor and Bond Room

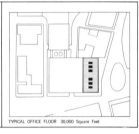

TYPICAL OFFICE FLOOR 30,000 Square Feet

NEW YORK STOCK EXCHANGE AND OFFICE BUILDINGS
Looking south on Broadway to Bowling Green, the Custom House, the Stock Exchange, with The New York Tower in the background.

Turner City

This rendering features 102 buildings completed during the year 1982 (right) by Turner Construction Company and its operating subsidiaries. It began in 1910 when they created the first drawing. The buildings built during 1920 are shown (above top), those during 1945 (above middle) and in the year 1965 (above bottom).

"Turner Cities" has been a company trademark for 75 years. Each year one is published in a special folder, with names of the owner, project, and architectural firm responsible for the design. They are keyed with a number in the published report.

PART TWO:
Projected Visuals

The Presentation Cycle

Marketing of professional services is an ongoing process. It shouldn't begin with an R.F.P. and end with a client interview. It should be an integrated system within your organization just like administration and production. In multi-disciplined firms, many layers of marketing activities are going on at the same time. The way these activities are integrated into the firm's organization is paramount to the success of the marketing plan.

Presentations are a vital function of marketing and occur at 5 major stages during the marketing cycle. Each presentation has similar objectives — mainly approval, yet they differ greatly in strategic approach. For example, each one must clearly identify the specific audience and address the client's needs.

The needs of the client remain similar in all 5 types, but the strategy for approaching those needs differs. The components used to express those needs change and even the method of delivery must change somewhat throughout the process. In addition, there are many variations within each of the 5 groups of presentation formats. The 5 major divisions can be roughly classified as follows:

1. Corporate Services Presentation

2. Interviews for Specific Projects

3. Design Competitions

4. Presentation to Public Agencies

5. Retrofit: Project to new uses

Each stage is dependent on the success of the previous one. As an example, if the corporate presentation doesn't stimulate a client to call the firm for a specific job, that is the end of the line. Interview presentations that are successful are pre-requisites for presenting to public agencies for approval of a project.

Design competitions oftentimes can come about without prior qualifications through presentations. Retrofitting a project presentation to new marketing use does require a completed presentation as the base, yet does not require a completed project for its success.

CORPORATE SERVICES PRESENTATION

OBJECTIVE: This type of presentation is designed to give an introductory overview of the firm to an unknown (or known) potential client. It is most often general in nature with focus on a particularly unique aspect of the firm's services. Since it may be shown to many client types it is often better to focus on the process rather than the product.

AUDIENCE: The client is a stranger (usually) to your firm and the thing he wants to hear is how you will relate to his project. Therefore, third party endorsements of your capabilities will be much more palatable to him.

THEME: If the program is designed for a particular market segment, then projects should be chosen that relate very specifically to that market area. It should describe your firm's process in relation to those market requirements.

COMPONENTS: Since the objective is to describe the firm and capabilities, most of the visual components must come from within the firm. These could include your location, pictures of the working environment, sketches, models, and pictures of the key people.

PRODUCTION: Many of these kinds of programs are produced out-of-house by AV producers. Many programs are produced with the use of a radio announcer's voice for the sound track. This makes it sound professional, but perhaps too much so. The client immediately equates your message with the words "canned presentation." By using natural dialogue for the sound track you can easily overcome this stigma.

TIMING: Since these programs are used over and over, and the image that is presented is critical, it should not be done in a hurry. The program should be perfected until it is less than 7 minutes.

DELIVERY: The majority of this type of program is pre-recorded with pulses on tape to run the show. It should be shown the same each time and should be designed so that anyone in the firm can run it simply by pressing a button.

PROJECT INTERVIEWS

OBJECTIVE: The primary objective is to be selected for the job, however, it is good to have a secondary objective, since all competitors share in wanting the job. For example, this secondary objective could be to position your firm for future work. Another might be to demonstrate how your capabilities match the client's overall needs.

AUDIENCE: Some review boards are made up of members of the client's ogranization of affiliated functions. The average size is 6 persons headed by a chairperson. Since this person, or review board at large, may not be the decision maker, it's essential that as much information as possible be uncovered prior to developing the presentation.

THEME: There should only be one primary theme for this type of presentation — how to satisfy the client's needs as expressed in the R.F.P. (request for proposal).

COMPONENTS: Since many of the firm's qualifications have already been evaluated in the proposal submittal, it is unwise to sell them a second time. Instead concentrate on material that relates to the client's site, his program, his schedule, and budget. Relate each visual to the project type.

PRODUCTION: Due to the short time frame, these presentations are mostly produced in-house. However, an outside consultant can often offer a more objective opinion as to how well the presentation answers the needs of the client. Pre-made visuals and generic material will alleviate the short time frame and keep it looking professional.

TIMING: Generally these presentations are longer than the corporate services presentations. In fact many firms use the corporate services presentation as an introduction to the interview. This can be risky since it is not specifically related to the project at hand.

DELIVERY: Usually these are given in person, spoken by the principal or project manager. On special occasions a combination of material may be used. In either case, rehearsals are necessary to perfect the timing and delivery.

DESIGN COMPETITIONS

OBJECTIVE: Even though there are two objectives in this type of presentation, the primary one is selling an appealing design solution. The secondary one is the capability of the firm to produce the project. Each type of competition has its own set of rules regarding program, site requirements, project delivery, or other pre-determined requirements.

AUDIENCE: In these instances, the audience, or at least the real decision makers, may not be identified. If they are known, it certainly will influence the solution to the program and even the design solution.

THEME: Since the program requirements must be spelled out, these very naturally become the theme of the design and the presentation. In this instance, the design process and presentation can be integrated for more impact.

COMPONENTS: The emphasis must be on the site and the design solution, as expressed in plans, sketches, elevations, models or other 3-dimensional simulation. The solution to the program, and the way the design scheme expresses that solution, should be the key elements of the presentation.

PRODUCTION: The major part of the design scheme drawing is done in-house. However, the way to present the scheme is often more effectively accomplished by a presentation consultant. They can objectively portray what the design team has in mind.

Good designers do not always make good presenters. In fact, the reverse is usually true.

TIMING: The scale and scope of the project will have a direct effect on the timing, at least it should have. Rather than waiting for the design to be completed, it is best to begin the presentation planning along with the designing. The two will then be inter-related. Oftentimes media decisions will affect design decisions, especially in the way they are presented.

DELIVERY: Full scale models and video presentations are not uncommon to this type of presentation.

PROJECT DESIGN PRESENTATION

OBJECTIVE: Primarily these are geared to seeking approval on a project, whether it be re-zoning or new land use. The primary objective is to secure as much in your favor to allow the project to continue.

AUDIENCE: Here, unquestionably, there are two groups that must be confronted: the agency itself and the community or constituency that the agency represents. Most often the second group will be the determining factor in shaping your presentation and in getting approval

THEME: To the agency the theme must be sound planning and economic viability. This is usually worked out in advance of the public hearing. Without their prior approval, a presentation is a waste of time.

To the audience the theme must be a respect for their concerns and a convincing plan that links benefits of the project to the community.

COMPONENTS: The proposed plan is most effective when presented in relationship to community concerns. Density, land use, traffic access, and infra-structure are all words that designers understand, but laymen may not. It's best to keep the design language to a minimum in the graphics.

PRODUCTION: The design material is best produced in-house, whereas the presentation is best produced by the consultant. Since human emotions often outweigh reason, the designer should let others, more experienced in making the message more palatable, tell the story to the community.

TIMING: Most public hearings are scheduled months in advance. Time should not be a factor provided the planning for the presentation is begun at the same time, or even before the design is started.

DELIVERY: Public hearings can be very volatile, even outright hostile. Therefore, one should be prepared for the worst. Pre-recorded messages are often an answer, since it's very difficult to argue with a tape recorder.

RETROFIT: PROJECT DESIGN TO MARKETING USE

OBJECTIVE: Previous presentations that were prepared for project submittals, or even interview submitals, can be re-used for marketing purposes. The original is usually project-oriented and can be used to seek other similar projects.

AUDIENCE: The presentation cycle is completed with this type of program, as the intended audience may not be familiar with the firm or the project used. Therefore, capabilities and general qualifications come back into play.

THEME: The message must be restructured around the introduction of the firm to a new client who would be interested specifically in this project type. Naturally, if the project shown has been built it would add credibility. Even if it hadn't, the material can still be used, highlighting some positive attribute of your firm relating to this project.

COMPONENTS: Most components come from the material prepared for the original presentation. Customizing can be easily accomplished by the addition of new graphics and some generic shots from the office.

This should include key personnel just as in the corporate services type. In fact, it becomes a hybrid of corporate services and a project submittal.

PRODUCTION: The costs to produce this can be extremely low if done in-house. However, a new script must be developed. Often it Is recorded for automatic showing, since the original program was most likely narrated in person.

TIMING: The time required to retrofit a presentation is short by comparison to some of the other types. It depends on how extensive a revision is made in the sound track, or even if a sound track is added.

DELIVERY: Most programs end up similar to the original corporate services, but geared towards a specific market, project type, or client. The use of this type of program extends use of the material into the future.

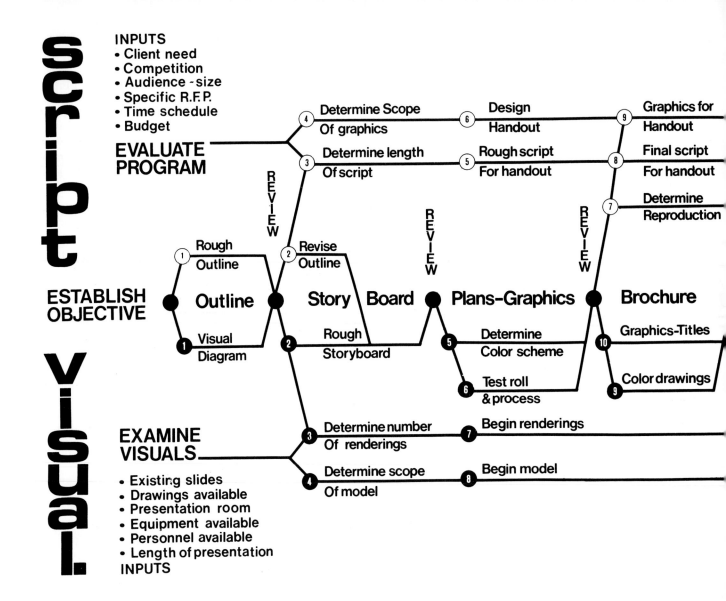

script

INPUTS
- Client need
- Competition
- Audience - size
- Specific R.F.P.
- Time schedule
- Budget

EVALUATE
PROGRAM

ESTABLISH
OBJECTIVE

visual.

EXAMINE
VISUALS

- Existing slides
- Drawings available
- Presentation room
- Equipment available
- Personnel available
- Length of presentation
INPUTS

REVIEW

④ Determine Scope
Of graphics

③ Determine length
Of script

⑥ Design
Handout

⑤ Rough script
For handout

⑨ Graphics for
Handout

⑧ Final script
For handout

⑦ Determine
Reproduction

① Rough
Outline

② Revise
Outline

Outline

① Visual
Diagram

② Rough
Storyboard

REVIEW

Story Board

REVIEW

Plans-Graphics

⑤ Determine
Color scheme

⑥ Test roll
& process

Brochure

⑩ Graphics-Titles

⑨ Color drawings

③ Determine number
Of renderings

④ Determine scope
Of model

⑦ Begin renderings

⑧ Begin model

Steps To A Successful Presentation

Planning a slide show can be a relatively simple job if there are only existing slides involved and the presentation is for a small audience or a small project.

However, the most successful presentation will be the one that is properly planned, and carefully organized in its preparation. A practical production schedule will insure ample time at the end to rehearse and make final corrections. Without these considerations you can be courting a disaster.

A chart will be useful when preparing a program from nothing more than the design sketches. Considering the total show at this stage is crucial, as the presentation now becomes a natural extension of the design program. Therefore, many of the concepts of the design solutions will influence your presentation. The end result will be a more harmonious visual

program. This cannot be emphasized too much, for the one single element that can raise a presentation to the level of excellence is a singleness of purpose. To achieve this quality you must begin to plan the show as early as possible.

The chart is divided horizontally into halves. The upper section relates to the preparation of the script. The lower half depicts the steps necessary to complete the visuals. Whenever they meet at the center indicates a review.

The chart is segmented in sequential stages. The main concern is that the rough outline and visual diagram for the show be started at the earliest possible date. This may necessitate several revisions along the way, but the results will be far more compatible with the proposed project than if you wait until a few weeks prior to the presentation to begin planning the show.

156

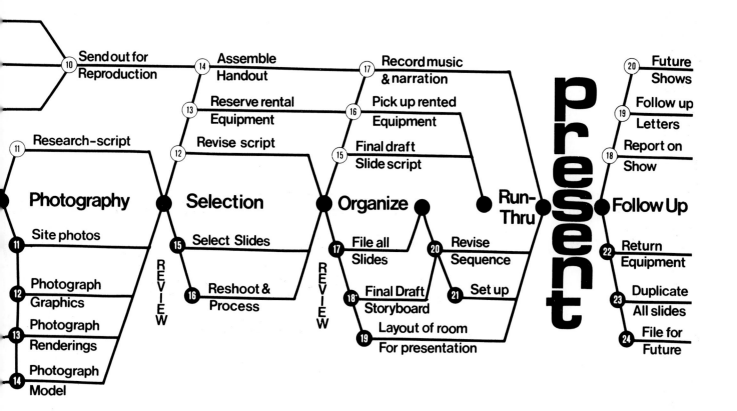

The person in charge of the script may work independently in producing a script or graphics to be used as a handout at the presentation. But it is generally a mistake to assume that the material used for a brochure will suffice for the slide show, or that slides can be used to produce illustrations for a handout or brochure. The two mediums are completely different.

Work which may be suitable for one may not be suitable, or legible, for the other. This does not mean that duplication of artwork is impossible; it merely indicates that one is a printed medium, usually 8½x11-inch format or larger, and the other is the production of 35mm slides. The same legibility standards do not apply.

Whereas the handout may attempt to summarize the slide presentation commentary, it most often will have a different message. The text material that is developed for the handout may be too technical or lengthy to be used in the slide presentation.

Such graphic exhibits as the organizational charts of a company, or joint venture involvements, are much too complex to be shown on the screen, but go well in a handout. Cost breakdown, budgets, time schedules, and other charts, must be extremely simple in slide form, but not so in a handout brochure.

A key item to remember is the early consideration of the graphics and overall color scheme for the show. This should be followed by test rolls to determine how the color choices will look on the screen. This will also allow you to determine the proper exposures in copying the artwork.

Many times the artwork is prepared and photographed and it is only then discovered that a lighter or darker shade or different contrast in color would have been more effective. Many times this discovery comes too late to change the artwork.

The final slides should be taken and processed by the same lab that did the test rolls, at least 2 weeks or more prior to the final deadline. This allows you to group your slides and rephotograph any that did not turn out to your expectations.

While taking the pictures of the site or model, make sure to take more than you need. They will be a great deal of trouble to retake. This reshooting refers to the artwork, titles, or renderings, as exposure, cropping, and legibility are most critical here.

Be sure to allow for a number of rehearsals, as this is where flaws in the presentation will show up.

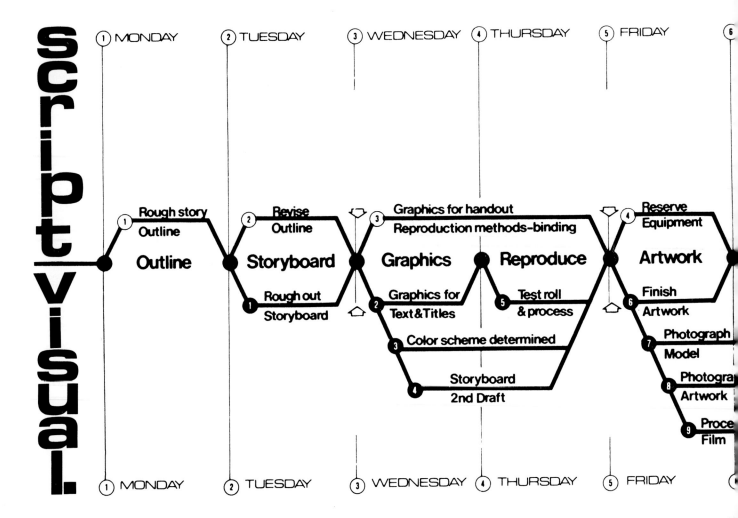

script visual

| ① MONDAY | ② TUESDAY | ③ WEDNESDAY | ④ THURSDAY | ⑤ FRIDAY | ⑥ |

Rough story
Outline

Outline

Revise
Outline

Storyboard

Rough out
Storyboard

Graphics for handout
Reproduction methods—binding

Graphics

Graphics for
Text & Titles

Color scheme determined

Storyboard
2nd Draft

Reproduce

Test roll
& process

Reserve
Equipment

Artwork

Finish
Artwork

Photograph
Model

Photogra
Artwork

Proce
Film

| ① MONDAY | ② TUESDAY | ③ WEDNESDAY | ④ THURSDAY | ⑤ FRIDAY | ⑥ |

12 Day Chart

The basic assumption behind this time frame is that most of the material already exists in some form. There is no provision for long-range planning.

Unfortunately, most presentations are done within this time span. There are many who have tried to do it on even shorter notice. Out of necessity, they skip either one or both of the most important items in the entire process.

The first item overlooked is the storyboard. The plan of the show evolves either on a light box or in the projectors. Then, with little time at the end, rehearsals are cut to a quick run-through. If you fall behind in your schedule, the items at the end of the chart will have to be cut short.

Therefore, it is always a good idea to plan your show in reverse, using the presentation as the tar-

158

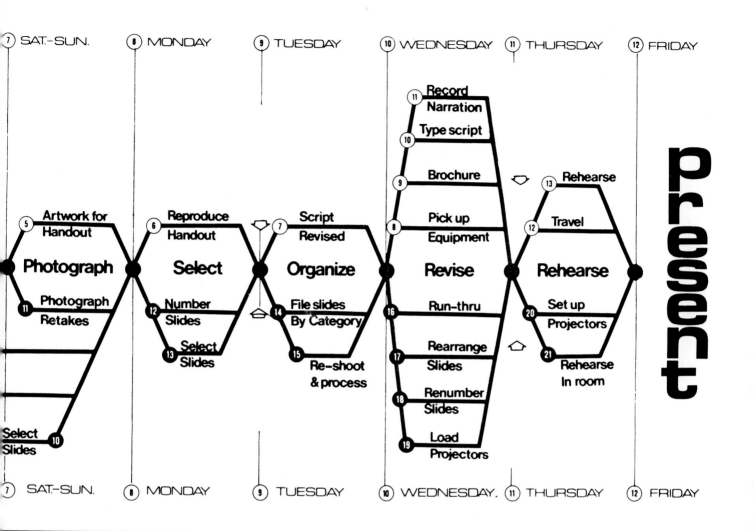

Artwork for Handout

⑤ **Photograph**

⑪ **Photograph Retakes**

Select Slides ⑩

⑥ **Reproduce Handout**

Select

⑫ **Number Slides**

⑬ **Select Slides**

⑦ **Script Revised**

Organize

⑭ **File slides By Category**

⑮ **Re-shoot & process**

⑪ **Record Narration**

⑩ **Type script**

⑨ **Brochure**

⑧ **Pick up Equipment**

Revise

⑯ **Run-thru**

⑰ **Rearrange Slides**

⑱ **Renumber Slides**

⑲ **Load Projectors**

⑬ **Rehearse**

⑫ **Travel**

Rehearse

⑳ **Set up Projectors**

㉑ **Rehearse In room**

present

⑦ SAT.-SUN.　　⑧ MONDAY　　⑨ TUESDAY　　⑩ WEDNESDAY.　　⑪ THURSDAY　　⑫ FRIDAY

get date. Start this reverse plan by allowing one day for rehearsals and possible minor changes. Be sure to allow time for rehearsing in the actual room, if possible. There may be many surprises in store for you if you do not.

Remember that the day prior to the rehearsal will be a busy one, with a great number of odds-and-ends to take care of. The basis of your show will be in the organization and selection of the final slides, so you must allow ample time for this endeavor.

As usual, you will be faced with at least one weekend during your schedule. This time can be put to good use if you plan to get all your film processed by Friday and retake any errors over the weekend. It is also a good time to begin filing your slides into various categories for selecting and final editing.

Media Comparison

There are many considerations that enter into selecting the medium and format for a particular presentation. At first it may appear that a number of choices are available, but many will be eliminated by specific limitations. For example, a formal proposal of a design scheme might rule out flip charts or the overhead in favor of more sophisticated means. Budgetary limitations and time constraints will also affect your choice. Other factors are the availability of equipment and the conditions of the presentation room itself. The size of the audience will contribute greatly to your choice, and the character of the intended audience will run a close second.

Another factor, which will affect your choice of medium, will be the length of production lead time. For most marketing interviews, lead time is short, which makes the slide medium a good choice because of the ease of changing a program to suit your client at relatively low cost. The production budget will also play an important role and possible hidden costs must be examined realistically. This can be done only by identifying all the tasks to be done, who will perform them, and how much they will charge.

The number of copies of the presentation required has a bearing on the media selection. Hard copy printing is easily accomplished, but extra copies of a slide presentation or a Super 8 film can become an additional expense. Another factor, which will contribute to your selection, is portability of the presentation equipment and visuals. Most marketing interviews and other client or public presentations are outside your own controllable environment.

Today, motion pictures and particularly video have made us very media conscious. And the more sophisticated the video media becomes, the more archaic the yellow tracing paper and other direct viewing presentations become. Remember, media and message must be integrated for maximum effectiveness.

ADVANTAGES	DISADVANTAGES
REAL OBJECTS Presentation can be spontaneous. Any material can be presented. Sequence of events can be controlled.	Hard for audience to see, unless large. Hard to transport; cumbersome to show. Audience can be distracted during show.
MODELS Gives excellent overview of project. Arouses audience interest in display. Visual display of inter-relationships.	Hard to relate to human scale. Can quickly prejudice an audience. Time consuming to build; hard to ship.
WALK-IN ENVIRONMENT, Gives experience of actual space. Saves costly errors on the real project.	Costly to construct. Difficult to move to another location.
CHALKBOARD Impromptu visual explanations. Inexpensive, easy to use, erase & reuse.	Visuals not permanent. Must be erased. Extremely primitive visual display. Presenter must turn back to the audience.
EASEL PAD/ FLIP CHART Impromptu, inexpensive visual sketches. Can be referred to again, or torn off pad. Color is possible using markers or pencil.	Presenter must turn back to the audience. Presenter has to have skill in drawing. Takes valuable time to write out.
OPAQUE PROJECTION Direct from opaque source to screen. No need for intermediary step or process.	Must be in totally dark room. Transition of visuals is not smooth.
OVERHEAD PROJECTION Can be placed in front of audience. Spontaneous, pace can be controlled. Can be used in a lighted room. Transparencies made easily, economical.	Bulky to transport (most models). Requires skill to present smoothly. Images cannot be sequenced rapidly. Art must be converted to transparencies.
35mm SLIDE PROJECTION Can be used for large or small audiences. Long/short projection distances possible. Transition between slides instantaneous. Easy to arrange, or re-arrange sequence. Professional appearance, controlled pace Easy to store and retrieve. Reproduction & distribution economical.	Not effective at high light levels. Material must be prepared in advance. Speaker cannot see image and audience. Sequence unchangeable while showing. Changes must be made on original.
REAR SCREEN PROJECTION CABINETS Show any slide program using same trays. Sound built-in, pulses make it automatic. Can be used in lighted room. Good for small groups, even one-on-one.	Unit is bulkier than a projector. Some cannot be transported easily.
FILMSTRIP PROJECTION Sequence will never be out-of-order. Images will never appear upside down. Compact, lightweight, easy to transport. Economical compared to motion pictures.	Production costs are higher. Synchronized scripts require sound.
MOTION PICTURE Can show motion, compress/expand time. Complete system, motion, sound & action. Highly motivational.	High cost/long production time. Must be processed, edited before shown. Sequences are difficult to rearrange.
VIDEOTAPE People used to seeing everything on video. Creates a special kind of reality. Images seen instantly and replayed.	Expensive to install, maintain, and use. Small screen limits playback.
COMPUTER GENERATED VISUALS Graphics/titles can be produced quickly. Special color effects are possible. Charts, diagrams, schedules, easy to plot.	Images must be generated from tapes. Technology changes very rapidly. Systems are expensive to install and use.

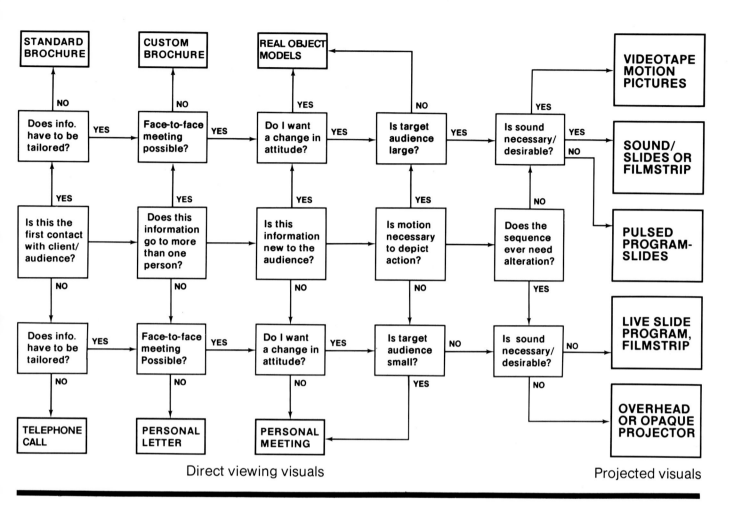

Direct viewing visuals · Projected visuals

There are a variety of marketing tools at your disposal today. Many are constantly being used for marketing by other businesses and industry. These tools can be divided into two classifications: hard copy and soft copy. Hard copy normally relates to printed matter and soft copy to projected matter. But for the design professional, a clearer picture would be to divide them into direct viewing and projected visuals.

Direct viewing visuals would include reports, proposals, brochures, board presentations and scale models. Projected visuals would include material shown on the overhead or opaque projector, filmstrip or slide projector, 8mm and 16mm motion pictures and videotape.

The decision about the proper AV medium to use for any communication usually comes too late in the design process. This negates one of the most unique advantages of any medium, that is,

being able to combine and coordinate "medium and message."

The choice of medium is based on many factors. On the chart above is a matrix listing items that will affect your choice. It is divided into direct viewing visuals, such as letters, reports, brochures, and real objects.

Real objects, of course, can include everything from a scale model to a full size mock-up of the object. On the lower end of the communications spectrum is the contact beyond the initial stage, where information does not have to be tailored, yet face-to-face meeting is not possible. These can be solved obviously by a simple phone call, or letter. If the contact is a new client, you may want to send a letter of interest and your general office brochure. For that special client, you will have to put together a customized brochure relating to his type of project.

However, once you leave the small audience, other considera-

tions enter into the media choice. Chalk boards and flip charts are all right when you want to ad lib, or talk and write, or draw diagrams. If sound is not necessary and the sequence needs to be altered on the spot, overhead projection is a good choice.

The medium most adaptable is the color slide medium, since it can be presented live with a prepared or an ad lib commentary. Slides can also be presented in pulsed programmed units in portable rear-screen projection cabinets. These units are becoming more widely used today. Of course, the criteria for sound and motion lead us to the medium we all know perhaps the best, though we use it the least for presentation purposes, that is, motion picture and videotape.

Today, there is so much advancement in the technology surrounding both film and video that they will definitely be the medium of the future.

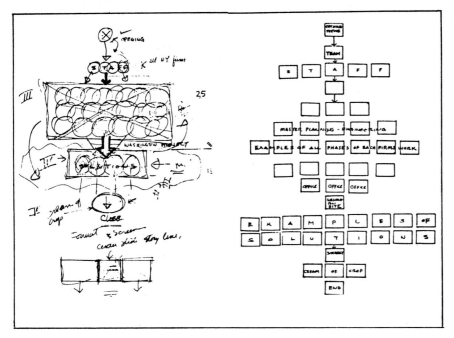

Concept Diagram

The question always comes up as to which comes first, the script or the visuals? One approach is to write the script with the visuals clearly in mind. Another is to organize your show based on the visuals, and write a commentary to fit your visual sequence.

However, the two elements overlap and must be developed together throughout the entire creative process. Your script is the mortar that will bind your slides together, and therefore it must relate to your objective, your audience, and your visuals.

The first rough draft of the presentation outline is usually drawn up by the principal of the firm or the person in charge of the presentation. This is usually in the form of an outline and organizes the basic points to be made in the presentation. This outline is reviewed by people on the staff or those involved in the presentation.

Next, someone will take the major points and begin to make a second outline which incorporates some indication of the number of visuals to be used. However, at this point there is still very little organization of the show and its structure is still not apparent.

As soon as one considers the show as a total entity, a diagram can be drawn depicting the structure of the entire show. This will be similar to a bubble diagram for a planning project and will outline the concept and structure of the program.

All too often this stage is overlooked, making the storyboard planning more difficult. Translating this concept sketch into a more refined structural diagram will reveal a systematic plan for the presentation. Here the objective is clearly defined in visual terms, the audience (client) is analyzed and so is the basic outline necessary to begin the script.

Just as a building cannot be constructed without architectural plans, a good presentation requires planning to build a good foundation. Every good presentation must begin with a concept. And then this concept must be expressed in concrete visual terms so that it can be comprehended by others.

A concept diagram for a project presentation is quite different in

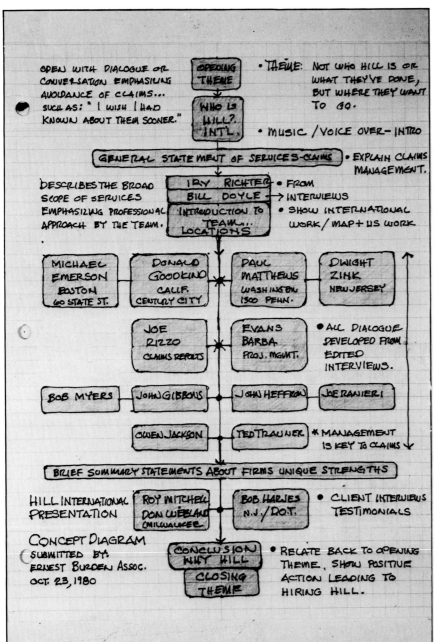

structure from that of a marketing presentation. The various forms of marketing presentations also result in slightly different diagrams in appearance. For example, the diagram for a corporate presentation looks very much like an organizational chart. There may be an opening theme, then an introduction to the key people in the firm. Next the services of the firm will be displayed. In summary, completed projects or testimonials by clients will summarize the firm's strengths and qualifications. The closing theme could echo the opening.

The diagram for an interview presentation (shown right and below) would focus on answering the items in the request for proposal (R.F.P.). It should follow the same sequence as the items in the request, if possible. It is an exercise in matching the qualifications of the firm to the needs of the client.

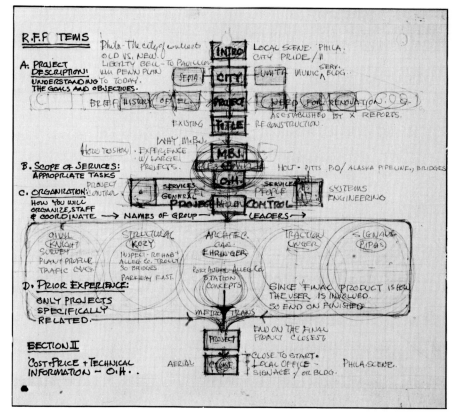

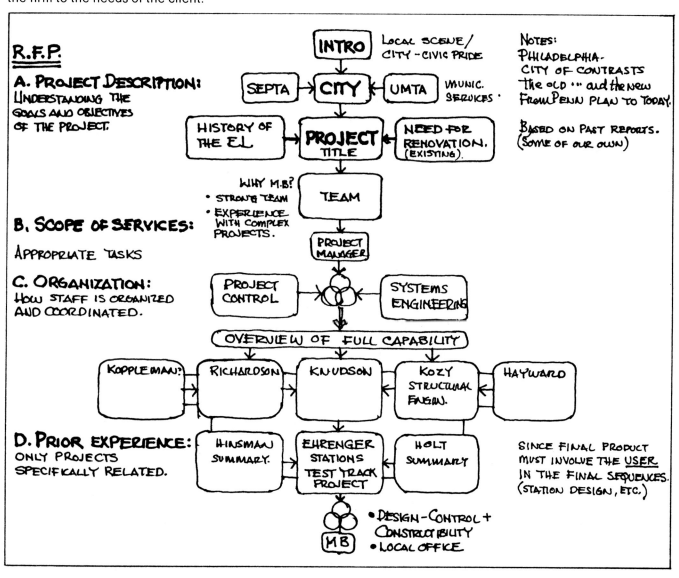

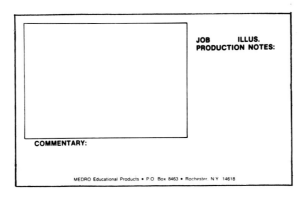

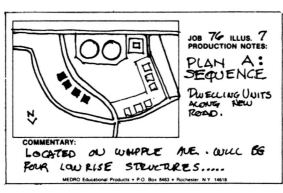

JOB 76 ILLUS. 7
PRODUCTION NOTES:

PLAN A:
SEQUENCE

DWELLING UNITS
ALONG NEW
ROAD.

COMMENTARY:
LOCATED ON WHIPPLE AVE. WILL BE
FOUR LOW RISE STRUCTURES.....

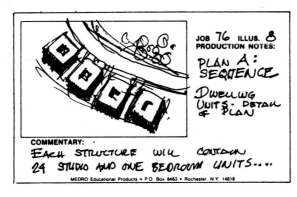

JOB 76 ILLUS. 8
PRODUCTION NOTES:

PLAN A:
SEQUENCE

DWELLING
UNITS - DETAIL
OF PLAN

COMMENTARY:
EACH STRUCTURE WILL CONTAIN
24 STUDIO AND ONE BEDROOM UNITS....

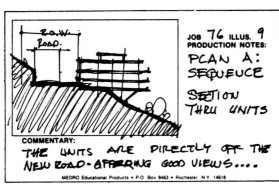

JOB 76 ILLUS. 9
PRODUCTION NOTES:

PLAN A:
SEQUENCE

SECTION
THRU UNITS

COMMENTARY:
THE UNITS ARE DIRECTLY OFF THE
NEW ROAD - OFFERING GOOD VIEWS....

JOB 76 ILLUS. 10
PRODUCTION NOTES:

PLAN A:
SEQUENCE

CLOSE UP
PERSPECTIVE

COMMENTARY:
BY CLUSTERING THE UNITS - OVER
50% OF THE LAND IS UNTOUCHED....

Planning Cards

There is a simple tool that is quite helpful in the early stages of organizing a presentation. It is called a storyboard later in the planning process.

An effective way to start your planning is to write on a plain card, one idea or point that you want to include to achieve your defined objective. Plain white index cards are used in this initial stage. The planning cards can be arranged on a board in any desired sequence. They are free to be previewed and rearranged whenever necessary.

Arrange these idea cards in some logical pattern or sequential order. You will discover at this point that ideas will be added or subtracted to smooth the program out. Cards bearing similar or over-lapping ideas can be grouped together to form sequences.

Once these basic ideas are approved, the next step is to develop a series of planning cards. There are some available on 3"x5" preprinted card stock. The large rectangle in the upper left corner provides a frame for a rough sketch of the planned visual.

The job number or other identification can also be entered on the card. The numbers should first be marked in pencil, then in ink once the arrangement is final. There is a space for commentary under the picture, which can be expanded later in the final script, if necessary.

One 3"x5" card per slide with one or two sentences per card is sufficient. However, don't number the cards, as you will want to edit them later.

For large group evaluation of the proposed presentation, a slide set of the visuals on the cards can be easily made. The entire prearranged board can be photographed and studied as an 8"x10" print.

Try to let the visuals carry the message. Use only enough narration to clarify what is being shown. As you edit the 3"x5" cards, organization of your presentation begins. Sequences will start to come together and the cards will be the starting point for developing the script. Before the script is finalized you should further expand the visual sequences on a storyboard form.

VISUAL FORMATS

SLIDES

35 mm

31 mm
(126)

SUPER SLIDE
(127)

FILMSTRIPS

35 mm SINGLE FRAME

(FILM)
MOTION PICTURES

16 mm

8 mm

OVERHEAD
TRANSPARENCIES

VIDEO

Media Formats

The choice of format is an extremely important consideration in the development of an effective AV presentation.

The most common type of slide is produced with color film which has been exposd in a 35mm camera. This size film is normally mounted in 2x2-inch cardboard mounts. The 2x2 inches refer only to the outside dimensions of the mount.

Slide mounts by different companies may vary. The important thing to remember is that every mount will cover up part of the slide image. Therefore, whenever you decide to use a special slide mount, you should shoot a test roll to determine the framing and alignment of the finished slide.

The most standard format can be used either in the horizontal or vertical position. The "half-frame" size is made to accept pictures made with a special half-frame camera and is the standard filmstrip format. There is also a square mount intended for use with a 126-roll film size. The opening in this mount is larger than the 35mm film, so it cannot be used with these mounts.

Some companies make special masks for standard 35mm film, such as the TV proportion format of 25mm x 31mm and a wide-screen mount of 17mm x 35mm proportion.

By using 120-roll film and a 2¼x2¼-inch camera, you can virtually create any format you may want. However, when using this size film you must hand-cut and hand-mount all the slides. The most common slide format produced by the 120 film is the superslide. When working with special formats and multiple-image effect, the large size is an advantage.

There are a number of standard masks available for creating special multiple-image effects. The choice of format should go hand-in-hand with your choice of projection and screen image.

Other projection formats are the 16mm and 8mm film, each of which has a 3:4 aspect ratio. This is the same ratio as the filmstrip, and video. Overhead transparencies can be masked to any aspect ratio, but the most common is 4:5 wherein the actual size is 8x10-inch transparencies.

Screen Format

The single-screen show is the most popular due to the inherent ease of use. However, continuity must be achieved through either well-planned, clearly understandable sequences — or through lap-dissolve projection. In this mode, one image fades out as the other fades in. Both projectors are aimed at the same screen and both images coincide. You are still dealing with a single image, one which dissolves from slide-to-slide.

In the case of a dissolve show, it is more important to control the use of varying formats. If you don't, the transition from vertical to horizontal and back to vertical can become distracting.

When more than one screen is used, the choice of format increases. By using two projectors, you can show a duplicate or double of what you could do on a single screen. You can also increase the number of combinations by alternating formats.

When utilizing a dual screen, you should design the show to accommodate your widest pair of slides so that they do not overlap.

If you mix horizontal and vertical formats within the same show, you have to plan the combinations very carefully.

The dual-screen is an excellent format for many types of presentations. First and foremost, you can make comparisons, or show examples of a situation discussed in the narration.

When using more than dual-screen projection the choice of format becomes a vital issue. Again, careful planning is extremely necessary to avoid a haphazard-looking program.

Even with such a wide choice of formats and combinations, it is still possible to plan a smooth-flowing and professional-looking show.

The ultimate way, of course, would be to have all projectors hooked up to dissolve units. This could become unwieldy for a presentation that had to be shown outside your environs. However, in a permanent projection room, it is very little trouble to set up and run.

Combining multi-screen projection with multiple-images on each slide makes endless possibilities for creating stunning effects.

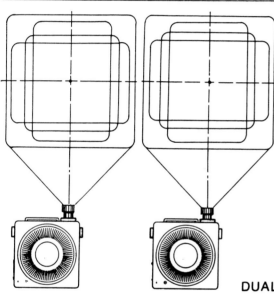

SINGLE SCREEN PROJECTION

DUAL SCREEN PROJECTION

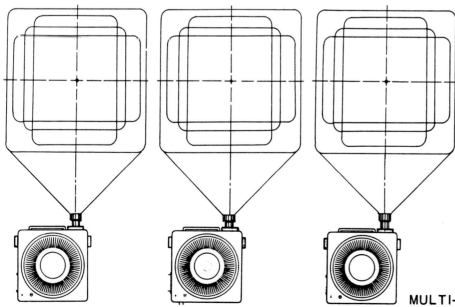

MULTI—SCREEN PROJECTION

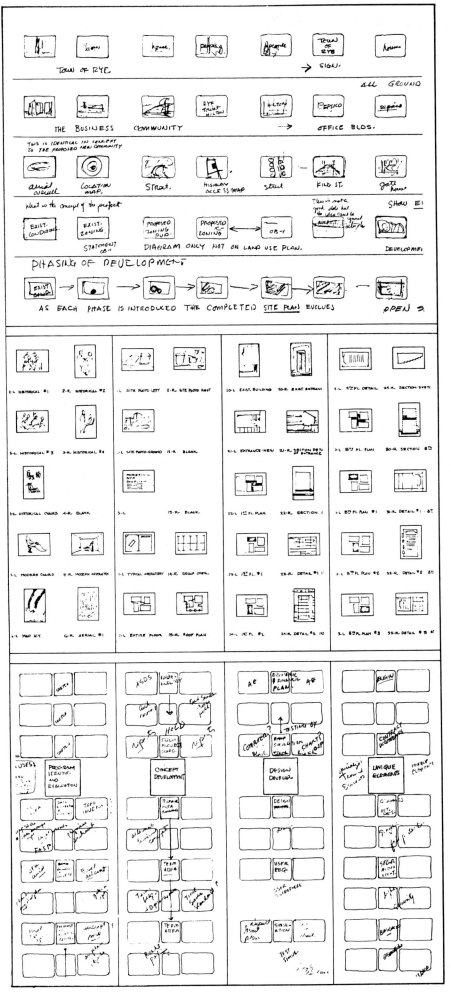

Storyboards

You can begin to plan your show by using a device known as the storyboard. The storyboard represents the entire program in miniature.

To plan one, simply rule off any number of 2x2-inch squares on a piece of paper. Draw in the horizontal, vertical, or super-slide formats (or any other format choice) within the squares. Using this as an underlay, you can begin to plan your show.

The function of the storyboard is to help you visualize how your show will look on the screen. Therefore, it is important to draw the storyboard to the exact format dimensions you have chosen.

The opening and closing sequences will be the hardest to plan, so you might begin with those and fill in between. After you have done your rough sketch, you will find some slides that you will want to eliminate altogether.

As you develop the storyboard, certain patterns will begin to emerge. By viewing the entire program at a glance in miniature, you will be able to consider an appropriate opening and closing sequence.

As the storyboard progresses, it will help you prepare a script to go with your slides. You will also discover what additional slides you may need to tell your story. By starting the storyboard at the very earliest stage of planning your show, you can save many hours of preparation later when time is short.

As you will discover, the usefulness of the storyboard will diminish as you begin to sort and organize the actual slides that will be used. However, the storyboard still has a useful function up to the very end of the planning.

It can be used to record the material that was selected for presenting. It is useful in numbering sequences — especially for the more complex three-or-four projector show. If the storyboard is drawn or sketched on tracing paper, then ozalid prints can be run to hand out to others involved with the presentation.

Once you have outlined the entire program, you can transfer the images to an 8½x11-inch sheet and work out a script for each group of slides.

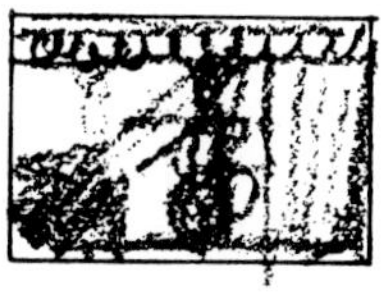

BETWEEN THE OLD....

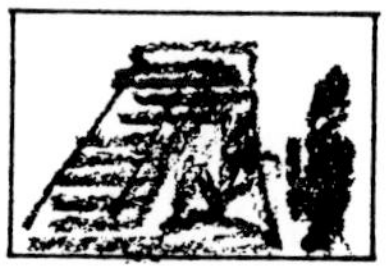

AND THE NEW.
(MUNICIPAL SERVICES BUILDING.)

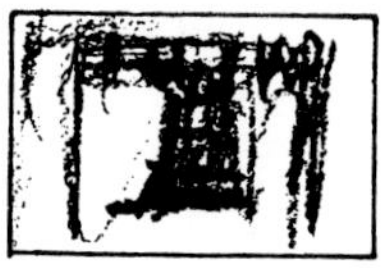

LIKE THE OLD LIBERTY BELL....

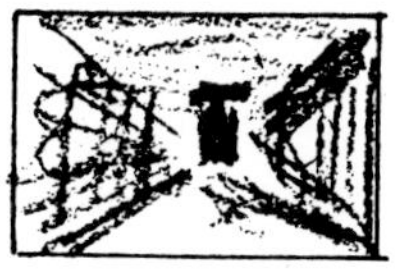

AND THE NEW LIBERTY BELL PAVILLION.

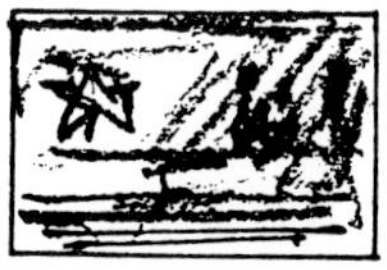

THE NEW STATION AT LIBERTY — PK.
LINK TO

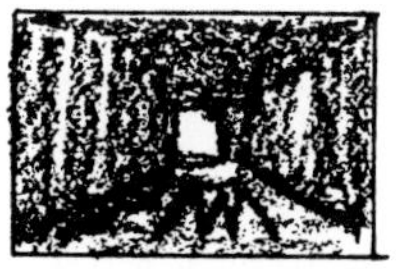

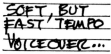

THE BEGINNING OF THE FRANKFOR EL.

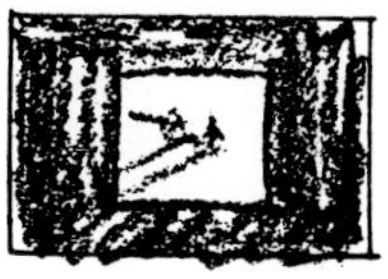

MUSIC BEGIN.
SOFT, BUT FAST TEMPO
VOICEOVER...

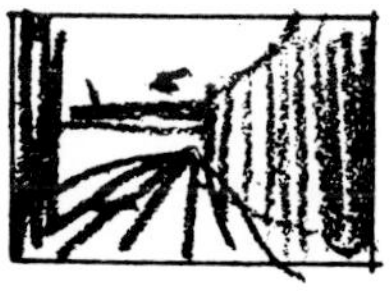

BRIEF STATEMENT ABOUT THE EL TODAY

HOW IT GOES THROUGH AND SERVICES — NEIGHBORHOOD ETC.

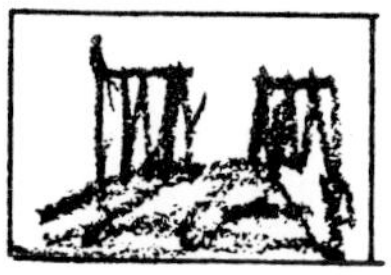

CROSSING X NUMBER OF BETH ROADWAYS WITH BRIDGES

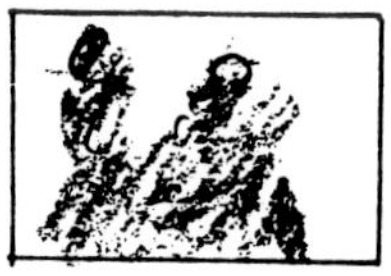

THE EL HAS HAD A LONG HISTORY.... IN A CITY WHICH BEGAN...

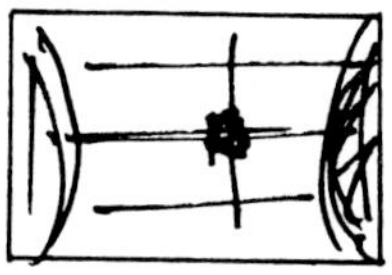

WITH THE PENN PLAN OF 1682.
AND DEVELOPED INTO THE MODERN CITY OF TODAY

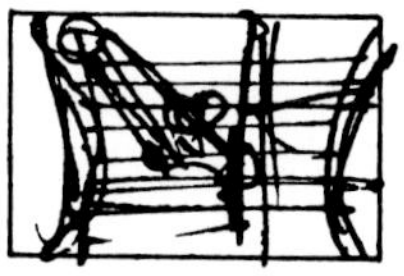

WITH ITS NETWORK OF ROADS + SERVICES

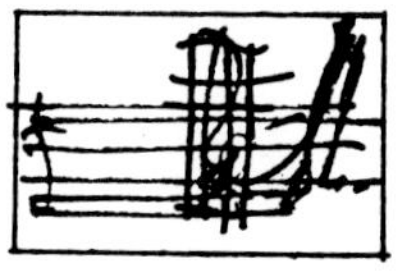

DETAIL OF PLAN. AT LIBERTY PARK

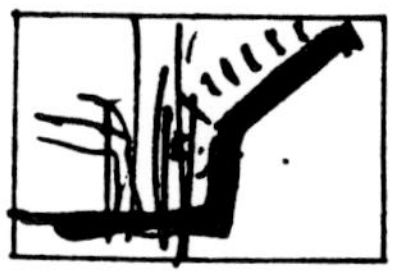

AND WITH ITS METRO SYSTEM.

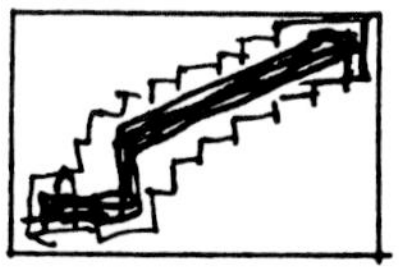

THE PROJECT ENCOMPASSES AREAS FROM — TO —

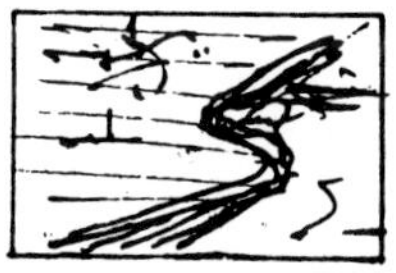

AERIAL VIEW ON THE WAY, THE DESIGN OF THE OLD EL

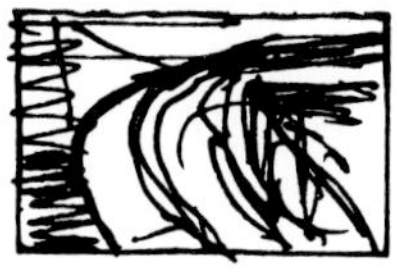

AERIAL VIEW
PASSES THROUGH AREAS NOW COMMERCIAL ETC.

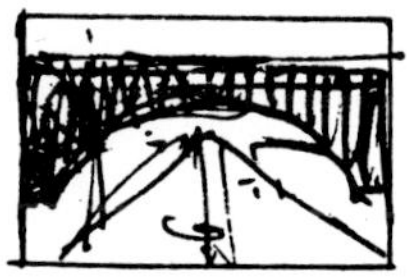

OVER. ARTERIES OF TRAFFIC THAT CANNOT BE INTERRUPTED (LEHIGH.)

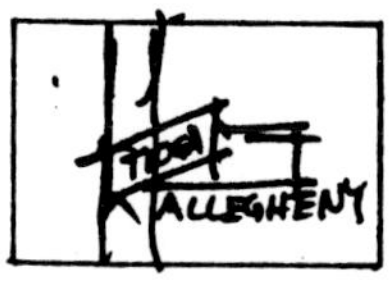

GROUND VIEW AND THROUGH BUSY INTERSECTION OF COMMERCIAL ZONES,

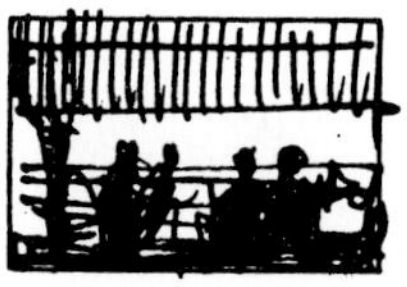

WE ARE AWARE OF THE RESPONSIBILITY OF COMMUNITY SATISFACTION.

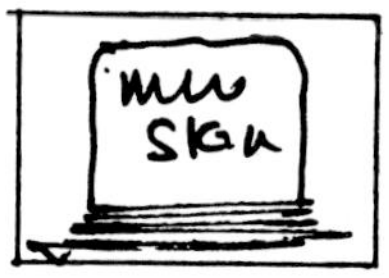

MICHAEL BAK JR. HAS BEEN ACTIVE IN RAIL PROJECT ETC.

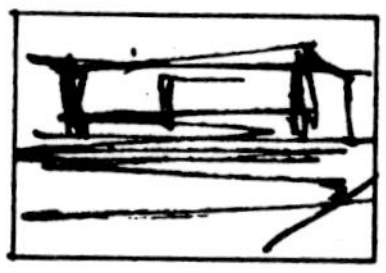

OUR HEADQTR IS LOCATED IN BEAVER, PA.

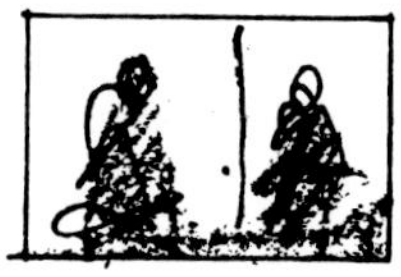

PRINCIPALE ARE M.B. III R.S.

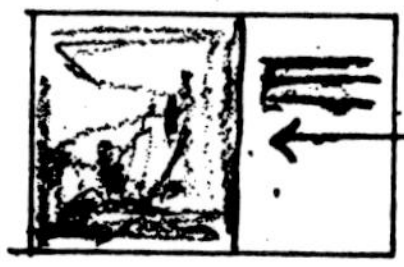

DOOR-TO LOBB W/SIGN.

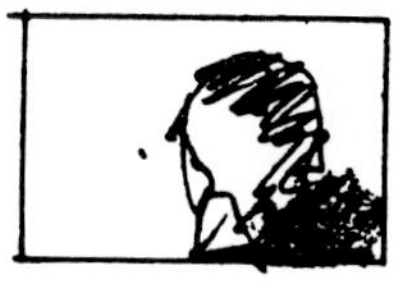

M.B. III IS IN

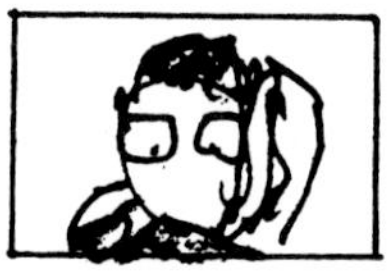

RICHARD SHAW —

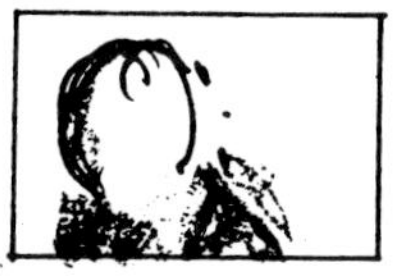

E. RICHARDSON IS OUR TRANSPORTATION GROUP VICE PRES

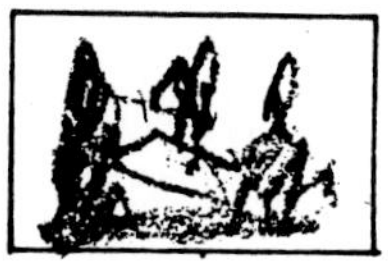

OUR SERVICES ARE QUITE COMPREHENSIVE FROM — TO CONSTRUCTION MANAGEMENT

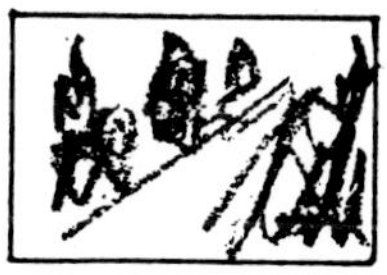

OUR TEAM IS COMPRISED OF — PROFESSIONAL ENGINEERS. WITH SPECIAL EXPERTISE IN TRAFFIC ENGINEERING OUR PRIMARY CONSULTANT TAD IS REPRESENTED BY J. KOPPLEMAN

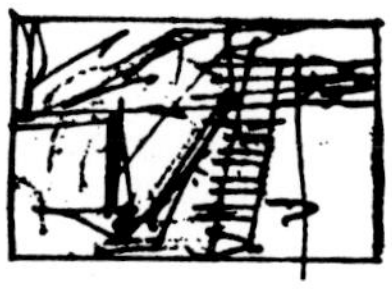

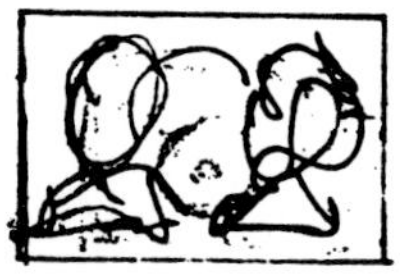

SUBCONSULTANTS SUCH AS — AND — . .

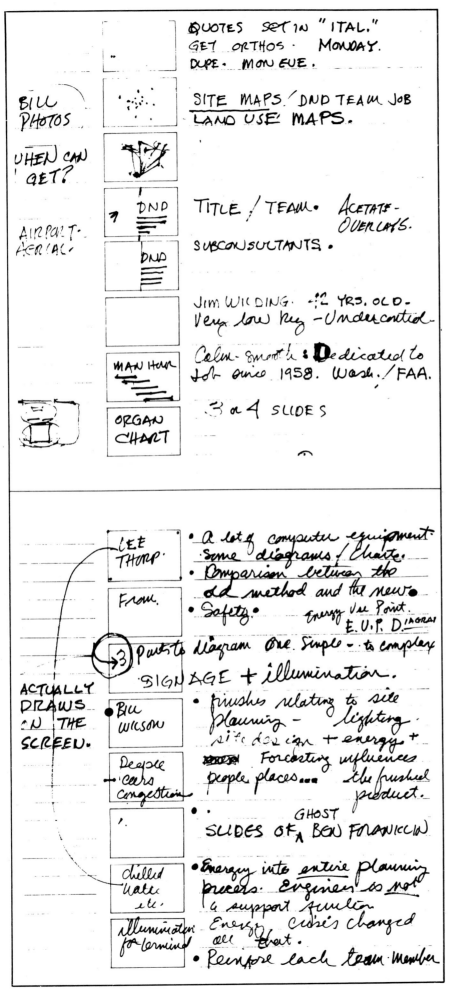

Script Sheets

Script sheets are very helpful in developing your ideas on paper. Rough notes will spark ideas on the visuals and the program can remain flexible at this stage of planning. It is still an easy task to move images and sequences around. However, as the script becomes more solidified it will begin to dictate which visuals will be needed.

As the words become finalized they will control the whole show as the visuals must now follow what is being said. However, the visuals should not be simply a literal translation of the script. They should contribute to the flow of the material and each visual should advance the storyline to where the script picks it up again and the process is repeated.

First-time script writers are inclined to make one of two mistakes: (1) they write words that do not relate to the pictures or (2) they say exactly what the picture on the screen is saying. Rather, you should use the picture on the screen to advance the plot and create continuity by leading into the next picture.

For a show of 80 to 120 slides that will run from 12 to 14 minutes, you will need a script of a maximum of 1500 words. More words will overpower your pictures instead of underscoring their meaning. Figure 120 words or more per minute and plan to show 6 to 7 slides in that time.

Before you begin writing the final script, arrange all the cards in the order that you plan to show them. Look at them alone the first time through. Then ad-lib a commentary as you go over them. This will get you involved with the material. You will begin to sense how long each slide should remain on the screen. At this stage the overall pattern and timing of your show will begin to emerge.

Once you have a rough caption for each picture, read the script aloud. It will sound choppy at first. Smooth out the writing by analyzing the slides as you read. You will discover many flaws this way. Strive for clarity and continuity. The first draft may be too long, so edit it down leaving only the essentials.

The amount of time devoted to slides during a presentation

should be kept within reasonable bounds. A darkened room can have an anesthetic effect on the viewers, especially after lunch. During a long meeting it is not advisable to let your film presentation monopolize the program.

Reading one's speech verbatim can be highly impressive, but it is usually anesthetic as well. First, the speech should be written to be read out loud. That calls for literary talent, and the speech must be rehearsed to be effective. Talking from notes has advantages over reading the comlete speech. To talk "ad-lib" from a list of main points is the simplest method.

A presentation is a combination of planned or programmed visuals and live participation. Every presentation needs an introduction and a summing up.

The opening and closing of a speech can make or break what is sandwiched in between. The opening should be direct and attention-getting and should set the stage for what is to follow.

The close of a speech is often a painful experience to both audience and speaker. The fear that one has not said it all, or well enough, brings about a reluctance to let go and sit down. Endless conclusions and lack of finale allow many a good talk to simply fade away.

Organizing a talk with an effective opening and a dramatic close is not easy. But when armed with a positive slide show, or other visuals, success is generally assured. The primary reason being that in developing a set of visuals, one is compelled to devise a sensible opening and a positive closing.

A rehearsal or "dry run", preferably before an audience capable of evaluating the presentation and making suggestions for improvements, will increase your confidence. Flaws or weak points can be discovered and corrected. Questions can be anticipated and answers prepared for them. A rehearsal will also help you find the proper points to place emphasis in the delivery.

A slide presentation can present a lot of material in a short period of time; that is its inherent strength. However, it will pay off to re-state your main objective at the conclusion. This will leave no doubt in the minds of the interviewers as to the course of action you want.

PAUL MATTHEWS

● MORE AND MORE WE'RE NOT ONLY HANDLING THE CLAIM ITSELF, BUT WE'RE ALSO PICKING UP THE REST OF THE PROBLEM THAT REMAINS AFTER YOU SETTLE THE (LITTLE) LEGAL RESPONSIBILITIES. 7.5

● (IN THE CASE OF THE VETERAN ADMINISTRATION,) WE FIRST ESTABLISHED THE AUTHORITY FOR A TERMINATION FOR DEFAULT FOR THE GOVERNMENT.

CONSTRUCTION- SEQUENCE (1)

● THAT LEFT A PROJECT WITH NO CONTRACTOR ON BOARD. AND WE ASSESSED THE REMAINING COST OF THE WORK

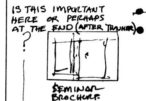
CONSTRUCTION- SEQUENCE (2)

● AND THEN WE PUT PEOPLE ON SITE TO REHIRE AS MANY PIECES (OF THE OLD) EXISTING CONSTRUCTION TEAM THAT WAS NOT INVOLVED IN THE ACTUAL LAW SUIT. 6.8

CONSTRUCTION- SEQUENCE (3)

● WE'RE CURRENTLY COMPLETING THE PROJECT AND WE SHOULD FINISH IT FAR UNDER A RELETTING OF A NEW BID BY THE GOVERNMENT WOULD PRODUCE. (PROBABLY) 50% (AT LEAST) CHEAPER THAN COULD HAVE BEEN DONE HAD COMPLETE NEW LETTING OF THE BID OCCURRED. 12.9

IS THIS IMPORTANT HERE OR PERHAPS AT THE END (AFTER TRAINER)
?

SEMINAR BROCHURE

● WE ALSO PUBLISH LITTLE HANDBOOK ON CLAIMS.

● WE HAVE A LOT OF SEMINARS THAT ARE GEARED COMPLETELY TOWARD THE OWNER. WHERE THEY'RE TAILORED FOR THAT OWNER'S PARTICULAR TYPE OF BUSINESS. 10.5

WE WOULD LIKE TO HELP PEOPLE AVOID CLAIMS, GET PROJECTS DONE ON SCHEDULE,

WITHIN BUDGET WITH MINIMUM DISRUPTION

MORE AND MORE WE'RE NOT ONLY HANDLING THE CLAIM ITSELF, BUT WE'RE ALSO PICKING UP THE REST OF THE PROBLEM THAT REMAINS AFTER YOU SETTLE THE LEGAL RESPONSIBLIITIES FOR WHO PAYS WHO AND WHO OWES WHO. AT THAT POINT SOMEBODY'S GOT TO FINISH THE PROJECT.

COMPLETE THE CONSTRUCTION, AND DO IT IN AN ECONOMICAL MANNER.

WE HAVE A LOT OF SEMINARS THAT ARE GEARED COMPLETELY TOWARD THE OWNER.

Room And Screen

Presentations are designed for one purpose. They consist of a few individuals trying to communicate and present their ideas to a group. Therefore, the group must be comfortably seated, they must be able to see and hear well, and there must be a minimum of distractions.

There are many considerations to be observed when planning facilities for presentations. First, you must determine the size of the audience and the unit space per person, which is about 6 square feet.

Considering that only 50% of the room area will be suitable for seating, you can arrive at an approximate size. The closest seats should be no closer to the screen than two times its width, and no further than six times its width. This is the two-and-six rule of thumb.

Most rental projectors come with zoom lenses, which greatly facilitates placing the projector and screen in an advantageous spot.

However, when giving a presentation in an unfamiliar room, there are any number of things to contend with. Unless you visit the room in advance, there may be many surprises in store for you.

The first consideration is the screen, if there is no flat wall to project on. The screen must be arranged so that all can see it. In a board room or city planning meeting room, the audience faces the council. So if you want both to see the show equally, you have to do some preplanning of the location of the screen such as placing it on a diagonal.

Check the ceiling height for obstructions, such as, hanging chandeliers, microphones, speakers, or other devices. Check the location of all switches and make sure that none of them turn off the power to the projector. Also, check how the room lights are to be controlled. Make sure there isn't stray light in the room, which will reflect on the screen.

Since most presentations are given in unfamiliar rooms, it is imperative that you check these conditions ahead of time, preferably the day before. This will give you some time to correct any situation that you hadn't counted on. If possible, check the room weeks in advance. The physical arrangements of the space will greatly affect your presentation.

Even with the proper preplanning, there are still items that will some up at the last minute. Take the case of a very important presentation put on by a joint venture organization composed of architects and engineers to demonstrate their expertise and capabilities before a review board.

The preliminary reconnaissance trip to the room yielded a sketched-out plan of the room showing door locations, dimensions, and approximate locations of the outlets (1). It also showed that there was a 2-foot-square column right in the middle of the room.

Along the front wall there was a low stage, and right in the middle of the wall there was a pilaster protruding out several inches. The plan called for an arrangement of desks by the reviewing board that would allow projecting on the side wall rather than on the front.

The three-screen show, out of necessity, had to include both horizontal and vertical formats. Therefore, the blank wall was the answer. Even the column in the middle of the room was an obstacle that could be worked around.

The presentation was on Monday morning. The team was scheduled to present at 11 o'clock and figured they had the situation well under control. However, the room was not accessible over the weekend and certain changes had been made between Friday and Monday.

One team was rescheduled to present Monday morning prior to our show. This meant that there was no time to set the room until 30 minutes before a presentation. In addition, the review board decided to move their desks to the front of the room at the last minute.

Therefore, our storyline would have been projected upon the pilaster. The column in the center was still a problem, but somehow the projector stands were set up to go around it

The review board had one screen in the room and that saved the day. The center slides were projected onto the screen, which covered the pilaster, and the two side slides were shown on the flanking walls. There was a difference of 8 inches or so between the images, but the overall visual effect of the multiple-screen show

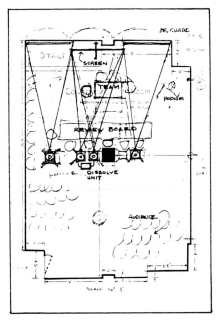

The plan on the far left shows the presentation arrangement as it was planned initially. The room had a two-foot square column in the middle and one blank wall. The program was carefully studied utilizing the blank wall as the screen. The unknown in this situation was not the fact that the room would be locked over the weekend, but another design team presented first on Monday morning.

They completely rearranged the room to suit their presentation and had positioned the review board carefully in an opposite direction.

Last minute adjustments were necessary to even show the presenttion on an uneven wall with pilasters, mouldings, pictures, and clocks. The answer was a roll of white paper (used to make prints) which was held up with tape, and which provided a long clean surface for projection.

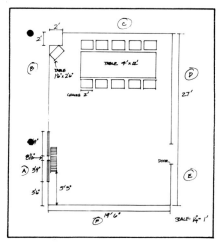

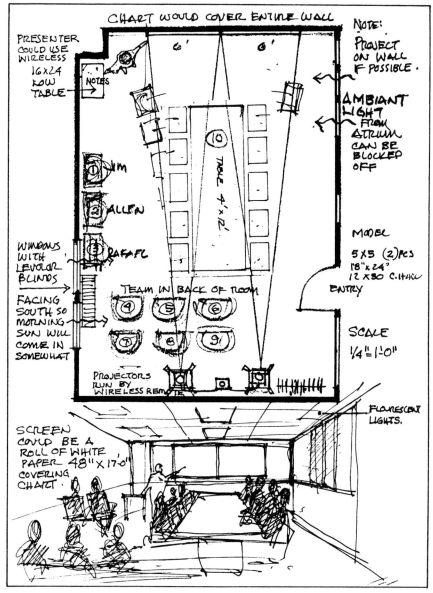

was sufficient to make up for it.

When surveying a room for a critical presentation, it is a good idea to take Polaroid pictures for reference back in the office. Also, a human scale can be very helpful to those who have not had the benefit of a site visit. Oftentimes light from windows can be controlled by placing pre-cut styrofoam panels over them to reduce glare. Similar panels are useful for placing under flourescent fixtures with double-stick tape.

When checking the acoustics, remember that they will be much different in an empty room than in a room filled with people. Then,

too, you should remember that the noise of the projectors can be very troublesome, especially in a small conference room. Check the room for potential outside noise and for noisy heaters or air conditioners.

Check the location of electrical outlets. Tape all extension cords to the floor, wherever people walk, to prevent the cords from being pulled out of the outlets. Most equipment comes with three-pronged plugs, so you may have to use adapters.

If you have additional graphic material other than slides, don't let the audience view it until the time comes to discuss it.

Try to visit the room at the same time of the day as the actual presentation, so the lighting conditions will be the same.

Once the room diagram is drawn, you can sketch the presentation set-up on a tracing paper overlay. This helps others to visualize the format you have in mind.

Arrive as early as possible in the room for setting up and to rehearse the program. Nothing contributes to the success of the presentation more than rehearsal. If the presentation is truly designed for the room, it will make a noticeable difference in the overall quality of your performance.

Planning An AV Facility

First, if the client has an existing AV Department, it may be called public relations, media communications or something similar. The best source of information is the people who work there. The people who actually take the photographs, record the sound and program the shows, will know more about the real needs of the department than anyone else. Spending some time with them will give you some real insight into what they do and how they do it.

Following your homework with the user, it is time to take a look at the building in which the facility is to be installed. If you are working with a new office building, chances are you will be dealing with a building standard ceiling height of 8—9 feet. This one fact will do more to set the design criteria for the audio-visual systems than anything else. With a nine-foot ceiling, the most you can probably expect, the size of the screen is established for either front or rear projection. The size of the audience area is set, the type of sound system is determined. And a number of other options are restricted.

The reasons for this are simple. Assuming the bottom of the screen needs to be 4½ feet off the floor, so those in the rear can see over those in the front, and you need 4—6 inches on the top of the screen for framing and trim, that only leaves you about 4 feet for the screen itself. One of the several audio-visual rules of thumb developed over the years for the size of the screen (or alternately, the size of the audience area) states that the nearest seat to the screen should be about 2 W away, "W" being the width of one screen image. The last seat in the rear should be about 6 W away from the screen for front projection or about 8 W away for rear projection.

To find the size limits of the audience, another rule of thumb states that the audience should be within about 35 to 50 degrees either side of the screen center line. The person in the seat nearest the screen should be able to see the top of it without looking up more that about 30 degrees.

Good planning and knowledge of basic rules of audio-visual functions are important in coming up with designs that are environmentally pleasing, cost effective and give the highest level of technilogical performance.

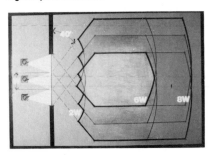

With these simple rules of thumb and several different furniture arrangements you can determine the number of people that will fit comfortably into the viewing envelope.

Getting back to the screen itself for a minute, its size for either rear or front projection should be established early in the design process. If a single slide is to be used, provision must be made for either vertical or horizontal formats, meaning a square screen area. If more than one image is being shown simultaneously, two, three or more square areas are required. For overlapping formats, a screen length-to-height ratio of at least three-to-one is needed. With proper masking and other production techniques, many combinations of images and full screen panoramas can be used for even greater versatility and impact.

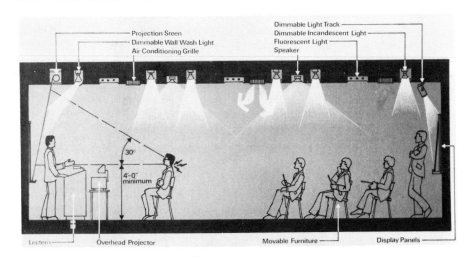

Section – Typical Audio-Visual Room

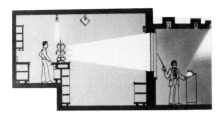

For rear projection the equipment room should be about 2½ or 3 times as deep as the diagonal of our original W. That is, if W is four feet, the equipment room should be about 12—16 feet from the screen to the wall behind the rear counter, including again the 3-foot aisle for the operator. The floor must be elevated so the projectors are at the screen's center line with the projection counter top about 3 feet above this raised floor.

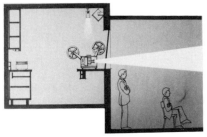

With front projection, a projection booth and equipment room, to avoid conflict with building code, is placed at the rear of the room and elevated so the projected light will clear the audiences' heads. The counter must be deep enough to hold all the projectors and other equipment. A rear counter allows for storage and preparation. Maintain a 3-foot clear aisle between for the operator. The glass can be tilted.

Two other aspects of the equipment room, which cannot be overlooked, are the electrical and mechanical systems. With multiple slide projectors, movie projector and other equipment all on simultaneously, electrical loads of 100 amps are not at all uncommon. It is recommended that an electrical subpanel for the AV system be installed in the equipment room. Similarly the heat loads generated by all this equipment, plus the operator and any room lights, can easily amount to some 30-50,000 BTU's per hr. In the conference room itself the ceiling is often the area of most concern.

Each consultant has specific requirements, which in addition to the designer's intent, must be provided for.

- The lighting consultant has both fluorescent fixtures and dimmable incandescents.
- The mechanical consultant must provide for air handling.
- The acoustical consultant needs so many square feet of absorption.
- The audio consultant needs multiple speakers so everyone can hear properly.

The design of the ceiling takes as much time and coordination as any other aspect of the room. If a lectern is needed, it may need a reading light, microphone, clock and perhaps a control panel.

To avoid having to run an exposed umbilical cord across the carpet, a floor box can be used. Here coordination with the structural consultant may be required. Control of the room's lighting, drapery, audio-visual systems, and other devices should be provided either on the lectern, on the wall, or both.

Finally, when all the design elements have been accounted for, it is time to begin preparation of working drawings and specifications. During the work on these contract documents, the audio-visual consultant will complete all the schematic documents for each system.

He will work with the other consultants and the architect to coordinate his final finishes and equipment locations and he will prepare written specifications including installation methods, testing procedures, equipment lists and many other details. He will also assist the owners and architect in preparing bid forms and in many cases will assist the owner in pre-qualifying bidders for the very specialized work. During construction and installation, he will work with the architect to review shop drawings and other submittals. He will make periodic site visits to assure himself that the work is being installed according to the design intent. When the installation is completed the audio-visual consultant will assist the contractor in making all final tests of sound and projection systems. And he will assist the owner in training personnel in the operation of the installed equipment.

All this and more is required to get that original slide image up on the wall. The finished facility may be as simple as a projector at one end of the room and a screen at the other. Or it may be a sophisticated computer-run multi-projector, quadraphonic sound, multi-media extravaganza with special effects and art work. Whatever the case, with prior planning, insightful design and attention to detail, the audio-visual environment can be a reliable tool to its users, a source of pride to its owners and most importantly a means of quality communications.

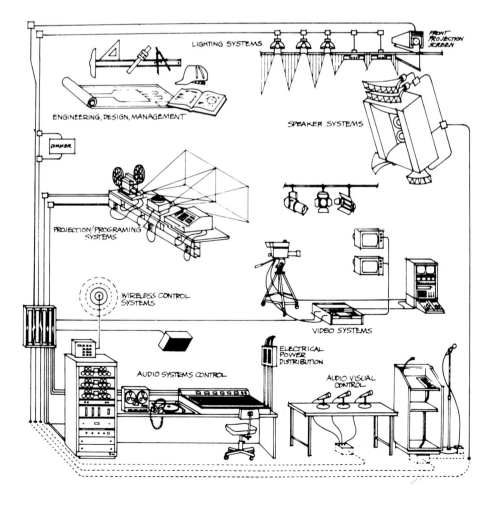

Presentation Environments

The Gruzen Partnership's conference room (below) is designed for slide presentations and model viewing. 3D/I Houston's conference room has a rear projection system (top right) and a convertible wall display (bottom right).

The physical environment of the presentation is a contributing factor to its success. Many times the actual interview is held in the client's environment. Most often it is selected for the client's convenience, not for presentation ambiance. A large factor in preparation for an interview can involve working your presentation around unforeseen obstacles.

When you are lucky enough to have the client come to your office for the interview, will you be ready for him? Probably not. Most design conference rooms were set up for meetings, not presentations.

Architect Robert Morris demonstrated the detailed planning necessary to achieve a workable presentation environment. Two large firms, The Gruzen Partnership in New York and 3D/International in Houston, demonstrate how their presentation rooms work.

According to Gruzen's Design Director Peter Samton, all their presentations are custom designed, either using slides, renderings, or board presentations. They have even made a 16mm film. In the old days, they would use one or two photographs, a rendering or a crude model. Today their competitors go to great lengths and leave them no alternative but to keep up.

The Gruzen conference room pictured is equipped with a multi-projector cabability system and a retractable screen. Photographs, renderings and plan drawings can be pinned to the softboard walls. Models can be set on a table in the center. Refreshments can be served from a nearby pantry unit. The atmosphere is informal and comfortable.

By contrast the 3D/I Houston conference room is controlled by push button consoles, which can be operated from three different locations, including the speaker's lectern. A credenza can be opened electronically to display plans, renderings, or color and material samples shown in the photo. A highly sophisticated AV system can project films, slides or video.

Frank Douglas, Director of Graphics for 3D/I, feels it is important to use every possible visual method to explain a design project. Even though some of their presentations have been felt tip markers on yellow tracing paper, most involve some combination of slides, video, models, renderings, and photos.

While both firms are capable of producing most of their work in-house, models, renderings, and films are done by outside consultants. 3D/I has some in-house video capabilities.

Can smaller firms compete with this level of sophistication? Peter Samton and Frank Douglas seem to think so. They also admit that some clients may be put off by a fancy presentation when one is not called for. You have to know the client and his level of sophistication in terms of presentations made to him. Technial staff will need one level of information presented, whereas a CEO will not have time nor interest in the detail.

The true value of a presentation is in the appropriateness of the concept to the client's program, and the concept is free. The presentation environment, however simple or sophisticated, should facilitate the delivery of ideas in a simple and believable fashion.

ROOM WITH A VIEW
An Architectural Concept Portrayed In A Presentation Environment

Rouse & Associates, Malvern, Pa., developers of commercial buildings, are using a dramatic new approach to rent space in Philadelphia's first atrium styled office building under construction at 1900 Market Street.

While atrium buildings are not new to some other sections of the country, this will be Philadelphia's first such structure and the developer wanted a new approach to introduce it to prospective occupants.

Appropriately, the eight-story building is called The Atrium. It is scheduled for completion in 1981. Since the new building is not finished, Rouse has set up a separate selling center in a suite occupied by their rental agent, Kennedy Wolfington Company, Inc. in the United Engineers Building.

To design a dramatic presentation, Rouse sought the services of Armstrong World Industries, Inc. Lancaster, Pa., which has wide experience in commercial interior design. Armstrong maintains a large commercial and residential Interior Design Center in Lancaster to facilitate the sale of interior products, including commercial ceilings, carpets and floors.

A special Armstrong task force, consisting of interior design and audiovisual specialists, undertook to develop the presentation. Their solution was a combination of redesigned conference room and a unique audiovisual presentation which dramatized the essence of the building's atrium design.

The atrium design itself, being unique to Philadelphia, was considered the most interesting and salable feature of the building. At the same time, it was the feature most in need of selling in a city where office buildings are largely traditional in design.

The new presentation consisted of three elements: 1. the redesigned presentation room, 2. a two-projector multi-image slide film, and 3. a spectacular visual transformation of the whole room into an architectural rendering of the interior of the Atrium's garden court as it will appear when completed.

Designing the Presentation Room

PHASE I

The first part of the plan was to make the 15 foot x 20 foot presentation room elegant.

In the center of the room is a built-in table with a recessed 1/16" scale model of the Atrium building encased in clear plastic. The model is dramatically lit while the rest of the room has more subdued lighting. Ash trays are built in.

Around the table are six modern leather covered swivel chairs.

The ceiling consists of a suspended structural stained oak module that conceals 12 Kodak slide projectors. Framing the wood module are fabric covered ceiling panels.

PHASE II

The presenter can press a button to dim the lights to any desired level, turn off the lights in the building model, and lower it into the table.

Two projectors in the ceiling then project onto a wall-to-wall, floor-to-ceiling motorized screen on one wall.

To help present the idea of the new Atrium building to prospective tenants, the two-projector multi-image film, produced by Armstrong's William F. Early, traces the atrium concept down through history, from its beginnings in ancient Rome to the enclosed courtyards of Renaissance Italy, and featuring some of today's most exciting atrium-styled buildings all over the United States.

PHASE III

In the final phase of the structured presentation, screens roll down on all four walls to the accompaniment of music as architectural renderings of the Atrium interior are projected on them to give the impression of being inside the actual Atrium garden court. The swivel chairs allow the visitors to swing around to see all four sides. The presenter can control how long the images are kept on the screen.

The conference table then can be used for laying out plans and papers to aid in the presentation.

The screen presentation includes commentary by the Atrium's designer, Architect Gerald M. Cope, as well as the voices of people who work in some of the featured Atrium offices.

Overview

A visual presentation means a live talk made before an audience with the aid of visual materials. These aids can be in the form of display charts or diagrams, overhead transparencies, slides, filmstrips, or motion pictures.

One approach to creating a visual presentation can include the use of existing slides to create a short, simple, and inexpensive show. Another might include full documentary coverage of a project. Or, following a written script or planned storyboard, where specific pictures will be required and new material created.

The basic elements that make up a good visual presentation involve photography on many levels and planning skills unlike any other form of communication.

The scope of the presentation will be dependent on many factors, such as budget considerations and the time schedule. However, preplanning can save many hours of wasted effort and make the most out of the budget dollar.

The key to preplanning is in recording the progress of the design development as it happens. If you cannot do this conveniently, at least keep a chronological record of the steps taken. Then when you begin to prepare your visuals, the material is ready.

Planning the rough storyboard is an essential part of any program, as well as writing the script. Then the script and the visuals must be organized to work together to tell the story.

The final appearance on the screen will be determined by the proper editing of the slides and the timing of the narration. Music can be added for continuity, provided that you coordinate the visuals and the script with the recorded music. Finally, after many rehearsals, you are ready to present.

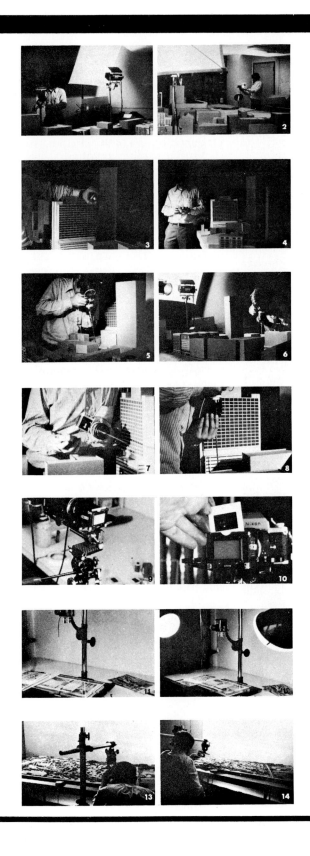
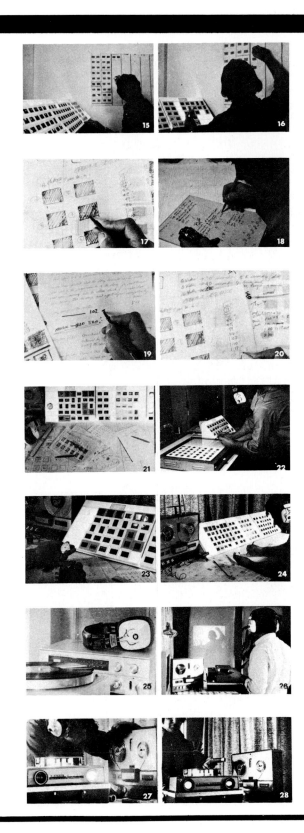

Selecting Visual Material

Visual materials used to create slide presentations can be gathered from many different sources. Since every project is set in some kind of environment, this is a good place to begin your search. The natural environment can provide many different moods.

Begin by making a reconnaissance trip to the site, and take the pictures as if you were relying on them to describe the place to others who have never seen the site. Surprisingly enough, you may discover many aspects that you might otherwise have overlooked.

Naturally, the most photogenic scenery may not be available to you at the time, but you can use other general shots mixed in with your site survey.

Avoid showing the site from every conceivable angle in the presentation by carefully selecting only those few pictures that really help tell your story.

Most presentations are filled with facts and figures, charts and graphs. It is a welcome relief to see people within a presentation. Therefore, when you are on one of your photo trips, take pictures of the neighborhood surrounding the project. Include action shots of people moving about, observing, playing, anything to help identify the setting or give the presentation some life. If the project is a school or a housing development near a school, take several pictures of school children playing or getting on a bus. Adding a human touch to a slide presentation, will convince your audience that you have taken the time to provide a well-rounded show.

To fill in the gaps you can add pictures from other sources, such as previous presentations. There are also many slide libraries with numerous listings that are available for special effects, although you may have to pay for their use.

Aerial Surveys

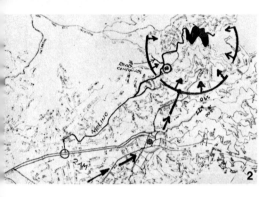

Don't limit yourself to ground views in your search for visual material. Most projects can best be seen from the air. A short trip by helicopter and a few rolls of color film will yield many views you probably had not counted on.

Aerial pictures of this sort are easy to obtain and in the overall cost of a presentation are worth the investment. Helicopter rates are charged by the hour and, if you are within range of a heliport, a 30-minute flight will take you a long way.

If you are averse to taking the flight yourself, or are not located near the project, try to find a freelance photographer to do it for you. If you cannot find one, there are many aerial photo services that will take the slides for you. This investment is usually reasonable and the pictures are often the most valuable and dramatic visuals you can include.

There is always something magical about seeing the project from the air. The informative value of the aerial slide is beyond compare. Entire tracts can be seen at a glance, or details otherwise impossible to show from the ground.

Once you have decided to order a set of aerial slides, you should prepare a map or flight pattern for the pilot and photographer to follow. To be certain of complete coverage, it is best to circle the site from a distance for overall general shots, then close the circle for the medium shots, and get closer yet if close-up details are required.

You can also use existing aerials of developments in order to emphasize a point or make a comparison. Certainly, when making a statement about large-scale planning concepts, aerial slide photography is a must. But don't overlook the possible applications to the small project as well.

Selecting Graphic Material

Graphic material can add a lot of variety to your presentation in the form of titles, charts, and diagrams. When combined with photographs of people or projects the graphics can provide a rich visual change of pace.

You should include titles and subtitles within your presentations. They can be used to introduce your program, answer questions, bridge gaps, or provide graphic explanation of points you are making in your narration.

In your search for graphic material, look for things that will have character on the screen. There is a wealth of graphic material right at your fingertips as you survey the site for pictures.

Once back at your office, you will have to translate your findings into graphic possibilities. Besides the natural or man-made titles, you can utilize many of the following: pictorial charts and pictograms, maps, charts, and graphs.

Maps, for example, contain almost all the elements used in the graphic language: scales, symbols, shapes, colors, captions, keys, titles, figures, text, and lettering. Overall, the map is the most complete communication device we have.

Flow charts are graphic and conceptual integration of all the various components of a project into a network. Organizational charts depict the structure of a group by delineating levels of authority and responsibility.

Charts are relatively inexpensive and are easy to make. They are usually used to explain the relationship of variables. Many pages of statistical data can be condensed into a few simple charts.

Remember charts and graphs can be delineated a dozen different ways. Select the one that gives emphasis and adds clarity to your story.

1. Lettering on an existing building can be used as the basis for a title slide. Trace over the outlines of the building from a projected slide.
2. Select a lettering style that goes with the type on the building and apply the title with dry transfer lettering over the sketch.

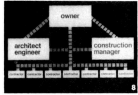

3. The existing road sign became the starting point for a title slide. The Old English typeface is available in dry transfer lettering.
4. The background was simplified in the new title slide. However, the size and shape of the sign was kept identical to the original.

5. When placing the title over a picture, do the lettering on clear acetate and...
6. move the lettering around until you find a good placement.

7. Experiment with contrasting approaches such as positive and...
8. negative views of the same subject.

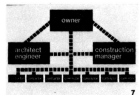

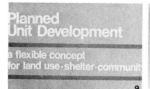

9. Titles can be professionally typeset by a printer in cold type or on film.
10. Or, they can be typewritten. An electric typewriter with a carbon ribbon makes the sharpest impression.

11. By utilizing a double exposure method you can combine title and picture.
12. Experimentation with exposures will be necessary to get the proper combination.

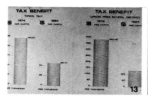

13. Make statistical charts interesting.
14. The $100 bill on top of the pile of money is more convincing than the stack of coins in 13.

15. Report covers make good title slides..
16. but they must be copied close enough for titles to be legible.

17. Maps can convey a log of information at one time.
18. They can show numerous locations at a glance and they can be visually appealing.

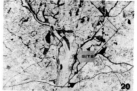

19. Do not use maps for visual appeal alone...
20. unless they convey specific information, such as the site location.

21. Some maps can be photocopied, others cannot. Check the copyright.
22. Re-draw the map, if necessary.

23. Concept diagrams must convey information clearly. Here the lettering is too small.
24. Targeted site areas are always effective.

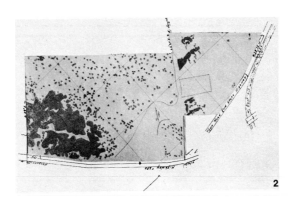

An inspection of the different types of visual illustration reveals that they all possess recognizable characteristics. These include line drawings, detailed shaded drawings, cartoons, photographs of three-dimensional models, and realistic photographs of an object. Some may be more effective than others in any given situation.

A visual realism continuum would extend from the object itself to a very simplified line representation of some aspect of the object. The more qualities the visual has in harmony with the object or situation which it represents, the more realistic the visual is. For example, a color photograph would provide the most realistic impression of the object. The visual spectrum can be outlined as follows:

1. Simple line representations.
2. Detailed and shaded drawings.
3. Photograph of a three-dimensional model.
4. Realistic color photographs of the object.

Color is considered to be a significant dimension in the realism spectrum for visual illustrations. Color used as a visual aid attracts the viewer and pleases the eye.

Color visuals definitely enhance a presentation and can be used to create emphasis, to identify, differentiate, and stimulate interest.

One example of a visual continuum is seen in the series of four illustrations depicting a vertical representation of a 60-acre parcel of rural property. The first is a simplified line outline; the second is a sketch of the property with evergreen tree growth patterns. The third is an aerial view in winter to emphasize the evergreen areas, and the final view, an aerial photograph of the entire property with full summer foliage. Each illustrated similar aspects of the overall site, but in a different way.

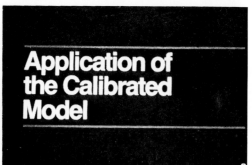

1

Application of the Calibrated Model

2

	PHASE I (1976 - 1983)		PHASE II (1983 - 1990)	
	U.S. $	Dr.	U.S. $	Dr.
AIRFIELD	74,154,800	2,224,644,000	47,808,800	1,434,264,(
PASSENGER TERMINAL	23,800,000	714,000,000	10,200,000	306,000,(
OTHER BUILDINGS	2,478,000	74,340,000	1,012,000	30,360,(
ROADS AND PARKING	9,750,000	292,500,000	1,950,000	58,500,(
MISCELLANEOUS	18,083,000	542,490,000	3,442,000	103,260,(
SUB-TOTAL	128,265,800	3,847,974,000	64,412,800	1,932,384,
ESCALATION	12,826,580	384,797,400	*	*
SUB-TOTAL	141,092,380	4,232,771,400	64,412,800	1,932,384,
ENGINEERING AND ADMINISTRATION	14,109,238	423,277,140	6,500,000	195,000
LAND ACQUISITION	50,000,000	1,500,000,000	0	
TOTAL	$205,201,618	Dr. 6,156,048,540	$70,912,800	Dr. 2,127,384

3

Pine Hills: cost/revenue

	conventional	PUD
Housing Units	2,350	2,350
Housing Type	single-family	multi-family
tax revenue	$1,750,000	1,800,000
education costs	1,318,000	608,000
road maintenance	60,000	20,000
other services	334,000	248,000
total costs	1,712,000	876,000
surplus revenue	38,000	924,000

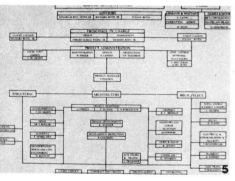

5

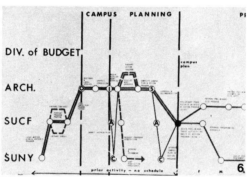

6

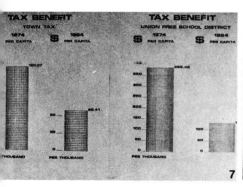

7

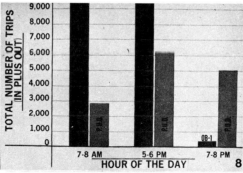

8

Legibility

The cardinal principle underlying the preparation of good visuals is simplicity. Each frame should deal with one central idea

In creating title slides, fancy lettering or an overelaborate background will result in confusion (1).

Keep the letters bold and simple at all costs (2).

Avoid the use of small typewritten characters on charts (3).

Reduce the amount of information and make the lettering as large as possible (4).

Avoid the use of complex interrelated diagrams unless someone is there to explain them to the audience (5).

Keep all flow diagrams bold and simple so that the ideas can be grasped at a glance (6).

Marking a bold and clear vertical scale on the side of the graph makes it more effective (7,8).

You can create simplicity and contrast in a title slide by photographing the lettering or graphics on ortho film. You can then place colored acetate behind the clear portion for colorful titles.

The recommended primary standard for the artwork is 10x12-inches with a working area of 6x9-inches. Although the lettering can ordinarily be a minimum of 1/50 the height of the information area, for average back row viewing distances the use of a letter height of 1/25 is encouraged.

Material that was not designed for projection, such as printed graphs, charts and maps, can be converted to a projected visual. Remember that contrast, colors, and viewing distances may change, but the requirements for legibility will remain the same.

It is a mistake to believe that enlarging the physical dimensions of a transparency improves the legibility. What counts is the size of the detail of the original artwork.

Renderings

Architectural sketches and renderings can be a valuable addition to any slide presentation. They can be used to tell a story and even create a mood.

Consider first the use of cartoons, executed by using colorful markers (1,2). They can be a marvelous storytelling device. Line sketches on acetate which have been painted on the back side with tempera or acrylic are highly colorful when made into slides (3,4). Pen-and-ink sketches colored with markers are also very effective (5,6).

When selecting material to use, look for a way to create interesting storytelling sequences; such as the ground-level view of an airport from the cockpit of a plane (5) and another view from inside an airborne plane (6).

When using a rendering or a series of renderings in a presentation, spend time to take close-up views. Sometimes a detail from a drawing measuring only a few inches or so can be very stunning when enlarged on the screen (7,12). You can build sequences and tell a story at the same time.

Study illustration 15 and then see how 16 and 17 relate to the overall drawing, which measured 30x40 inches in the original colored version. These details are only a few inches in length, yet on the screen they create more interest and hold more attention.

It is interesting to show close-up sequences and details of interior drawings (18-23). Here you have an opportunity to focus on figures and activity related to the function of the building.

Renderings and model photographs are not always compatible on the screen. The rendering will generally overshadow the model, since choice of viewpoint and dramatic angle are more readily achieved in the rendering (24,25).

Sequential Disclosure

To create a series of slides on the development of a concept sketch or rendering sequence is a relatively easy matter. Simply place the camera on a tripod or copy stand and place the artwork on the wall or copyboard. Secure the art in position with tacks or tape. Light it in the usual manner with two photoflood lights in reflectors.

Do not rely on any method of aligning artwork within the camera by eye. The ground glass is too small to be used for that purpose. Therefore, all alignment for over-lapping pictures must be set up in advance. If the plans are different scales, there will be problems keeping the images aligned.

To begin the sequence, photograph the complete plan. Then remove portions of the plan, one at a time, corresponding to each phase of development. Take several exposures of each phase until the final sequence is left. This last picture will be the initial site without the proposed development.

When projecting this sequence in the presentation, reverse the order of the slides, so that the initial phase begins the sequence. It is easier to remove portions of a plan in sequential order than to add and align each phase as you go.

A typical sequence showing the development of a plan is illustrated as follows: Contour map of entire property (7). Diagram of evergreen tree growth to remain as part of "open space subdivision" plan (8). Vertical aerial photograph in winter emphasizing evergreens (9). Rough sketches showing possible road and lot layouts (10,11). Final sketch of lot design (12). Overlay of sketch on contours and tree pattern (13). Vertical aerial of property, undeveloped (14). Final version with full development of property (15).

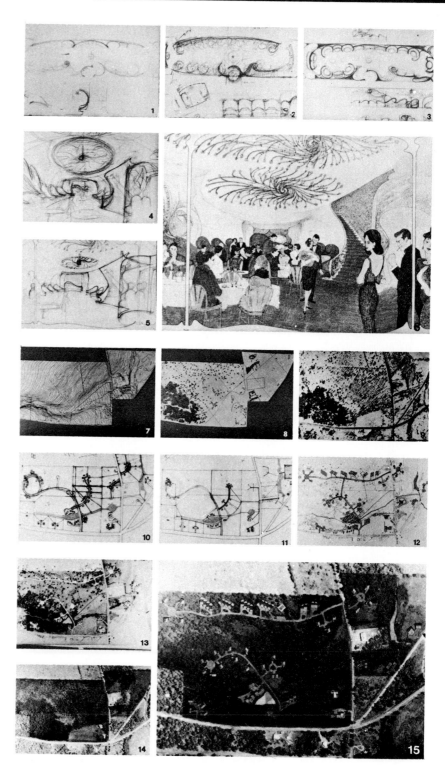

Progressive Sequences

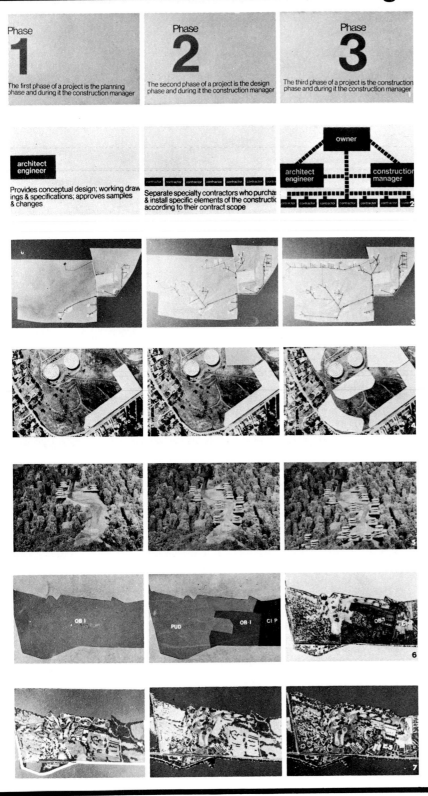

Phase

1

The first phase of a project is the planning phase and during it the construction manager

Phase

2

The second phase of a project is the design phase and during it the construction manager

Phase

3

The third phase of a project is the construction phase and during it the construction manager

architect engineer

Provides conceptual design; working drawings & specifications; approves samples & changes

Separate specialty contractors who purchase & install specific elements of the construction according to their contract scope

owner

architect engineer

construction manager

If you have compiled a short list of statements or graphic material, you can present them very dramatically using a technique called sequential disclosure.

The first slide will show a single statement, or part of a graph. The second slide will show an added statement, and so on until the final slide in the sequence will include all the statements, or the entire graph. It is much easier for the audience to remember one thought at a time, as it is added to the preceding idea.

You should design the artwork to make the photography easier and thus assure that the sequence will work well on the screen. For example, the lettering (1) can be designed to appear in a different spot each time. If certain individual items appear as widely separated ideas, however, the audience may not make the connection from slide-to-slide (2). Thus the main benefit of sequential disclosure will be lost.

This method works especially well for showing phasing diagrams for a dvelopment. The illustration here (3) shows a phased utility plan indicating the construction of sewer and water lines.

Broad planning concepts or land-use patterns for mixed-use are easily shown using this technique (4). Sequential pictures of a model are useful in demonstrating a phased development (5). And a large-scale development sequence can begin with a graphic sequence depicting the planning concepts of a plan (6). The final staging of development (7) is easily understood when depicting growth of a project over a ten-year period, and it helps in getting the audience involved.

The final concept in visual continuity is the development of combinations of sequences that build storytelling ideas.

In the first sequences (1,2), hypothetical growth patterns are examined in three-dimensional model form. The camera was stationed on a tripod and various model elements representing modular units were arranged and added to complete a progression of ideas. The same technique can be used in the elevation view (3), but you will be limited to a two-dimensional picture in this case.

You can also build sequences by using sequential portions of a rendering (4) to unfold, telling the complete story or setting the scene for something else.

The same thinking can be brought to almost any situation, such as the construction sequence of an airplane maintenance hangar (5). The airline symbol on the tail of the plane is followed by the name appearing on the hangar. The construction crane and open framework provide the continuity from slide-to-slide. The plane taking off in the distance is the cue to the last picture, which is an aerial view of the hangar taken from a plane during takeoff.

In developing a series of sequences you will have to provide links either in color, form, or subject matter.

The basis of an audio-visual presentation is continuity, both in storyline and visual images. Therefore anything that will help contribute to developing that element in your program should be played up. All too often visual presentations are made up of disjointed images that lack continuity of idea, form, color, or subject matter.

Examine your storyboard for potential areas where you can build sequences. This can be done either in two dimensional plans, diagrams or graphics, or three dimensional models and real objects. Whatever the mode it will greatly enhance your presentation.

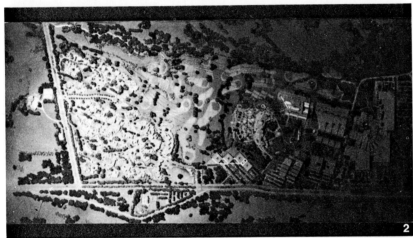

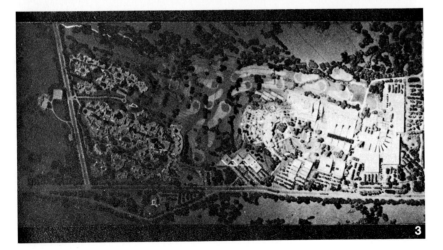

Slides of architectural models, when properly lit, can be very dramatic in a presentation. Of course, the more finished the model, the better the slide. However, even rough study models have their place in the presentation. The secret is in the lighting of the model.

There are many ways of lighting a model other than an overall even spread of light (1). The flat illumination lacks contrast and interest, and attention is not focused in any way. This is especially deadly if the light is aimed directly from the front without producing distinct shadows.

For a more effective result, light the overall model evenly with photofloods placed far enough away to provide a soft overall light. If you have access to a photographic studio, you can use an umbrella reflector which spreads light evenly over a large area (6).

One of the most versatile pieces of equipment in the studio is the focusing quartz light (5). It will focus a sharp beam of light onto a tiny spot, or spread to a bright flood of light. These lights are designed to hold conical "snoots" to further control and focus the light (4).

By aiming the light at a specific area, you can create dramatic highlights while the background of the model remains in darkness. In this case you should expose for the highlighted portion of the model to ensure that it doesn't get "washed out" in overexposure.

Another effective device that can be created with this light is shown in (2,3). Place the camera on a tripod in one spot, taking several exposures with the light in one position. Then, without moving the camera, move and focus the light on another area.

If these slides are shown in a lap-dissolve sequence, that light

will slowly shift from one area to another. This is extremely effective on the screen and can highlight portions of a development.

This intense light is also very useful when using a modelscope (7). The effective aperture of the modelscope is similar to a pinhole camera making viewing through the camera ground glass a difficult task (8). However, the small aperture requires a long-time exposure, and the camera and modelscope attachment must be placed on a sturdy tripod (9).

Since the function of a modelscope is to take pictures in areas inaccessible to other conventional lenses, it will be necessary to get the camera suspended well over the model (10).

While the model is in an upright position for the overall plan view, take closer details of portions of the plan. These can be coordinated later with plan graphics shot with similar framing. This device may be useful in making transition pictures from plan to model or back again. Then photograph the model from a variety of oblique views, again relating each shot to a particular sequence of plan and oblique view (11-18).

Another alternative to the modelscope is sub-miniature format cameras. These will yield a much sharper picture, but you may be shooting without being able to view the scene except through a viewfinder.

The ideal solution is to construct the model with photography in mind, but this is an added complication and it may prove to be too costly in most cases.

While the model is in the studio, take as many pictures as you can, and if you are unsure of the exposure, bracket them. The lighting set-up is a major portion of the work, and you should utilize it to the fullest advantage.

Photographing Buildings

Architectural photography presents problems that are unique to most photographers. Unlike the average photographic subject, architecture must be approached with somewhat specialized equipment but, more important, a highly selective and specialized way of "seeing".

The aim, of course, is to produce pictures for use in presentations, and the use of a 35mm camera is the easiest way to accomplish this. With the advent of perspective control (PC) lenses, the versatile zoom lenses, and the ever popular wide-angle lenses, most photographic situations can easily be handled by the small format camera.

When shooting sequences of a building, be sure to change camera angle and distance with each shot. There are times when you may want a special effect of zooming in on a building or portion of a building, and in this case the camera angle would not change. Generally, it is good practice to change both camera angle and distance with each picture.

When selecting pictures of buildings for the use in slide presentations, there are many factors to consider. If your slide file has been built around professional architectural pictures, then you have little to worry about. However, if you are trying to fill in gaps and decide to go out and take your own pictures, some helpful hints are in order.

Some books on architectural photography deal with the view camera only. However, there are some that deal with topics such as camera angle, composition, and lighting that apply regardless of size or format of the camera.

The following page illustrates what can be done with the hand-held 35mm camera equipped with a perspective control lens.

1. Modern architecture offers exciting challenges to the photographer.
2. Some buildings are naturally photogenic because of their unique and interesting form.

3. Sunlight enhances the form of a building and further emphasizes detail on the facade.
4. Some materials are brought to life by the play of light and shadow.

5. Frontal or elevational views often lend an interesting and abstract pattern, but oblique views are the most common.
6. A low camera angle can add drama and compositional interest. (7,8)

9. Water can add another dimension to a building through its reflective quality,
10. and in a general scene it lends an element of change and movement.

11. Today, environmental sculpture can be found in most contemporary sites.
12. The abstract shapes are dynamic elements and offer many new and dramatic framing and compositional devices.

13. When photographing an interior of a building, take some extra time to shoot the lobby.
14. Interior pictures are always more difficult because of light limitations, but they contribute greatly to photographic coverage. (15,16)

17. Frame all views with foliage for a softening effect. especially in long overall views.
18. Don't overlook the foliage frame for close views as well.

19. Overall shots can be followed up with details by using a zoom lens from the same location.
20. The effect is different than walking closer to the building where perspective changes with every step.

21. Dramatic compositional elements can be obtained from low level views looking directly up a building.
22. Nearly every city now has an observation deck on top of the tallest building and there are numerous possibilities for aerial views of the urban scene. (20,24)

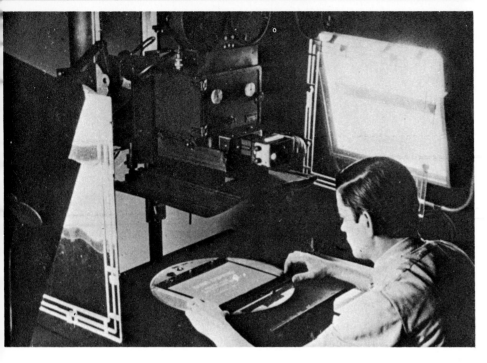

Slide Copying

The best method for copying slides is done by using a piece of equipment (1) made specially for that purpose. This unit has a built-in electronic flash balanced for daylight-film. The camera is permanently attached to a bellows and can copy a wide range of reductions.

Thus, you can crop portions of an existing slide by enlarging the original in copying. The color of an original slide can be changed in duplication by placing color correction filters under the slide to be copied.

A method called transillumination copies the slide directly, not the projected image (2). Cameras can be equipped with extension tubes and bellows (3) that will permit same-size (1:1) copying.

You must increase the f stop when using this method. You can then copy a slide by placing it in the accessory copy holder (4) and placing a light source behind the unit.

You can also copy slides by taking a picture of a projected slide (5). Use a mat-white screen and set the projector and camera as close as possible to the center of the projector beam. You can move the camera closer and crop the projected image, if desired.

You can also use a rear-screen projection method (6), but you will be shooting a reversed picture. (The slide can be turned backwards in the projector.) The illumination is somewhat greater in the center of the rear projection screen causing a "hot spot" effect. By shooting off the central axis, you can eliminate this hot spot.

Each illustration shows the use of a single projector, but the same technique can be used with two or more projectors, thereby making it possible to create multiple-image effects, double-exposures, or superimpositions.

There are many ways of utilizing existing slides in a new presentation, either by straight duplication of the originals, or by superimpositions and multiple-images.

When using duplicates, consider the following: a color duplicate of an original camera transparency is merely an approximation of the original transparency, just as the original is an approximation of the original scene in all respects.

When you view an original slide, the "scene" is rarely available for comparison. However, when you compare a copy of a slide with the original, it may not always look exactly like it. Color may shift and contrast may increase somewhat. However, the audience will never see the original for comparison.

Therefore, if the copy is to your liking, use it in your show. A dark slide can be lightened considerably in duplication, but a light slide cannot be intensified in color or value.

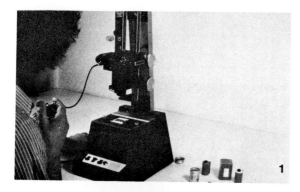

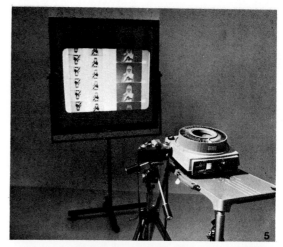

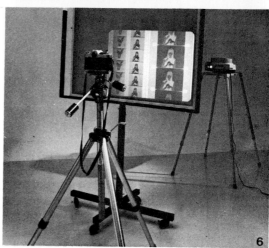

Back Projection

Several other useful techniques can be accomplished by using projected slides. The easiest of these is the simple tracing or copying of a projected slide onto a piece of drawing paper. Simply enlarge a slide to the desired size and trace off the images you want, making sure to include the slide frame. Use this picture as the basis for a sketch or colored rendering.

Then copy the rendering back onto a slide, being careful to frame the original format outline on the ground glass of the camera. The result will be a new slide that can show your proposed design side-by-side with the existing scene. You do not necessarily have to duplicate every detail in your sketch, since the comfparison on the screen will be very effective (1,2,3,4).

There is a variation of this technique which can provide an astonishingly realistic effect on the screen. Simply back-project a slide of the site onto a rear projection screen. Then, place a model of the building in front of that screen. Take care not to light up the back-projected image, and aim the lights only at the model.

If you do not have a rear projection screen, you can create one quite easily. Simply stretch a piece of tracing paper over a frame of any sort, or tape the paper to a window frame. Translucent paper makes a very good rear screen.

The projected image will be a little less sharp that the model in front, but this is an advantage. The softer background will not distract from the new project. In addition, you can enlarge or reduce the background to your own liking, by moving the projector in relationship to the screen.

This technique can provide a sense of realism on the screen that is impossible to obtain by any method other than back-projection.

Superimposition

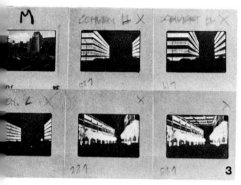

By combining several of these techniques you will find a number of startling effects that can be created by combining projected images. For instance, suppose you are attempting to show how your proposed new design would relate to an existing building.

First, take a picture of the site from the best vantage point that would show your new design (1). Project the slide up on a wall and trace the perspective vanishing lines and any other data that you need to construct a sketch perspective (2). Make sure to include the outside frame of the site slide in relation to sketch.

After you have done sketch perspectives of whatever schemes you are planning to present, have these sketches reproduced in negative form. Then take slides of these negatives, taking care to frame the sketch so that the same format will be maintained as in the original site picture. (Hence the need for the slide border.)

What you will end up with is one original site photo and several slides with sketches in white lines on a black background (3). Since light will not pass through the black portions of the sketch slides, it can be projected directly over the site photo.

This requires two projectors and the size of the projected images must be identical. Then you can take a picture of this superimposition by using methods described earlier in slide-making techinques.

There is yet another method of producing the same effect. By using the double exposure feature of a slide copier (4), you can expose the site picture first and the negative sketch second. The result will be the combination of the two images on one slide (6,8). These techniques are both graphic and realistic at the same time.

Editing The Script

The first step in organizing an effective slide show is to know exactly what visual material you have to work with. This necessitates a plan for sorting, organizing, and filing all the slides for consideration.

Don't throw any slide away. The slide you are tempted to reject at first for photographic reasons may bring a positive response for quite a different reason. File each slide carefully so that you can locate it when you want it.

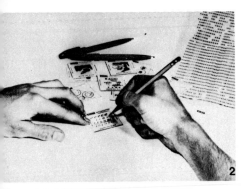

Sorting through hundreds of slides requires that you use a light box of some sort. Commercial viewers are inexpensive, hold up to 80 slides at a time and can be folded up for easy storage

People who work regularly with slides use illuminators which hold 200 slides at one time. You can make one yourself by taping tracing paper across a window pane. Then you put the window across two chairs and place a table lamp underneath the pane.

One of the most exciting parts of photography is viewing your pictures and selecting those that you want to best tell your story. This editing process can also be the most challenging step in constructing a slide show.

Select only those pictures that will assist you in communicating your message without the need of a lot of narration.

The slides you select should follow your outline closely and require no apologies for any technical weakness.

While grouping your slides in a storytelling order, give some thought to how you can lift your presentation out of the ordinary run of slide programs. You probably have many more good slides than you realize. Don't throw away any slide just because it is a bit off center or shows too much sky or foreground.

The narration is used mainly to prepare the audience for what is coming up next. It creates continuity.

Keep your narration simple and to the point. Good narration ties the pictures together and puts the emphasis where you want it. It can also round out the story. Avoid saying "in this slide we see", or "here we have a picture of"

Talk to the audience in a conversational tone. This arouses interest and adds a personal warmth to your presentation.

A combination tape-live program sometimes makes an interesting presentation. Live narration can be interspersed with the recorded portion.

If you give the show yourself, the live part can be a question-answer session at the end. If the program is all on tape, using two people for narration adds variety and a change of pace.

For most presentations, you don't need a professional writer to prepare a script or narration or a professional announcer to deliver it. It's your audience, your subject, and you are the authority.

For one-time meetings there is no substitute for the speaker in the flesh. The advantages of the live presentation are many. The cost can be kept down to zero if need be. It can be planned and staged on short notice. It offers endless flexibility. It permits audience participation. It can also be terribly dull

You may find it desirable to tape record your comments, either to permit a precisely timed delivery or to have the program presented without you.

A canned presentation is any form of artifically reproduced voice — by tape or film track. Canned sound offers the advantage of allowing the voice part to be perfected offstage.

However, it can lack the warmth of human presence. On the other hand, a voice in a dark room can become just as impersonal as a loudspeaker. The pace of canned presentations is fixed and cannot be varied, but live presentations are under the control of the speaker.

In making the recording, speak slowly and distinctly in a conversational tone. Speak directly into the microphone. Pause about 2 seconds after finishing each frame to allow the audience to catch up before recording the change signal. Rehearse the entire procedure at least once before recording.

Follow manufacturers' instructions for use of the recorder and in setting and adjusting recording and playback levels. Read the script directly into the microphone, speaking slowly and naturally.

The best type of recorder to use has two separate recording channels, one for the speech and the other for the synchronizing signal (if used). The two channels are completely independent. Any portion of either may be erased and re-recorded without affecting the other.

In preparing a canned talk, the copy should be written to be read in sections, one for each picture frame, typed double-spaced for easy reading. If the talk requires periods of speech without frequent changes of slides, an opaque slide or map or situation slide may be made up.

The easiest way to record narration and sound simultaneously is simply to have the background sound on as you narrate. Both are recorded at the same time through one microphone. The quality of the background music depends on the quality of the speaker.

You can fade music in and out of the recorded narration by holding the microphone just inches away from the speaker and moving it to within inches from your voice. This puts the music way in the background. Or use volume control.

You may want to use a single musical theme threading throughout your entire presentation to bind it together. However, to change pace or mood, choose several different selections, as long as they relate. Repeat a selection if it isn't long enough to cover a complete section of the show. You can also repeat a selection to help tie the mood and content of one section to that of a similar section.

Decide where you want a musical background and what selections you are going to use. Run through your program and mark the places on the script where the music should begin and end. Sound effects taken from special records on "location" can add drama and realism too.

If you want to gain impact by having certain bars of music emphasize certain words and pictures, time the music and the dialogue so that the emphasis will come where you want it. If you want music without narrative or vice-versa, you can record it on a separate tape and splice it into the master.

A slide flashing on the screen at just the right moment can mean the difference between a strong point well made or just another slide on the screen. Make sure the cue marks for slide changes are accurately marked on your script.

For split-second timing you must push the advance button slightly before you want the slide because of the mechanical time lag. Get to know the timing of your projector. The best time for a slide change might be right in the middle of a sentence.

Continuity

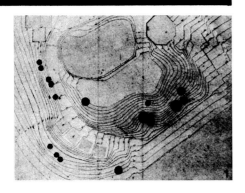

In developing an outline for a slide show, try to plan sequences that will use various devices of continuity. The outline, or structure, of the show itself should be a natural continuous unfolding of ideas disclosing the basic concepts behind your proposal.

The project illustrated here was presented to a planning board for approval of a mixed-use development, consisting of medical offices, a hospital, and apartment units.

The opening close-up views of trees on an otherwise barren hillside showed that this sentinel hill remained untouched by development, in the midst of a developed suburban area. This sequence ended with aerial photos of the entire property.

The title slide appeared next, introducing the name of the project and the designers and engineers. The mixed-use concept was described by a series of alternating sequences. First statistical data was given in support of the particular land use. Then the plan view illustrated which portion of the property would be developed with that particular use.

A sequential development of plans, from existing topography through various stages of development, culminated in a plan view of a finished model, which was followed by details of various portions of the project which echoed the same development pattern.

At the end the entire project was shown in an overall aerial perspective view which dissolved into aerial views of the model. The final sequences were distant ground-level views of the model.

The storyboard format is the best method for working out sequences in the planning stage. Once you have the slides they can be arranged on a light table that simulates a storyboard.

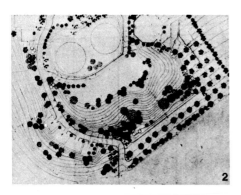

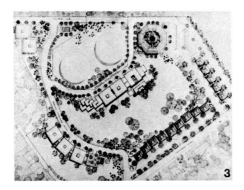

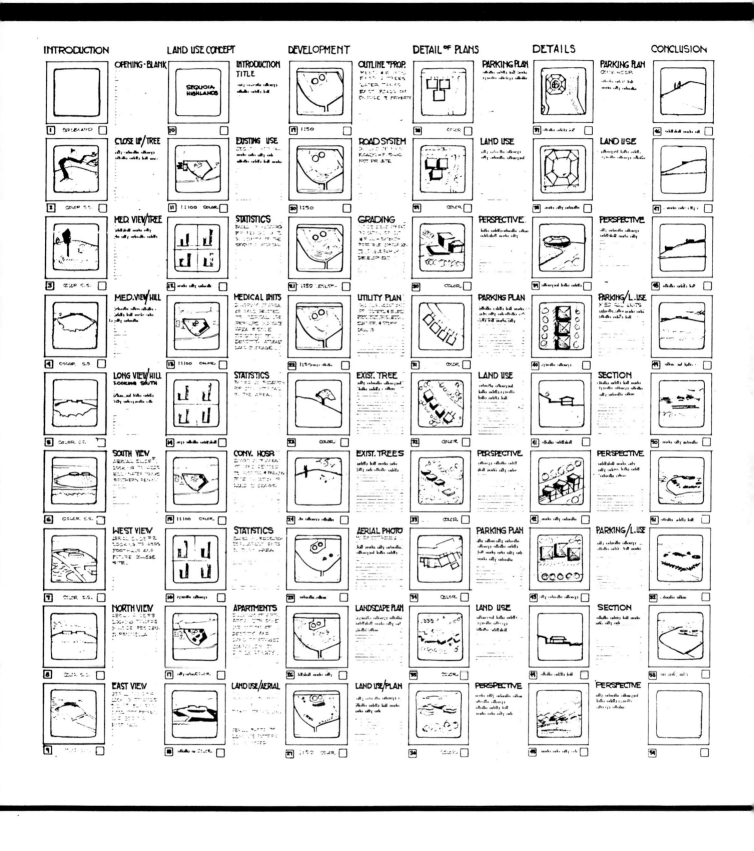

Pan Am

In the presentation for the new Pan Am terminal expansion there were many devices used to create continuity. Most were planned in the storyboard stage prior to the actual production of the drawings or the photographing of models.

The presentation opened with an aerial map of the entire JFK International Airport. The Pan Am terminal was identified by its unusual oval shaped roof. This shape became a symbol which was repeated in all the visuals to establish continuity. This was particularly true in the sequence of graphic plans. Another device of continuity was made evident in the alignment of the plans with the existing oval shaped roof at the top of each diagram. It was also evident in the alignment of the model photographs to match the plan.

There was an architectural model available that was built in sections so that half of each floor could be removed to see the relationship to the floor below. By alternation between plan and model, an interesting succession of images was created. The model was also photographed in detail, since removal of the floor sections made easy access for the camera.

An aerial photograph of the existing terminal was used as the basis for a color perspective. The background of the perspective was simply painted over, thus providing a very realistic effect. In the actual show the rendering followed the site photograph in a 10-second dissolve. The new building appeared on the screen as if by magic. The final view of the overall model, which had been dramatically lit with a focusing light, faded out in a slow dissolve to darkness.

Multiple-Image Techniques

Multiple-image projection is not as difficult to achieve as it may appear on the screen. Multiple-image refers to any slide which has more than one image per frame.

There are several ways to achieve multiple images. The easiest one to accomplish is the actual cutting and mounting of original pieces of transparencies within one slide mount. This is a very valid method of producing more than one picture per frame, since the composite slide can be made from original transparency material.

However, when working with 35mm slides cut apart, you must be extremely accurate in cutting and taping. If there are any errors, they will be magnified on the screen. One way to overcome the size limitation is to work with a larger film size, say 2¼x3¼ inches, 4x5 inches, or even 8x10 inches. Then you can have the composite reduced to a 35mm slide for use in the presentation.

There are several masks for multiple-image slides available. If you plan to use them, the artwork can be set up in advance to conform to the slide mask.

There is another method of producing multiple-image slides, using reflected copy and color or black-and-white prints instead of transparencies. Working with large prints is far more convenient than small pieces of film.

Cut the pictures out in the desired size and place them on boards to form the composite picture. Photograph this composite picture with color film (even for black-and-white composites). Take the slide that you get as a result, and use an opaque tape to mask off separations between pictures.

If you mount the pictures on black mat board and expose the slide properly, you can sometimes avoid the need for the tape. By utilizing multiple-image projection, images can be any size on the screen or located in any position, a great device for storytelling, animation, or just providing a change of pace within a presentation.

The slide show "Facade" (right) depicted a group of old Victorian and "carpenter gothic" buildings that were slated for destruction.

The opening section was in color, contrasted by the middle section in black-and-white, which depicted the destruction in vivid detail. This entire black-and-white section was done in a super-slide format to futher emphasize the devastation.

The epilogue which followed was in color. The crane which destroyed the buildings was now replaced by a construction crane. Following a series of construction sequences, the final section was a series of fast-moving images depicting the new buildings, the new face of the city.

To portray this amount of material on the screen would have required multiple-screen projection. All the pictures were selected and prearranged, cut out and mounted on black mat board. Then the composite of two or three pictures was reshot on one single 35mm frame. This meant that 250 pictures could be shown on 80 single 35mm slides.

The end result was a multiple-image presentation using a single projector and a single slide each time. The possibilities of combinations using this approach are endless.

Before making a multiple-image presentation, the sequences and positioning of the images should be planned using techniques that are described earlier in this chapter. These would include the development of the images on some form of storyboard.

The Joint Venture Presentation

This 3-screen presentation was designed to reflect the design process for an airport. The introduction outlined the problems of the existing airport, and then developed according to very explicit patterns. These included: (1) program identification, (2) concept development, (3) design development, (4) unique requirements, (5) construction management, and (6) implementation.

The total show consisted of 236 slides with 54 slides in the center projector, 95 in the left, and 87 in the right. The entire show ran for 23 minutes, which averages 10 slide changes per minute.

The storyline center slide was designed as a square image with the square dimensions matching the vertical dimension of the flanking ones.

The lettering for the major divisions within the show was done with white lettering on the sky-blue background. The secondary titles, also on a blue background, were done with a smaller, lower-case black lettering of the same type style.

The blue background became the unifying color element in the whole show. And each pair of slides was selected by the way it looked with the blue color title. In addition, the two flanking slides matched each other in color, hue, and intensity so the unit of three slides would not appear unbalanced

The end result of this planning culminated in a smooth-flowing and homogeneous mixture of visual images. The three images on the screen almost touched to further emphasize the careful color study.

The screen was created by using a 5-foot-wide roll of white paper streched over one end wall of the presentation room. This continuous screen accommodated the combination of three images that was nearly 18 feet long.

Total Design Packages for Japan

Donald Clever, designer, tells how he prepares total presentation packages for restaurant projects he designed for a Japanese food franchise.

A typical presentation consists of a cover sheet and title block for the slide presentation (top). Other items include uniform designs, color and material display boards, and graphic designs (bottom). Architectural plans (top right), sections, exterior elevations and models. At bottom are two views of the finished structures, one exterior and one interior.

Typically, meetings are recorded and written meeting notes are prepared after each week long session. Returning to San Francisco with excellent references, we prepared an architectural design concept and preliminary planning, colors, materials and graphics. The total presentation included the following items, and this procedure has prevailed for the past few years, for a variety of projects:

- Namemark design.
- Floor plan and reflected ceiling.
- Elevations, interior and exterior.
- Roof plan/plot plan.
- Engineering and structural concept (in Japanese).
- Materials and colors.
- Scale model.
- Typed review of the design precepts and philosophy.
- Graphics and signing.
- Uniforms.

The scale models are particularly helpful to executives and management people not familiar with engineering or architecture. All designs and plans are mounted on foam board here in the USA. I check them all with my luggage on the plane and take a set of slides in my briefcase in case the luggage and packages are lost or misdirected.

I return to Japan for the presentation, which is usually made to a committee of approximately twelve persons, including Mr. Fujii and his design staff, structural, electrical, and mechanical engineers, also sales and merchandising people. If the presentation concerns building programs involving large sums of money, the president of Fujiya and his Board of Directors attend the meeting and they each respond with questions and suggestions.

I sometimes request incandescent flood lights to correct color distortions to our presentations of colors and materials, caused by total fluorescent illumination typical in Japanese conference rooms.

The chairman introduces the subject, reviews the purpose and objectives of the presentation. I usually begin with a statement (through an interpreter) thanking them for inviting the presentation and for the excellent input and explicit parameters provided by their dedicated staff and management.

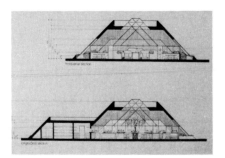

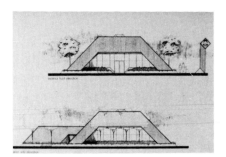

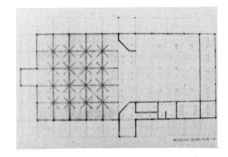

**Above: Models of various other Fujiya restaurants, and a confectionery store.
Right: Presentation sequence for Fujiya Peko Burger restaurant.**

All planning and dimensions are metric and space designations are in "tsubo". One tsubo is 3.3 square meters. Plans are dated by both Western and Japanese calendars.

In my early presentations in Japan I noted that the chief executive and board members became impatient if slides did not pertain exactly to subject at hand, or if slides of conceptual and development sketches were too numerous. Therefore, now we do not show development sketches in our slide presentations in Japan.

Our presentations are exceedingly well prepared and severely edited to provide rapid, explicit design information and illustrations pertaining precisely to the subject of the conference. The presentations are well received and no impatience or disinterest is apparent.

Upon completing the presentation, each department is invited to provide questions or suggestions pertaining to their section, i.e., structural, electrical, mechanical, merchandising, etc. after which Mr. Fujii pronounces his judgement and instructions which usually result in a decision to proceed with Phase Two: plans and details, following by construction of the first unit.

All of our working drawings were redrawn by the client's engineers. They don't make nice big blueprints like we do, but little books. They fold every plan up into an 8x10 folder.

Presentation drawings are not redone. I keep the tracing and send them reproducibles. I usually leave presentation drawings over there and sample boards of materials.

- One set of duplicate slides.
- The scale model.
- One set of reproducibles of architectural, interior, and engineering plans.
- One set of prints of above.
- The color and materials boards.
- The graphics and uniform designs.

Communication between our office and our clients in Japan is almost instantaneous through telex and facsimile whereby we transmit plans and drawings via RCA satellite systems.

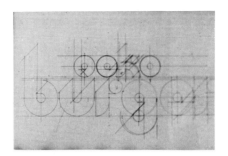

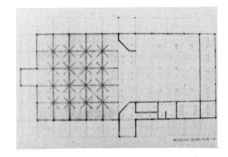

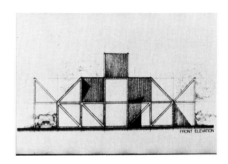

Fujitec America

KZF, a widely respected American architectural, engineering, and planning firm prepared this slide presentation. It was designed to present to Fujitec for a new manufacturing plant in the greater Cincinnati area.

FUJITEC AMERICA, INC.

Some of you are already familiar with KZF, and through earlier meetings with our professional staff, have determined that KZF is qualified to provide the design services that you require. Our key people are now here to meet you face-to-face, to discuss and understand your specific concerns, and to give you an opportunity to learn what KZF can do and how we will approach this important project.

We know that your time is valuable. Therefore, we have structured as much of this presentation as possible in Japanese to convey a large amount of important information directly and succinctly. Hopefully, this will aid you in making a rapid decision as to how you will proceed with this aspect of your project.

So now, we would like to tell you briefly who and what KZF is and why we think KZF is the best and most logical firm to design your industrial plant.

The KZF team offers Fujitec overall management simplicity since only one firm will be involved, encompassing all of the required areas of knowledge. We also have the familiarity and competence to design large scale building complexes, and with our 100 person staff, a commitment of the required manpower to accomplish the job with your desired schedule.

KZF has performed successfully on numerous complex projects requiring sophisticated phasing and scheduling of both the design and construction portions of the project. This means that KZF can meet your need for an accelerated schedule in a proficient and responsive manner. Our staff is also sensitive to ways to design and document decisions to maximize Fujitec's ability to take advantage of Federal business incentives, such as the investment tax credit.

KZF has the total in-house capability of providing.....

- Architecture
- Master Planning
- Interior Design
- Industrial Engineering
- Mechanical Engineering
- Electrical Engineering
- Structural Engineering
- Civil Engineering
- Landspace Architecture

Located in Cincinnati, convenient to the various sites you are considering for this project, KZF is a major design firm with a reputation built on unsurpassed service to its clients. Since its founding in 1956, KZF has grown steadily as a mature, stable organization, organized for continuity of operations and equipped to provide the latest in state-of-the-art design technology.

Our team is well experienced in the design of industrial facilities as this brief look at a few of our past projects will demonstrate.

Good design, however, does not happen by accident. It results from the coordinated, systematic, and realistic approach that KZF brings to complex projects like yours. To produce quality architecture that gets built on time and within budget, strict attention must be paid to the realities of your:

- Program
- Site
- Schedule
- Budget
- Quality expectations

To ensure that our design responds correctly to these factors, an effective design management system must be utilized. KZF's unique "matrix" management concept was instituted to provide the type of management system that industrial clients like Fujitec deserve and expect. The matrix approach provides a simple system of control that ensures that our designs are not only functional, efficient, manageable and aesthetically pleasing, but can also be built in accordance with your schedule and your budget. The KZF Project Manager, who is key to this system's operation, will have total responsibility for coordination, scheduling, budgeting, communications and liaison with your key people.

KZF establishes an in-house quality review panel to provide a "hands-off" critique by a selected group of professionals who are not otherwise involved in the project. This group evaluates how well the design team is addressing the client's program and quality expectations. Many unique alternatives have been generated by this system, and in many cases, by minor design or program changes, substantial cost savings to the client have resulted.

Our design approach to your project will respond to the proposed site, the Fujitec process, and the needs of your employees. The land will be shaped and landscaped to define an appropriate entry to the plant. The roadways will be designed to provide ease of access for private automobiles and truck traffic. We will strive to compliment the industrial process with the most cost-effective building, systems and finishes to promote employee comfort and enhance productivity. We will share more of these ideas with you in a moment. But now, let's meet the KZF team:

George Kral, President of KZF and a Fellow of the American Society of Civil Engineers, will ensure the total commitment of our team to your project and assume ultimate responsibility for seeing that KZF's work is done to Fujitec's satisfaction. Mr. Kral founded the KZF organization 25 years ago and is an engineer with well over 30 years of experience in the design profession.

The key individual in bringing together the KZF team and coordinating its day-to-day efforts with Fujitec is Dick Lenz. As Project Manager, Mr. Lenz will have single-point responsiblity for seeing that we keep to your program and schedule by anticipating, rather than reacting to, problems. Mr. Lenz is an engineer and a Vice President of KZF and has a great deal of experience in the management and design of industrial projects for major clients like Procter & Gamble, Emery Industries and Container Corporation of America.

Del Strickland, KZF's Chief of Architectural Design, will have primary responsibility for taking your preliminary plan and making it respond to the unique factors of the site, budget and local building code requirements.

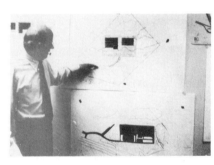

All the major titles, including charts and diagrams had caligraphy in reverse lettering (color on black background). These titles added a professional look to the program. The remainder of the program depicted the usual elements found in most KZF presentations. Photos of their key people intermingled with projects depicted through models, or completed installations. The graphics were the main customizing element, the most effective, and the easiest to achieve on a modest budget.

Accompanying the slide presentation was a script of the narration in both English and Japanese. The narration was spoken by a female Japanese, and many of the slides had titles in caligraphy superimposed over them.

Jon Bennett will be your structural engineer.

Geoff Hill will be your mechanical engineer, and

Bob Redmond will be responsible for electrical engineering on the project.

KZF's staff also includes a full-time construction cost estimator, Rick Hampton. Mr. Hampton's daily contact with the construction industry and with suppliers and vendors assures that the budget toward which we design is indeed realistic and reflects the latest in the volatile present-day constructtion marketplace.

So, to give you the opportunity of meeting with key members of the KZF team in person, they are here to share further specific information with you about your project. But before they do, we would like to summarize the KZF advantage with three words and hope you will continue to think of KZF in this way...

KZF is competent. We have years of experience in the major areas of expertise required by your project. The team we offer you is experienced in working together on projects such as yours and will be able to commence immediately on the solution to your program.

KZF is creative. We will charge our design team to create for you a flexible, functional, expandable and aesthetically pleasing facility which can be constructed in a short time and at moderate cost.

KZF is compatible with the Fujitec team. At KZF, the client becomes an integral part of the project team and throughout all phases of your project, KZF will work with you not merely for you. We are ready when you are.

River Walk

Four developers presented their development schemes in public hearings, held within the community where the project was scheduled to be built.

SCENARIO: The Public Meeting

Each developer was given 30 minutes to make their presentation to the public. Questions would be addressed after all four were completed. As part of New York State law, each developer was represented by an attorney who made the introductory remarks. As professionals who appear before the public often, they have much to learn about presentation techniques.

As the public came into the exhibition space, the models were on display. (This is a mistake in our opinion, because people can quickly become prejudiced against a project looking at a model.) Brochures for each project were handed out as people entered the auditorium. (Our illustrations were taken from those brochures.) People circulated through the audience with cards for those who wanted to ask questions, or make a statement about the proposals. The capacity crowd stayed until close to midnight.

RIVER WALK: The Winning Design

River Walk presented their story with a color slide dissolve presentation, utilizing an automatic advance on the sound track. When the "canned" program began with music the audience began to giggle. Then the narrator's voice came in with "Old New York, a waterfront community. The audience quickly quieted down and became intent on the program. After a brief opening, the camera surveyed the existing site: "This is the waterfront now"...barges, broken down piers, a burned out hull of a dock building... on the sound track SILENCE.

The music returned, this time with a soft upbeat sound and details of colorful sketches showed the activity of the proposed development; tennis courts, the marina, fountains, shops, the boardwalk and the River Walk community. The presentation concluded with an aerial sketch of the entire development. At the end of the presentation was a second 2-minute "canned" program about Cadillac Fairview. How they intend to build, own and operate this project and how they will complete it within 38 months from day of approval. "We will not sell the project, we live with what we build." (Applause)

EAST COVE:

Rose / Macri Joint Venture
I.M. Pei & Partners, Architects
Zion & Breen, Landscape Architects
Isamu Noguchi, Sculpture
Chermayeff & Geismar, Graphics

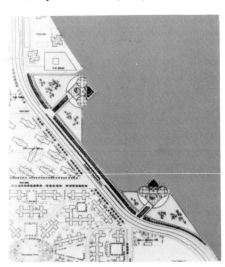

The presentation consisted mainly of photographs of the model. However, most of the views were aerials and made the project (especially the 70-story twin towers) look very big. The slide presentation was very short, but it was followed by a 16mm movie, produced by Project for Public Spaces, which featured children playing, people sunning themselves on piers, fountains, sculpture, people jogging, some sitting, looking, eating in cafes, and in general walking on riverfront esplanades.

The project also ignored the R.F.P. and presented a 100% residential scheme. They did not believe that any commercial scheme was economically viable based on past experience on adjacent property.

This project was chosen as number one by the Community Board 6 and ranked last by the adjacent Waterside Tenants' Association.

Developer: River Cove Development Co.
Architect: Ulrich Franzen & Assoc.
Construction Manager: Geo. A. Fuller Co.

**This project was selected as the number
two choice by Community Board 6
and first choice by neighboring
Waterside.**

RIVER COVE:

This scheme purposely did not follow the R.F.P. based on the philosophy that the waterfront should have an active role in the fabric of the city and a commer-cial development would provide this. The presentation followed this theme by showing slides of old engravings of waterfront areas such as the Quincy Market in Boston and the old New York waterfront. This was followed by slides of the model from an aerial viewpoint. Next, pictures of sketches were used to relate it again to the scale of the old pier-like waterfront atmosphere. The entire 20-minute presentation was narrated in person.

EAST RIVER VILLAGE:
Calico Corp. Michael O'Keefe

This presentation was perhaps the least effective of all for the following reasons:

1. The slant was towards selling the benefits of living in such a project: the energy systems, the orientations, all directed towards selling units. (The community was only concerned about the impact it would have on them.)

2. Some slides were on the screen up to 10 minutes.
3. Vertical slides wouldn't fit on the screen. (Remember the 10 x 15 foot horizontal screen?)
4. Rather than presenting it on its own merits, it always alluded to being like something else.

This project was not recognized by Community Board 6, but was ranked second by Waterside.

HARVARD SCHOOL OF DESIGN

**Harvard Graduate School of Design
Urban Design Program/Community
Assistance Program**

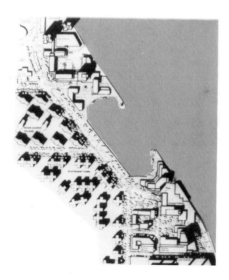

**The planning board of Community
Board 6 approached the university for
assistance in revising the draft R.F.P.
and, eventually, in evaluating the
developers' proposal for the site.**

AFTERMATH: East River Project

The Mayor's decision came as a surprise to everyone including the winning team. The community and Community Board 6 had clearly voted the East Cove project as their number one choice, the River Cove development as second and River Walk as third. There was no fourth choice.

However, in light of the only guidelines to follow, that is the R.F.P., River Walk was definitely the winner. The Mayor said he would choose the project that came the closest to the kind clearly expressed in the R.F.P.

Other things being equal, when it came time to decide on a winner, the team that did their home-work, the team that did the leg work and apparently followed up came away with the commission.

Bunker Hill

A reenactment of the design competition for the last major parcel of redevelopment area on Bunker Hill in downtown Los Angeles by the winning design team and representatives of the four competition finalists.

The evaluation criteria as set forth in the R.F.P. was quite extensive and carefully prepared to assure a good design plus a marketable development. The team that had prepared the R.F.P. was multi-faceted. Six were design oriented, two were real estate specialists, one real estate attorney, and one economic consultant. Between four and five months were spent in reviewing all the proposals.

The format for review of each developer's proposal was well structured. Besides the questions of the quality of the design and the marketability of the project, there were concerns for the relationship to the surrounding neighborhood. They wanted to know what special amenities would be provided, and how the open spaces could be used by pedestrians. Also important was the proposed linkage to the rest of the city.

To be objective in evaluating the designs, each model was set into an existing model of the surrounding buildings. Then each scheme was photographed from the same vantage point, from an aerial view, and a ground level view.

The Community Redevelopment Agency visited each developer, looked at their work and how their plans developed into completed projects. They were interested in the developer's experience in mixed-use development projects because there are not many good examples around.

Of the five schemes presented, two received recognition. One presentation consisted of an elaborate fabric with historical examples of architectural and planning schemes quite contrary to those requested. The sense of inappropriateness was felt (and expressed) by the entire audience. The other schemes were not so far off target, but neither had the spark to fire the client's imagination. There were adequate proposals featuring good planning and design that simply did not get a rise out of anyone (including the CRA). The two remaining were the focus of the controversy as the Maguire team presented a star-studded cast of world recognized designers, architects, minority consultants and developer. It featured a creative site plan, a variety of open spaces, grade changes in all manner of configuration, a museum which projected boldy over the street, and an overall design that was exciting, dramatic, playful and would create the true center of the city. Developer Maguire would contribute $15 million to the museum, plus a proposed guarantee of $300,000 in annual operating funds. His award of the commission of the $100 million plus office building to a minority architect was the largest ever awarded in California.

The Maguire Partnership's scheme featured a star-studded cast of designers, architects and consultants.

The Bunker Hill Associates scheme offered a complete development package, including financing

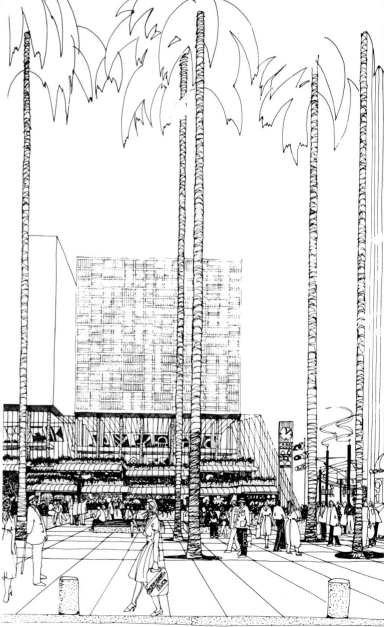

Union Terminal

This dual-screen slide presentation was made to present a two-project scheme to the owners of the Denver Union Terminal and the City of Denver. The total scheme involved constructing a new hotel and convention center over the existing railroad station and using land presently owned by the city, where the existing convention center was located. The existing convention center would be remodeled into a commercial and office complex. The dual-site proposal inspired the dual-screen presentation, so the two sites could be geographically and photographically connected.

The introduction to the project was delivered by the key individual in the development team. Pairs of panorama scenes introduced the site and project team.

Stephen W. Brener Associates, Inc.
Jeffrey C. Carter, Director of Consulting and Valuation Services

Individual joint-venture team members were introduced using a Kodalith slide on the left screen and an illustrative example on the right. The projects selected for the right screen related to the particular hotel and convention center expertise each team member would bring to the project.

One of the development team members showed a major renovation project that was recently completed adjacent to the downtown area. The project was the renovation of an old brewery into an attractive specialty commercial venture. Parking was one of the biggest concerns in the downtown areas adjacent to the project site.

A panorama covering both screens was made by photographing an illustrated city map of the downtown business district. The map was drawn in isometric projection so the heights of buildings could be seen. The two sites appeared at opposite ends of this map, the convention center on the left and the terminal on the right.

• PLANNING CONTEXT

Title slides were used throughout the program to identify the major subdivisions within the presentation. At each of the major points the visual on the right screen summarized the section. In all the overall aerial scenes both sites could be seen so that one never lost the sense of the 2-site concept.

The convention center project was depicted in an aerial view on the left screen, showing the configuration of the existing hall. Along side of it appeared a photomontague showing the new towers drawn into the aerial. The orientation was similar to the view of the existing hall.

One of the towers is featured in the vertical shot of the remodeled convention center. The right screen depicted oblique views of the two office tower structures. The photos of the model were taken with dramatic side lighting to emphasize their curvilinear shape, and from a low camera angle.

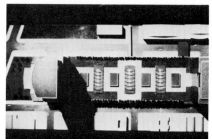 

The existing railroad terminal became the focal point of the new hotel convention center complex. The existing lobby would remain intact as the lobby for the new hotel. A vertical cross section shows the relationship of the lobby to the new hotel which would be constructed over it.

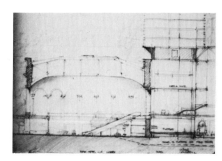 

The layout of the hotel complex is explained by pairs of slides showing the floor plans on the left and a model photo on the right. The plans were Kodalith pictures without colored gels. The simplicity of the white line on the black background was very readable and complimented the model shots.

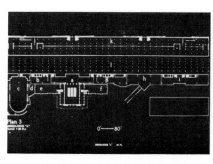 

At the conclusion of the story about the two-site project, the attention was focused on the terminal and convention center part of the project. One reason for this was the proposed schedule by the developer to completely finish the new convention center before moving to the other site.

 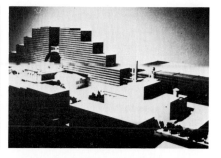

The final scene in the presentation was the completed hotel and convention center model. It was photographed to be used as a panorama and showed how the new hotel would encompass the existing terminal. The slide presentation ended with an aerial view of the two sites as they would look when completed.

Countryside Acres

This presentation was made to seek approval of a 60-acre development of rural property. Opposition to the project came from a strong environmental group protecting the water courses and fish streams. The presentation was designed to answer the objections of this group through sound planning techniques.

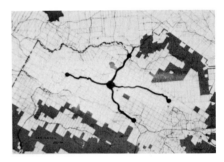

The property is very conveniently located at the crossroads of two county roads connecting four towns. In addition, it is immediately accessible to New York City by bus. It is a short 3 hours from the Port Authority bus terminal to this corner. Therefore, it was certainly prime property for development.

People would come to the Catskills to see wildlife in a natural setting or to fish in its many famous trout streams. The rural nature of the community was gradually disappearing as evidenced by the ski slope on the mountain.

The skiers were coming by the thousands each weekend, to build new houses for the future, and the farm community was rapidly giving way to new condominiums and new development.

As a result of a landowner study, it was found that 60 percent of the people who lived here owned second homes. This was not a primary residential area. Therefore, many planning studies were necessary to effect good planning.

Some people came to this area to build second homes that blended with the landscape, others did not. However, without local zoning, the local town government really could not control it.

All the houses had one thing in common; they were built on soil that was totally unsuitable for the individual septic systems that were allowed by the state and local communities, thereby putting all the trout streams in jeopardy. The proposed planned development utilized a balance of single-family and townhouse dwellings.

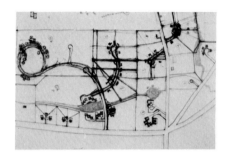

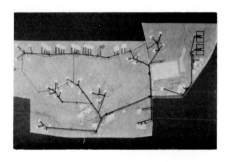

All utilities would be put in a central system; none of the sewage or treatment would ever end up in the stream. The architect also pointed out that the land-use concept of cluster housing, single-family dwellings mixed with townhouses, would certainly preserve much of the open space of the property.

Only 15 percent of the property would be developed, thereby preserving the beauty of the Catskills for future generations. Opposition was withdrawn and the project was approved.

Rye Town Community

This presentation was prepared to gain planning commission approval of a large, mixed-use PUD. The mixed-use included 1000 luxury condominium units, an office park, a conference center and a large retail complex.

There was every reason to expect strong opposition to the project, as many other proposals for the same site had been defeated in the past.

The developer first presented his case armed with many graphic aids; maps, charts, and a fully detailed architectural model of the 300 acre development. The only slides he had of the site were taken in the winter and were very drab. He lost control of the presentation as soon as he began discussing the traffic diagrams. The confusion that resulted from the audience participation forced the developer to close the public hearing and retreat.

The developer then decided to utilize a color slide presentation designed to prohibit interruptions from the audience. This was achieved by using a pre-recorded voice track with a soft musical background throughout the entire script. At the public hearing. the lights were turned out, the tape recorder turned on, and the entire presentation was made without interruption.

Visual material for the presentation was carefully selected to minimize the impact of the development on the neighboring community. The traffic issue was only mentioned briefly, whereas the benefits of the development to the town were stressed, including tax revenues generated by the new project.

Material for the color slide presentation was carefully planned. The site was photographed at the height of the fall foliage, on the ground and by a series of aerial views taken from a rental helicopter. The graphic maps were re-colored to match the site photos and the colored sketches were rendered to match the site and model photographs. The professionalism of the presentation was made possible by the selection of elements in the slide presentation and the coordinated story line which accompanied the pictures.

The Village of Port Chester and the Town of Rye are people-oriented communities.

Pride in a heritage dating back to 1660 is still felt by people who take time to care for their town.

This can be seen in the character and dignity of older homes

that so amicably blend with the newer residences...

in its children as they learn, play, and mature

and in the concern for relating new architecture to the community.

The property encompasses a 350-acre tract of land.

Many large-scale corporate offices have been planned for the immediate area

and many other new developments are immediate neighbors.

To the south is the prestigious headquarters of Pepsico,

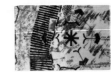
incorporating the grace and character of the site in its design.

To the west is the newly designed campus of the State University of New York.

Projected student population by the year 1980 will generate traffic greater

than can now be handled by the existing roadways.

This has led many local and state agencies to make detailed traffic studies.

The devoper has made his own traffic studies,

which will turn some existing streets into private roadways within the neighboring communities.

The property is characterized by gently rolling topography

sprinkled with clumps of mature trees

and traversed by long tree rows following old stone walls.

Preservation of these natural elements is a strong feature in the design.

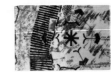
Special emphasis will be placed on High Point gate house and the majority of existing structures,

such as the High Point Mansion, that will be retained as a club and park.

From High Point there are dramatic views in all directions.

Other environmental considerations include the Westchester County Airport

immediately to the north of the property.

A safety landing zone has been provided on the property

limiting development to commercial use.

DESIGN CONCEPT
The design concept is based on preservation of open space within the new community.

The existing zoning on the property would permit extensive office building development.

By considering the entire property as a creatively planned community,

a one-third reduction in the present zoning can be achieved.

Careful studies were made merging all the requirements for development

The plan was developed stage-by-stage until the final design was realized

The ultimate plan would be a gradual buildup based on the acclimation of the project into the community.

By 1980 there will be a new 18-hole golf course.

By 1990 the fashion center will be operating

and a large portion of the housing units will be occupied.

By the year 2000 the entire project will be functioning as a total entity,

providing a great fiscal benefit to the town, the county, and the state.

Students generated by this development will not exceed the planned school capacity.

CONCEPT DEVELOPMENT
Balance is the key to the success of the community.

There will be a variety of uses, ranging from cluster housing to professional offices,

a conference center and a fashion center.

This balance will be oriented around a complete recreational environment.

Existing lakes on the property will be retained for use in the residential areas.

Houses will be terraced down the hillside and built into the landscape

to reduce the appearance of density.

Many of the luxury townhouses will overlook the golf course.

A new conference center will be built near the existing High Point Mansion.

The unique feature here is an existing tree bosque

that will be developed into an outdoor fashion boutique leading to the fashion center.

Here, lakes and waterfalls will provide an exciting visual focal point

for restaurants and other community facilities.

The 'fashion galleria' will become a community space

for town meetings and other large gatherings.

This truly creative environment will be for all the residents to share in harmony

with the overall character of the Town of Rye.

By working closely with the community,

a landmark of creative design will be created.

Computers In Presentations

The computer explosion among design professionals is everywhere, as evidenced by articles in every major trade journal.

One pioneering and progressive firm using computers for architectural design is Everett I. Brown Company of Indianapolis, In. They are not only leaders in the use of computers, but are always on the lookout for new techniques utilizing the computer's capability to depict space. They became intrigued with the presentation possibilities of their computer on one of their recent proposal submittals for the Farm Credit Bank.

To help visualize the dramatic setting of the Farm Credit Banks' building and the interior design as it would be seen by a visitor, Everett I. Brown Company developed a videotape sequence of computer-generated drawings simulating the approach to and a walk around the building.

"We believe this is the first time a computer-generated building design has ever won a major design competition," said Joseph Brown, partner in charge of design for Everett I. Brown Company.

"Utilizing the computer, we have been able to combine excellence of design with energy and cost efficiency. Not only will this be an architecturally outstanding building in a beautiful park-like setting, it will be economical to build, economical to operate and maintain, and economical to expand."

"By using videotape in place of the conventional architectural model, we were able to show how the building 'works' at eye level so the Farm Credit Banks' people could put themselves into the design and see it from all angles, including an aerial view," said Brown. "This, to the best of our knowledge, has never before been done in a presentation."

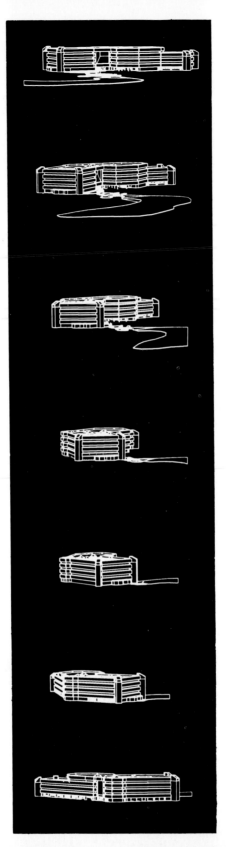

To establish the 3-D perspective of the Farm Credit Banks' new building, the 2-D conceptual design sketches were placed in a 3-D file in basic outline form.

Then, working with the designer, the appropriate square footages were established in accordance with the architectural design program. The various floor plans were manipulated within the file to check proportions.

Once the desired square footage and proportions were established, the 2-D file was projected into the third dimension. The 3-D file was then utilized to conduct massing studies.

The building was scanned utilizing sophisticated software to eliminate hidden lines. The building was then rotated through 360-degrees to check 3-D proportions, perspectives and symmetry.

The building was then dissected to check the structural framing plan. Cross sections were reviewed for proper square footages and utilized in the space planning efforts. Eventually a color table was created in-house from scratch to examine potential color schemes.

The 3-D file of the building was created early in the preliminary design phase while program changes affecting the overall building shape and size were still occurring. These changes were easily accomplished in the graphics 3-D file.

First, they put the design of the bank building in their computer in a 3-D mode. Someone suggested taking slides of the 3-D images and using them in the presentation in place of a model. They already knew that one of their competitors was going to use a model.

After they took a closer look at the slides they had taken, partner Joseph Brown suggested videotaping a slide sequence to see if they could add motion to it. This would give the client a display of how the building looked from all angles.

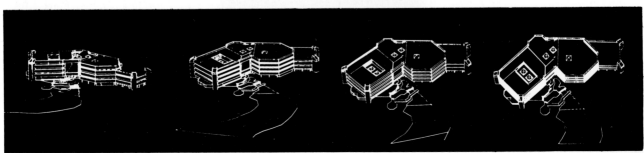

The videotape was created by photographing a number of views of the Farm Credit Banks' building directly off the CAD system workstation screen, utilizing a 35mm camera.

"Once we had the slides, we set up a procedure in-house to transfer these images to video tape. We used the technique called "off the wall" where we simply copied the projected slides with a home video camera in the ½" (VHS) format. Each slide was taped for about 6-7 seconds. As soon as we video taped one slide we would wait until any "ghosting" disappeared on the monitor, and then we projected the next slide. In taping the 60 or more slides we came up with a minute of video tape."

The videotape was utilized for presentation to the client in lieu of a model, an artist's rendering or both. It was felt that the dynamics of the videotape would have a favorable impression on the client, and they believe it did.

Additionally, it was a means of presenting our extensive CAD efforts to a client who was approximately 800 miles from our office and the CAD system.

The videotape was carried to the client's office for showing as part of Everett I. Brown Company's presentation during the architects' competition. On request, the client willingly provided the VHS recorder and the TV monitor used during the presentation.

This type of presentation of a proposed design to a client has considerable merit. With the advent of dynamic rotation, it will literally be possible not only to take a client on a trip around and over a building, but also on a walk through the interior.

The total effect of the motion and simulated viewing of the building from all angles impressed the client. The dynamics of this type of presentation will very likely make the use of models and renderings obsolete.

One advantage to this form of presentation is the immediacy of the visual images. Other methods of visualization require extensive work to produce more than one view. A three-dimensional model can, of course, be photographed from many angles but the percision required in constructing the sequential views would have been much more time consuming.

Another plus is the apparent willingness on the part of the viewer to watch a less than picture-perfect image as long as it is shown on a video monitor.

"The client provided the TV monitor when we went in for the final presentation. We had requested this in earlier discussions with the client. Since it was produced on home video equipment, the quality was not as smooth as a larger format and professional equipment would yield. However, the total effect of the motion and simulation of the completed building really impressed the client, and we got the job. The client also liked the design, so the video simulation just added to his decision to have us do the work."

Everett I. Brown Company plans to continue and to expand the use of this form of design presentation to clients.

The latest treat for designers is the 3-D graphics capability which will undoubtedly change the course of all visualization. Once the coordinates are programmed the possibilities for studying the design from all angles can be realized. In essence renderings and model techniques are combined into a single graphic image. This new technology will eventually alter the course of architectural design. Using these new electronic tools one can draw, study design schemes, compare, evaluate, and even present solutions in a fraction of the time. A far more important factor than the reduction of time is the unlimited variations and possibilities for exploration that are finally available to the designer, engineer, and artist.

Kuwait News Agency

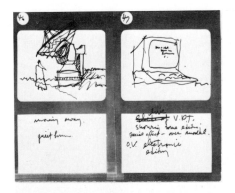

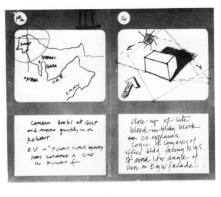

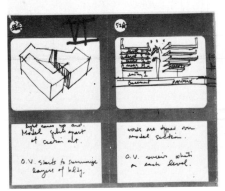

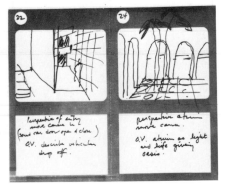

THE CLIENT

The videotape was for a paid competition to design a headquarters building for the Kuwait News Agency (KUNA) in Kuwait. We had a comprehensive team including engineers, local associates, as well as United Press International (U.P.I.) as special consultants on news and news editing.

THE DECISION TO DO A VIDEOTAPE

We had developed our design to the extent that we knew pretty much what the building was going to do. The team was talking about how we would present the project and we had covered most of the traditional methods of presentation: drawings, perspectives, models, technical reports, slides, and one of the people from the team in our graphics department had been involved in a video course, as well as making a film for the Jubail project (an industrial city in Saudi Arabia master-planned by TAC). It was suggested we might make a videotape or a movie. After interviewing several video and film makers, we decided to use video rather than film because of cost, the tight time schedule, and because we felt we could participate more directly in the making process of videotape as opposed to a film.

HIRING VIDEOCOM

We hired Videocom, even though they were not the least expensive firm we interviewed because we felt they would provide the kind of quality we wanted in the short time frame, and we felt they would work with us as a team.
The budget for this program was $10,000.

TIME FRAME

From the time we first talked to Videocom until we went to Kuwait with the finished tape, the time span was one month. The production time was 2 days — one for the "shoot" and one for editing .

The first thing we did was the storyboards. We had certain presentation materials developed and we had decided that the videotape would not be our entire presentation but would complement the technical report and the drawing boards we were submitting. The weekend before our first team-meeting with Videocom, I took home a T.V. pad and did the "storyboards". Since I had no previous experience with this sort of thing, I didn't worry about how things would be done but concentrated on the best way to tell the story we wanted to tell.

Then Videocom hired a script writer. While the script was being written, they gave us several voices to choose from for the narrator. They also hired someone to do an original musical score for the production. At the same time, the TAC team was building study models, doing graphics, perspectives and collecting things for the "shoot". We were surprised to learn from Videocom that the sound track would be done first and that the "shooting" would be done to the completed sound track. The two production days were very full days going well into

the night and the experience was terrific —— like magic. We were able to see everything instantly as it was being shot, as well as being able to participate in the editing.

PROBLEMS IN THE PRODUCTION

Although nothing happened that detrimentally affected the end product, there were several mini crises, such as finding that Arabic translation was longer than the English version and getting format converted to the PAL system so it could be shown in Kuwait.

The videotape was a new presentation technique for TAC, and we feel it is very effective. We have received uniformly positive comments from both professionals and nonprofessionals. The third party presentation allows the architect not only to express in a focused, concise way the design concept, but also to express the client's highest ideals without sounding conceited. And the ability of the camera to move against the perspective drawings, coupled with the background sound, allows the viewer to really be in the spaces.

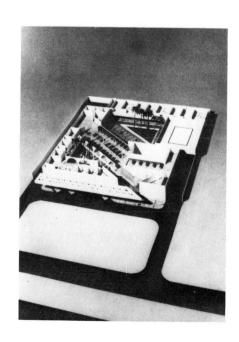

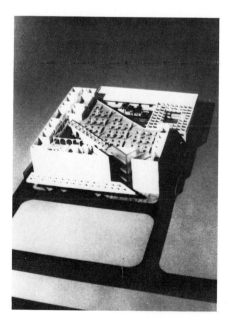

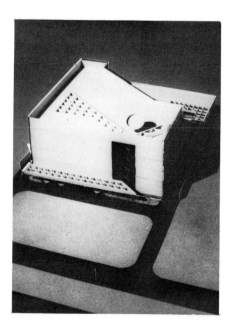

Superior Oil

This presentation was the winning entry in a design competition for the prestigious headquarters building in Houston. The elements of the site, access and vegitation were explored using two-dimensional graphics.

The plans and diagrams were copied on the videotape with minimal animation. The following sequence involved an animated build-up of the building's elements, the parking, the core structure, and the massing concepts.

Then the visitor is taken on a tour of the facility from the front entry through the interior functional levels of the facility. This was accomplished through the use of the video camera moving across the drawing. It created the sense of three-dimensional space.

At the conclusion of the tour the visitor was outside the building looking at the three-dimensional model. As the video camera took a tour around the structure, the exterior surface materials were described and final design comments were made.

The entire program was narrated using a soft-sell approach. There was no background music either in the introduction or in the closing. The sophistication of the voice carried the message of quality design.

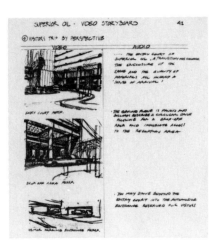

Copley Place

This elaborate videotape was submitted to the developer to present interior design concepts for the Copley Place development.

TAC is acting as master planner for a 3.2 million square foot complex in Boston's Copley Square. Occupying 9.5 acres adjacent to (and using air rights over) the Massachusetts Turnpike, the development includes two convention hotels, office and retail space, restaurants, theatres, 100 units of housing and parking for 1,800 cars.

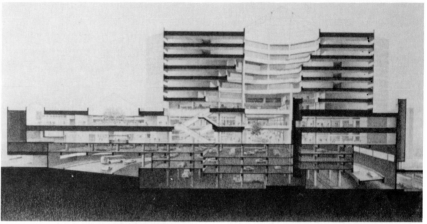

A spacious skylighted and landscaped retail gallery links all of the complex's buildings and connects to parking and rail service. The 100,000-square-foot prestige department store, Neiman-Marcus, and 200,000 square feet of specialty shops, create a strong retail focus which will add to the activity and visual excitement of the complex.

TAC is architect for the 1,000-room Western International Hotel and planner for the 900-room Marriott Hotel. These two high-rise towers form the anchors at each end of the complex. The four office buildings overlook the interior gallery, as well as the surrounding Back Bay area of Boston.

The film utilized a camera panning in on interior renderings giving the effect of movement. Those sequences dissolved into camera movements through the model giving the illusion of the space as it would look when completed.

Model photos by: Most Media

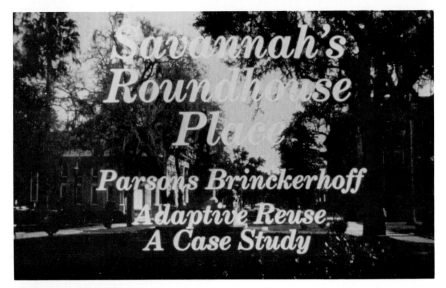

Roundhouse Place

This program was originally prepared in 35mm slides for the City of Savannah to explain and sell the project to the City Agencies. It was then modified for use with new clients to illustrate Parsons Brinkerhoff's services and capabilities on adaptive re-use projects. The modifications included the addition of a taped narration and musical introduction.

The existing structures of this old railroad complex form the basis for the discussion of the new uses. Both interior and exterior views were necessary to show the scale of the existing structures, which are listed in the National Register of Historic Places. They are imposible to duplicate today.

Many planning sessions were held during the course of the development of the project. Key individuals were photographed while they were making presentations. These were used to point out how the local community was involved. A headline from a local newspaper added further emphasis to their case.

Generic photographs of existing similar projects were mixed with sketches of the proposed design to create the illusion that the project was already built. Photos selected were similar in nature to the proposed new uses in the project, and added a sense of realism.

Renderings were created of the new development, both from aerial viewpoints and from ground level. These were used throughout the presentation. They were also photographed using cropped details so that one drawing would yield several slides. The aerial view provided as many as six details.

Our analysis showed a substantial untapped market for specialty retail items. Sales are expected to increase by 12 percent from 1980 to 1985.

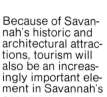

Because of Savannah's historic and architectural attractions, tourism will also be an increasingly important element in Savannah's economy.

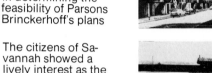

The marketing study was a prime element in determining the feasibility of Parsons Brinckerhoff's plans

The citizens of Savannah showed a lively interest as the plans took shape.

When completed, Roundhouse Place will be home to a fascinating mix of tenants in a unique complex combining carefully restored and renovated old buildings with new structures.

Serving as the focal point of the retail and restaurant area and as a visual symbol for Roundhouse Place is the brick smokestack.

Railroad cars and railroad memorabilia combined with carefully designed landscaping,

will create an active outdoor public area in the courtyard surrounding the tower.

Adjoining the Roundhouse is the machine shop, virtually a ruin, that will be rebuilt and transformed with the addition of a fabric roof.

Bright canopies, flags, and carts will add to the festive atmosphere,

attracting families and tourists of all ages to the colorful shops.

The old boiler house will be the focus of a children's entertainment area.

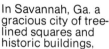

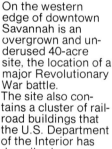

In Savannah, Ga. a gracious city of tree-lined squares and historic buildings,

Parsons Brinckerhoff is undertaking a major restoration and redevelopment project, Roundhouse Place.

On the western edge of downtown Savannah is an overgrown and underused 40-acre site, the location of a major Revolutionary War battle.
The site also contains a cluster of railroad buildings that the U.S. Department of the Interior has described as the finest surviving example of railroad shop architecture in America.

Many of the structures built in the 1850's of brick and heavy timber, have a scale and esthetic quality almost impossible to reproduce today.

The Romanesque revival brick buildings are listed in the National Register of Historic Places.

Deteriorated and underutilized structrues like these in Savannah can be refurbished and returned to economic vitality.

In cities large and small, Parsons Brinckerhoff's architects, engineers, and planners are designing the adaptive reuse of such buildings.

It will become a children's theatre, with a cast of four-foot-high animated puppets,

enacting scenes that will bring to life the romance of the old railroad.

Adding another kind of urban vitality, the train sheds on the northern end of the site will be developed into townhouses,
with a character similar to these restored homes in the nearby historic district.

An outstanding tourist attraction will be the history orientation center,

to be located in the long train shed attached to the Chamber of Commerce and Vistors Center.

Sophisticated audiovisual techniques will be used to depict the battle of Savannah.

and witness the Vanderbilt Cup Race held in Savannah in 1911.

The history orientation tour will culminate in a realistic train ride, in a vintage railroad car,

The focus of the site and the major pedestrian access to Roundhouse Place will be through Battlefield Park.

The City of Savannah has approved Parsons Brinckerhoff's conceptual plans for Roundhouse Place and Battlefield Park, and has selected our real estate development subsidiary to develop the site.

Our architects, engineers and planners are now working to implement the transformation of these neglected railroad buildings,

preserving the historic buildings and bringing vitality to a neglected site.

Corporate Services Presentations

Planning a presentation should always begin with a concept diagram which outlines the basic storyline in graphic form. In a program about the services of a design or consulting firm there are many approaches, of course. The one we chose for Hill was based on a structure similar to an organizational chart. There was a brief and rather formal introduction. It told who they were, where they were located and what their major services consisted of. This was followed by an opening statement first by the President and then by the Chairman of the Board.

Then each key principal began to unfold the story about the firm. First, from one angle, then from another, although still rather general in tone. Once into the middle of the program the dialogue des-cribed the nitty-gritty of what the firm does, and how their services benefit the client. At the conclusion, two clients would give testimony to the value of Hills services as it applied to their particular project. The program would close with a short musical passage behind a summary narration emphasizing the role that the Hill people contributed to every project.

Any program about a company and its services revolves around the people who provide those services. We prefer to let the people tell their own story about their role in the organization and how this will benefit the potential client. The technique used is not necessarily new. However, its use in the field of design professionals and consultants makes it quite unique.

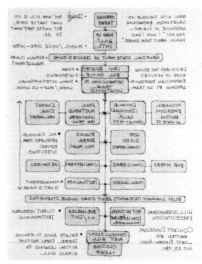

The concept diagram (above) is helpful in organizing the basic structure of the program, in terms of the major elements and their linear sequence in the story. The storyboard (below) defines the slide-for-slide sequence and facilitates the planning of the whole program in miniature. It depicts how each sequence relates to each other sequence so the entire program can be visualized in advance.

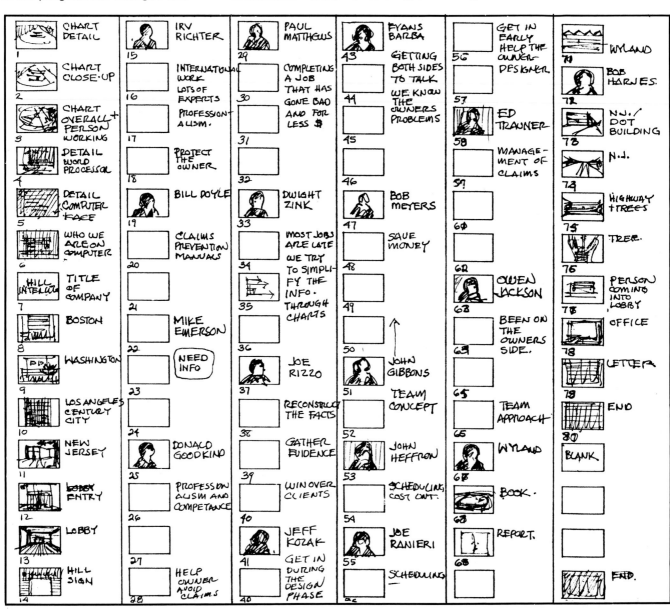

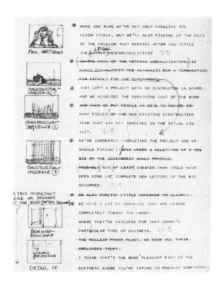

Stuart Richter
Director Business
Development

FROM CONCEPT TO SCRIPT

The first draft of the edited script combined with a sketch of each slide is when the program first begins to take on its final form. This script represents the first cut of the taped conversations. It is still too lengthy, but now it can be accurately timed and edited further. The illustrations can now be selected to relate to the edited script.

The final script is typed and illustrations of the actual slides can be made by reproducing them on a color xerox, cutting them out individually and pasting them next to the corresponding part of the script. Cue marks can be added at this point to indicate the slide changes, whether done manually or pulsed on an audiotape for automatic synchronization. This color version can then be photocopied in black and white.

Title slides for the key individuals in the program were made by using press-on lettering on acetate overlays. The titles are in two colors, white for the major title and yellow for the subtitle. The acetate is placed over a 3x5 inch color print. The resulting slide is a combination of the picture and title done inexpensively, without the need of a photo lab. This method gives control and accuracy at low cost.

Develop the storyboard.

The storyboard is an indispensable item in the planning of any audio-visual program. It gives you the opportunity to sketch out your entire program and view it on one piece of paper. Frames for the slides can be drawn with an empty slide mount or laid out on a drafting table. The most workable size for same size illustrations is a 24"x 36" format. For a single projector program or single screen dissolve — remember — you are only going to use horizontal slides.

The storyboard for Hill first identified the opening and closing sequences. Then space was left for two client testimonials at the end, one slightly longer that the other. Next, the 14 individuals who would appear throughout the program were placed in sequence, according to the structure of the concept diagram. Additional space was left for each person, depending on the length of the edited interviews. The main value, of course, is that you can show others your intent and they can visualize the finished product much easier than from a verbal description.

Do the audio first.

Most presentations talk *at* the listener. This one talks *to* the listener, in natural conversational dialogue. The dialogue was not planned or scripted. It is spontaneous and unrehearsed. The effect is

that each individual is personally telling you their part in the story of the company. Each person is interviewed in a relaxed situation, and their comments and conversation and response to posed questions are recorded. These recorded sessions are then transcribed word-for-word. This is the working script. From 20 minutes of conservation, we are looking for 20 seconds of dialogue. So every word, every phrase, every pause, becomes an important cog in the development of the final script.

This approach is somewhat different from programs where the narration is done from a written script which usually follows a predetermined visual story line.

Follow the 7 second rule.

The material gleaned from these interviews will be the basis for the entire audio track. Therefore,you should edit the narrative down to the desired length, then carefully time each section in seconds. Then follow the "seven second rule" whereby the average length of time that a slide is on the screen does not exceed seven seconds. You simply time the length of each statement, sentence or paragraph, and divide by 7. This will tell you how many slides you should show in that time period. For example, if a sentence turns out to be 15 seconds you should change slides twice during that interval.

Create meaningful sequences.

In the Hill program the visual sequences were selected to follow a conversational plannned dialogue. A word of caution is in order here, as one remembers a cardinal rule regarding slide presentation scripts from our workshops in VISUAL MARKETING, "Don't tell them what's on the screen...tell them what's not on the screen". However, with the type of program like Hill the exact opposite is true. You shouldn't illustrate in exact visual terms what the dialogue is saying, instead, you show something that is related in concept. You reinforce the dialogue with a related visual sequence.

Editing is the key.

In editing for a written message, every rule must be followed in terms of grammar,punctuation and the like. It's the writer's objective to boil down the dialogue to its factual essense, tighten it up and enliven the sentence structure, speed up and keep the verbal action close to the point of the material being written.

In real life, people don't speak like that at all. They always use more words than necessary. They digress. Their speech is interspersed with "uh" and "well", and a host of other expressions. They repeat themselves. They use voice inflection to reinforce the meaning.

Hill International

The factors that went into the planning of this story are described on the preceding pages (234-235). The following depicts the final version of the audiovisual program in both script and visual content.

Stimulate interest

What we look for in the editing is the most natural, the most interesting, and the most stimulating part of the conversation. We select passages that will keep the interest high during the entire program. We also look for the most positive statements. We eliminate everything that is not clearly directed to the client or anything that could be interpreted as a negative in any way.

Sometimes that means giving up what one might think is explanatory dialogue for that which stimulates interest. This approach is designed to encourage the client to want to know more about the company. This becomes the perfect lead-in for the person showing the program. They can seek additional response from the client and then direct comments to the client's own project or need.

Identify the theme

Once you have identified your primary audience (coupled with your overall objectives), you will be able to develop the theme for your program. What emerged as the central theme in the Hill presentation was not a description of the services they offered in representing an owner or contractor in a claims situation but in claims prevention. This main theme is underlying each statement by each of the individuals who speak in the presentation. The identifying of the theme is a primary concern.

Customize the approach

A general marketing program does not need quite so much fine tuning. Once you have settled on the specific audience you want to reach the rest will fall into place. Keep in mind that no general marketing program can be the same to all your clients. So you must decide on your most important audience and direct all your efforts to them in every detail. Every slide, every word, all must relate to that client and his project. It will pay off in the long run.

Hill International is a group of professionals dedicated to the resolution of problems in the construction industry.

Hill International's world headquarters is located in Willingboro, New Jersey, with other branch offices in:

Boston

Washington

Los Angeles

Our services include:

SCHEDULING, where we develop workable and effective construction programs.

PROJECT MANAGEMENT, where we utilize our field personnel to complete projects within time and budget

CLAIMS MANAGEMENT, where we minimize construction risks and potential claims exposure, and

CONSTRUCTION AUDIT, where we provide reliable and factual financial data.

Our company is headed by Irv Richter, President and Chief Executive Officer.

Today, if you look at all the companies in the industry, you'll find Hill has the highest level of professionals.

That's the biggest thing about Hill is our people.

Every project owner needs to control costs and time overruns.

We know the kinds of problems the owner's going to have in a contract. So we start out by helping him write a good set of specifications.

There's nobody that specializes in protecting the owners. And that's the function we serve.

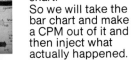

We're very proud of the level of competence that's offered here.

We would like to help people avoid claims, get projects done on schedule, within budget with minimum disruption.

More and more we're not only handling the claim itself, but we're also picking up the rest of the problem that remains after you settle the legal responsibilities.

At that point somebody's got to finish the project.

Complete the construction, and do it in an economical manner.

Most jobs are late today. Most construction claims have a large element of dispute concerning who was responsible for that delay.

A lot of the projects we get involved with, there isn't any CPM. There's a bar chart.
So we will take the bar chart and make a CPM out of it and then inject what actually happened.

So as to determine what caused the as-planned schedule to become the as-built schedule.

We start in the simplification process by distilling a great mass of data.

We've carried the level of expertise we think to the forefront of existing technology.

What they want from you is the facts. Try to put together what happened

We go out to the field. We gather all the copies of all the daily reports.

We copy the superintendent's reports. We copy all the correspondence.

You've got to be more aware of what happened than the people who actually ran the job.

The object is to try to improve the client's position and to back him up in any way that you can.

In dealing with the design and specification from the engineering standpoint, I have that owner's experience.

I know what the contractor's looking to do, what the owner's looking to do.

We try to get in during the design phase and try to help them out in the earliest phase possible on the job.

We're pretty much up-to-date on the latest happenings in terms of construction law.

Claims management from one aspect would be working with the designer or the owner in terms of his contract documents at the very beginning and attempting to minimize the chances for disputes.

Well, the most important thing that we have here is the team concept.

I mean I don't think there are too many companies that have the talent that Hill has.

We'd like to get in as soon as somebody thinks they'd like to build something before they even have it on paper.

Assisting them in hiring an architect, then working with the architect on the design aspects.

My outlook with claims and the whole business is very different. It's really a management problem.

We can effectively manage projects on the front end, because we've seen the back side of them so often.

If I can save them some money, that's one of my major objectives. I want to be just as cost effective as I can.

It's the type of company that has combined a number of very unique skills.

Hill is in a unique position of calling upon these different individuals.
And tailoring that team to suit the owner's needs.

The sanitary district has been involved in two decisions on some of our construction projects that were carried through to litigation.

We decided that Hill International would be best suited for our project.

They're preparing a manual right now.

They've been very good to work with. The recommendations are such that they can be easily followed.

Hill International assisted us on several projects where we had major claims from construction contractors.

And their work was really excellent and gave us a lot of help in settling these claims.

I feel very good about having them on our side in any litigation or in trying to settle any claim.

Our company obviously is based on the talents of our people.

We do a better job of putting together our people and final product than anyone else.

They keep abreast of technology and equipment to give our client every thing we can;

but it all centers around people. You know it really does.

Easy to customize

A similar approach to this method of letting the story tell itself through the words of those involved in the project has been used successfully in specific project design submittals. It focuses all the attention on the client and the project. It is extremely effective by customizing the presentation in the editing process. It is not so easy to use the same program for other clients or projects, especially if you did an effective job at customizing it to begin with.

Easy to store and retrieve

Active slide programs can be stored in their carousel trays (with the rings glued on) preferably under lock and key. There should be only one person responsible for the safe keeping of these important programs. The best insurance, however, is to have several duplicate sets made immediately. Then the "original" program can be stored in acetate sleeves in three ring binders. There are some sleeves that will hold up to 80 or more slides in one package for convenient storage.

Easy to reproduce

Duplicate slides are inexpensive and, if done properly, it would take an expert to tell them from the originals. In many cases duplicating can actually improve an original by changing the color balance, adding contrast, or by lightening up a dim slide.

Large or small groups

The program for Hill was designed to be shown most often in a rear screen projection cabinet such as the Kodak Audio-Viewer. The audience would be mostly small groups. For larger groups they would use a regular projector coupled with a cassette recorder. (The Audio-Viewer has its own automatic playback.)

Professional appearance

Nearly anyone can make a slide show that looks good as long as they use good photography and legible titles. To get the same professionalism in film or video, a good deal more technical knowledge is necessary. And for the beginner a lot more time in planning and producing is also required. There are many films and videotapes that are not very much more effective than they would have been in a slide format.

The Sidwell Company

After they planned their program and wrote the script they hired a professional to record the narration. It gives the program an air of authority to have a practiced voice that puts the emphasis where you want it, while not sounding unnatural.

When The Sidwell Company produced the winning entry in the 1979 Society for Marketing Professional Services Marketing Achievement Award, it was a name familiar to the society. They had won the award the previous year in the newsletter competition.

The 1978 winner was "Map News" a quarterly newsletter developed to help make the firm's potential clients aware of the variety and extent of their services.

Their 1979 winner in the slide presentation competition was a filmstrip used by the company's representatives when calling on clients.

The Winner Was A Sound/Filmstrip

The presentations of The Sidwell Co. use both slides and filmstrip. Each representative is equipped with a compact filmstrip projector and several programs. These are capable of being shown on the projector's built-in rear screen or projected onto a large front screen for a group.

Most of the photography is done in-house and the quality of pictures is evident in the illustrated script.

But just exactly how they got the images they wanted is important. They knew first of all that images do not magically appear on the screen. They must be planned, organized, examined and evaluated, and then tested.

They began their program by using a device called a storyboard or illustrated script. Here they were able to develop the script and the visuals simultaneously. They used a preprinted storyboard. Several types are available.

238

● Soft lead-in music.

● Airplane engine starting over music.

● "Clear for take-off."

● "The production of maps has changed rapidly in recent years."

● Large project areas can be covered in a matter of hours with photography that records every visible feature.

● These features are converted into maps for a variety of engineering projects.

● In earlier days, photographs were taken from ballons and kites.

● While aerial photography was being improved, most maps were still produced by traditional survey methods.

● These early maps provided the kind of information needed for our country's rapid westward expansion.

● During WWII there was a great demand for maps. The development of high altitude aircraft,

● ..new cameras and instruments established photogrammetry as a practical mapping method.

● Today, satellite photography provides info on land use, geology, pollution, etc.

● (Change music) But let's come down to earth. Photogrammetric mapping has four steps.

● These are, aerial photography.... Field control. Compilation. And drafting.

● Let's take a tour through Sidwell's mapping facility and see exactly.

● What goes into each of these detailed mapping steps.

● Each mapping area and use is different. Complete planning is done before actual mapping begins.

● New precision aerial photography is tailored to each project area and map scale and...

● Flight maps are carefully drawn to insure each area is fully covered.

● The actual flying height varies depending on the final map scale, contour interval and focal length of camera.

● The photos are then taken so that they overlap one another. This overlap area is called the stereo model.

● And represents the portion of each photo used for mapping in the stereo-plotter.

● Our flight crews use the latest in photographic equipment modified aircraft. And precision aerial cameras.

● In addition, the photography must be taken during the time the leaves are off the trees. Notice how the detail in the photo

● ..is obscured by summer foliage.

● The film is checked for quality and negatives are selected to cover the project area.

● We're now at step two in the mapping process, field control. The aerial photos must be referenced.

● To do this, visible ground features are selected and marked. Ground surveys are then taken.

Jim Lyons, of the Sidwell Co., at work on his light table. He has just completed their third slide presentation.

After Jim planned the program and wrote the script, he hired a professional to record the narration. It gives the program an air of authority to have a practiced voice that puts the emphasis where you want it, while not sounding unnatural.

- On large projects, the basic control is further expanded through the use of analytical aerial triangulation.

- Computer programs then translate all measured and surveyed control readings into

- ..adjusted values for each control point in the mapping project. This method saves valuable days of field surveying.

- The third step in the mapping process is compilation. First each control point is plotted on a mylar manuscript.

- The plotter operator views the overlap area of the two photos as a 3-dimensional image

- ..and using a superimposed reference mark, he draws desired planimetric and topographic information.

- At Sidwell, drafting is done using the negative scribe process which produces a master negative.

- Positive copies of the maps are then produced by contact printing on photo mylar. The final maps represent many hours.

- ..to make several sets of paper prints for field use and initial planning.

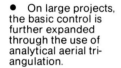

- Also, aerial enlargements provide an accurate record of ground features for engineering and planning uses.

- The Sidwell Company has developed a special type of topographic map called Topo-Plan.

- It combines the best features of precision aerial photography and topographic mapping.

- (Change music.) The range of mapping products is as varied as the applications and users.

- Planners... Highway departments and.. Private consultants all rely on photogrammetry for mapping needs.

- (Airplane sound fades to voice tower to plane, clear to land, etc.) (See tape.)

- For over 50 years the Sidwell Company has been providing precision aerial photography and mapping services.

- We offer an experienced mapping staff that makes the science of photogrammetry work for you.

- The Sidwell Company, serving your mapping needs since 1927.(Music fades.)

Putting It All Together

There are a couple of pictures that were taken by their free lance photographer. He did a lot of the work on the first mapping program. The second one was a combination of their work. They did a third program completely in-house.

The pictures of the people, especially the close-ups of them producing the maps, were produced by using a wide angle lens. Most of their maps are put on mylar, a reproducible plastic material. They have cameras which have large lighted back-boards on them. Some of them have a vacuum frame to hold the maps in place. They just put them in the frame and come in close with the camera on a tripod and shoot it, correcting for the fluorescent backlighting. In other cases they take the same map and make a black-and-white print of it, then light it from the front with regular 500 watt photoflood lamps.

To get the proper exposure they use the built -in meter in the camera and it has been very successful. It is necessary to be careful when metering. If there are highlights and dark areas, meter different areas and bracket those areas.

Metrocom

This script depicts a 16mm film produced internally for Turner Collie and Braden by Kay Lentz. The film was used to describe the benefits of METROCOM to city officials in other locations.

"Since this was our first effort, we wanted an individual we could both trust and share confidence in what we were doing. We toured studios, viewed numerous films, checked and rechecked references and past experience. But most importantly, we wanted someone who could understand and respect our opinions," she notes. Pearlman Productions, Inc., an independent film maker also based in Houston, fit the bill, and the team set out to produce a winner for $19,800.

Though Lentz and Porr essentially knew what should be described in the film, a freelance professional writer, John Davis, was hired to develop an integrated storyline. By joining the marketing staff for two days, Davis was able to better comprehend, verbally illustrate, and discuss METROCOM with interested viewers via the written script.

A 10-minute, 16-millimeter format was chosen because it could easily be converted into Super-8 or video cassettes to accommodate large and small audiences and offer better overall flexibility. Ten minutes proved to be an excellent length for a feature film detailing a technical subject since it allowed enough information to hold audience attention and still retain appeal.

Early in the project, it was decided that Lentz and Porr be the coordinating liaisons with the film team. Lentz explains, "It simply would have created too much havoc and confusion for more than two people to be involved in such a complex project. We were the only two representatives from the firm involved in the production from beginning to its end in only 10 weeks."

Fortunate to have cinema expert Pearlman, Lentz frequently relied on his special council. Lentz notes, "We didn't always accept his advice, but fully discussed every scene, word, musical note, and intonation. We were all pleased with the final result."

Soft lead-in music. Houston, Texas, but it could be any city in which people live, work and grow.

We're an urban people, but for the most part we have little knowledge of what it takes to keep an urban area working.

Take a look at the complexity of the problem. There are surface details such as buildings, streets, and structures.

Underground facilities, populations information and many other types of information installed and collected at different times by different people.

The city of Houston covers about 600 square miles.

The city maintains approximately 60 series of maps, plus over 25,000 tax block maps.

How can managers keep abreast of this expanding volume of information and be assured of getting all of the necessary data.

The city turns to Turner Collie and Braden for the answer.

Turner Collie and Braden has provided multi-disciplined engineering services to governmental agencies and private companies since 1946.

And employs a full range of technical expertise to address almost any engineering problem.

The city's charge was to design a data management system that combines the best of both engineering and computer sciences.

A system to reduce the very complex to the very simple.

An interactive computer system with both graphic and non-graphic storage and display capabilities was chosen for data base development.

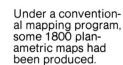

The result is METROCOM.

Under a conventional mapping program, some 1800 planametric maps had been produced.

These maps, plus the 900 maps produced later, provided the cultural geobase for the system.

When the maps are finalized, they're entered into the data base using a digitizing table linked to the computer.

This is done with the digitizing cursor which transfers points from source documents into the information storage files.

This is the graphic foundation of METROCOM.

Since this information will have numerous users, it is entered so output can be tailored to a user's specific need without displaying non-essential information.

Non-graphic information is entered concurrently with graphic data.

To put all of this information in the hands of the people who need it requires more than a single terminal.

In use some terminals will be without the data entry ability, so only authorized persons can modify the data base.

Now, let's take a look at METROCOM in action.

To get tax information, an operator calls up a map of the neighborhood.

Using street address, tax track number, or in this case, the electronic cross hair.

The non-graphic can be printed out while the data remains secure within the system.

Graphic information can be provided on hard copy or plotted map.

Pearlman also suggested music to accompany the film, and a local radio talent to handle the voice-over dialogue. The approved selections were chosen to best reflect the professional image of the firm. Though from a "sound library", the music's tasteful quality coordinates with the storyline. And it was considerably less expensive in comparison to an original musical score. Lentz also approved the nomination of Mike Scott, an area disc-jockey from a "beautiful music" station. An excellent investment, Scott's mellow voice helped maintain the overall warm professionalism desired.

Though the film is highly successful, it was not without its unique "challenges". For example, the movie deals with a highly technical data base developed for the City of Houston, one of the firm's major clients. Phenomenal growth in the last decade had created the need for the City to update its crowded record-keeping systems, yet the film could not cast the client's mode of operation in an unfavorable light. Instead, the focus of the film identified METROCOM as a unique and intelligent solution to a common problem and explained how Houstonians were benefiting from the system.

Another aspect Lentz kept foremost in direction was the avoidance of "dating" the film. "We didn't want to mention any items that could outdate our film prior to its circulation. It was crucial that care be taken in this aspect wherever possible," she states.

In filming the METROCOM system, certain precautions were necessary to insure quality footage. Effectively illustrating moving graphics in the system required acquisition of a "fast" lens, with the filming of the system's CRT screen being done in total darkness with a "pushed" developing process. As a result, the completed film was shown in "correct" tones and colors.

After final production efforts, the project was integrated with high-quality video sequences, contemporary music, and pleasant narration. Successfully blended in the production is a timely combination of marketing expertise and technical awareness.

Clients and staff members alike have seen the film and shared positive views regarding its content and marketing potential. And the film has provided other unexpected benefits. One such advantage was best expressed by the employee who remarked, "It's made me even prouder to be associated with such a progressive and capable firm."

When a water line leak is reported, a number of questions arise.

The user asks for information about water and other facilities in the area.

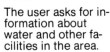

By using the systems scanning capability, the location of the water line and that of conflicting utilities can be determined.

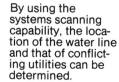

Today the uses of METROCOM are limited only by the imagination.

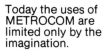

Police, fire, health, almost any department can take advantage of METROCOM's capabilities.

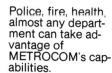

Private corporations, utility companies, anyone who must maintain and use large volumes of information can manage better with METROCOM.

When a new regional shopping center is under consideration, the system could provide information on areas of potential traffic congestion.

Think what this could mean to planners.

Recommend traffic improvements, changes to the shopping center, or other plan modifications could be developed.

METROCOM could be used to plan the location of new schools.

The same is true of parks, highways, hospitals and other facilities.

Increasingly we are an urban people, creating a steadily increasing volume of data to be managed.

But this doesn't mean that the data must become unmanageable.

Only that management tools and techniques must keep pace.

And as more and more applications are developed, METROCOM will continue to provide solutions.

Kirkham Michael And Associates

This ten-minute program was originally produced as a three-projector, multi-image slide program. It was designed primarily to explain the design process used by KMA in health care facilities.

It was shown to hospital administrators and board members of Western and Midwestern small rural hospitals prior to shortlisting.

The program was transferred to a videotape format for showing in local hospital facilities.

One of the key ingredients in the program was the emphasis on the people and the services provided to the client. The outline of the program followed very closely the design process used in planning medical facilities.

The dialogue used to develop the script utilizes medical terminology relating the services to similar functions performed in medicine.

The program features scenes from medical facilities and showed the firm's people with hospital people during the crucial planning stages.

It begins with people. With their need for life-giving, life-saving health care.

Faced with unprecedented challenges American health care institutions today are searching as never before,

for innovative ways to satisfy the rapidly changing demands of patients, providers, and the public.

To comply fully with codes and joint commission's standards, to allow for more efficient diagnostic and treatment space,

to accommodate new equipment and procedures, to design efficient work flow patterns,

to ease crowded conditions, and to apply sound economics to the expansion

and improvement of health care facilities. Challenging? Yes. Impossible? No.

At Kirkham Michael, & Associates, we deal in ideas that bring people and possibilities together in our uniquely creative design process.

Kirkham Michael, serving primarily in the western and midwestern states,

has achieved an outstanding record of success, growth and leadership, in planning, architecture, and engineering.

Our health care facility design division is a specialized unit drawing upon the talents

and training of health care architects, mechanical, electrical, structural and civil engineers and interior designers.

It's a multi-disciplinary team, committed to the idea that health care design must be as much an art as it is a science.

Within the framework of these cost conscience times, Kirkham Michael designs encompass short term

and long range strategies to keep capital expenditures within your budgets today

and equally important to minimize operating costs far into the future.

The objective, quite simply, to help you provide more and better patient-centered services for less money.

Let's take a closer look at the people and processes that set Kirkham Michael apart.

First and foremost — communication. We place a premium on personal relationships with our clients.

Setting up shop in your facility enables us to talk with you, but more important to look,

to listen and to learn first-hand about the unique characteristics of your institution.

During the preliminary phase, our in-house engineers conduct a thorough physical examination

...a check-up designed to diagnose any deficiences in your facilities

...to suggest interim remedies and to propose permanent solutions.

 Simultaneously, your goals for the long term future of your facility take shape in the form of a master plan.

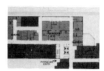 An indispensable guide that outlines a proposed course for your institution in years to come

 Block drawings, single line drawings, site analysis, and schematics form our initial design process.

 And serve as valuable tools in communicating our concepts to you.

 A preferred design option evolves. And additional study sharpens the focus.

 Your reactions and those of your staff serve as our guide for further fine tuning.

 We learn how the various spaces will function, by including your staff members in the development process.

 Meantime, Kirkham Michael's interior designers are assembling colors, fabrics, finishes and furnishings,

 creating an atmosphere to complement the character of your hospital and your community.

 Throughout the certificate of need review process, Kirkham Michael serves as a reliable source of information for you.

 With the individual components of the design now fully realized, we prepare your construction documents,

 the drawings and specifications which will guide your prospective contractors in establishing their bids.

 The precision of Kirkham Michael construction documents allows bidders to estimate their costs more accurately.

 And that means more reliable figures to base your contract decisions on.

 Many of our clients have found positive results with the construction manager approach,

 a problem solving method that can offer significant time and money saving benefits, especially in fast-track projects.

 For other clients, conventional bidding or negotiated fee have proven to be

 the most appropriate means of contracting for construction.

 We'll look closely at the alternatives, and offer the most efficient and economical method for your project.

 With construction underway, the Kirkham Michael design team continues to represent your interests, conducting periodic...

 and final on site reviews to demonstrate that the contract specifications have been met.

 Since your health care facility is a major investment, and a major asset for your community,

 we feel the community should share in your progress on the way. And your pride on the day the doors open.

 So your community relations department can call on us any time for help in carrying your story to the public.

 Now that the certificate of occupancy has been issued,

 we're as determined as you are to see your facility delivers the improved performance designed into it.

 So you can count on Kirkham Michael follow-up. We'll check in by phone regularly.

 And visit your facility to review the improvements with your staff, to field questions,

 From need identification to concept, to preliminary and final design stages,

 on thru construction and into full operation, we at Kirkham Michael commit ourselves to work not just for you, but with you.

 We've built our reputation on our unique ability to respond quickly.

 And to address your concerns completely. To deliver your project on time, on target;

 These challenges bring out the best in Kirkham Michael.

 So whether you're building in, on, out or up, we urge you to look closely at our record of success.

 Because it all begins and ends here. If the needs of people create the challenge,

 the resources of people — yours and ours — working together, offer us the means to master it.

Design Credits

Index